CREATING WEB APPLETS

WITH

JAVA™

David Gulbransen
Kenrick Rawlings

201 West 103rd Street
Indianapolis, IN 46290

Copyright © 1996 by Sams.net Publishing

FIRST EDITION

International Standard Book Number: 1-57521-070-3

Library of Congress Catalog Card Number: 95-072940

99 98 97 96   4   3   2   1

Interpretation of the printing code: the rightmost double-digit number is the year of the book's printing; the rightmost single-digit, the number of the book's printing. For example, a printing code of 96-1 shows that the first printing of the book occurred in 1996.

Composed in AGaramond and MCPdigital by Macmillan Computer Publishing

Printed in the United States of America

Trademarks

Publisher	Richard K. Swadley
Publishing Manager	Mark Taber
Managing Editor	Cindy Morrow
Marketing Manager	John Pierce
Assistant Marketing Manager	Kristina Perry

Acquisitions Editor
Beverly M. Eppink

Development Editor
Fran Hatton

Software Development Specialist
Merle Newlon

Production/Copy Editor
Heather Stith

Technical Reviewer
Sue Charlesworth

Editorial Coordinator
Bill Whitmer

Technical Edit Coordinator
Lynette Quinn

Resource Coordinator
Deborah Frisby

Formatter
Frank Sinclair

Editorial Assistants
Carol Ackerman
Andi Richter
Rhonda Tinch-Mize

Cover Designer
Jason Grisham

Book Designer
Gary Adair

Copy Writer
Peter Fuller

Production Team Supervisor
Brad Chinn

Production
Mary Ann Abramson,
Ginny Bess, Carol Bowers,
Michael Brumitt, Jeanne Clark,
Mike Dietsch, Jason Hand,
Sonja Hart, Mike Henry,
Clint Lahnen, Donna Martin,
Laura Robbins, Bobbi Satterfield,
Todd Wente, Colleen Williams

Overview

Contents

D   What's on the CD-ROM   **281**

Index   **287**

Dedication

To Stephanie, for your love and support.

And to my father, for never losing faith in me.

David Gulbransen

To my father, for always being there.

Kenrick Rawlings

Acknowledgments

Thanks to Andy Granger, for putting up with us. Thanks to Jim Causey, for putting up with us. Thanks to the Dynamic Duo, for putting up with us. Paul, Clarence, and Alabama, thanks for the CDs! Thanks to our families: the Gulbransens, the Berlins, the Rawlings, the Morefords, and the McKees (Whew!).

Fran Hatton: Thanks! Thanks! Thanks! Thanks to Beverly Eppink, for the opportunity. Thanks to Dan Friedman, for showing that programming is more than just coding. Thanks also to Mark Lynch, Mark Tabor, and John December.

Thanks also to the Java Development Team, Sun Microsystems/Javasoft, the ACCESS MicroCenter at Indiana University, and the Henry Radford Hope School of Fine Arts.

About the Authors

David Gulbransen (dgulbran@indiana.edu) is currently the Computing Specialist for the Indiana University school of Fine Arts. He is also a principal partner in Grey Associates, a Java software development and consulting firm. Occasionally, Dave likes to put down the mouse for a movie camera to pursue his hobby of cinematography. He wants Ken's cats.

Kenrick Rawlings (krawling@bluemarble.net) is currently employed at Indiana University as a software specialist at the ACCESS MicroCenter. He is also the Principal Software Architect for Grey Associates. In his copious amounts of spare time, Kenrick enjoys coding Scheme, coding Delphi, and listening to the soulful sounds of James Brown. He has two very popular cats.

Contributing Authors

Billy Barron (billy@metronet.com) is currently the Network Services Manager for the University of Texas at Dallas and has an M.S. in Computer Science from the University of North Texas. He has written and technically reviewed such books as *Tricks of the Internet Gurus*, *Education on the Internet*, and *Accessing Online Bibliographic Databases,* as well as written for periodicals.

Lay Wah Ooi (ooi@pobox.com) is a Computer Systems Engineer at Titan Spectrum Technologies. She graduated with a Computer Science degree from the University of North Texas. Lay Wah was a contributor to Sams.net Publishing's *Internet Unleashed* and was a technical editor for *Java Unleashed.*

Introduction

What Is Java?

The question, "What is Java?" often leads only to more questions. Some people see Java as yet another bit of Internet hype. Others see Java as the future of the Internet and Internet applications. In truth, Java probably lies somewhere in between the extremes.

We hope that this book will begin to show you what Java is and what Java is not. Java is new, and Java is exciting. But Java is not the solution to every computing problem. Java is, quite simply, a new object-oriented programming language. With it come the advantages of object-oriented programming and several other advantages that have been created through Java's development process.

Java has been presented in many different ways by many different interests, but at the heart of all the Java hype is the language itself. Many people are confused or scared about what using Java means. What we hope to accomplish with this book is to provide you with some answers.

Part I takes a first look at Java. You'll see where Java has been and where it's headed. You'll also take a look at what Java is capable of and hopefully you'll finish these chapters as excited about Java as we are.

Part II approaches Java from a user's standpoint. How do you view Java applets and applications? What are the limits of what Java can do? What are the real-world uses for Java, and when is Java not enough?

Part III discusses how you can start using Java applets in your own Web development projects. You'll learn where to find Java applets, how to add those applets to your Web pages, and how to customize them.

Once you've seen what Java can do and have started adding Java to your pages, Parts IV and V will teach you more about the language and take you through the basics of programming your own applets.

Finally, Part VI provides you with some real-world applet examples. You can see the development of two working applets from beginning to end. Use this part as a starting point for developing your own applets and as a general guide for programming.

We've also included a CD-ROM to provide in a convenient format many of the tools and applets we talk about. The CD-ROM contains the Java Developer's Kit, all the applets developed in this book, and a host of other applets ready for you to use on your Web pages. In the end, we hope you come away with a solid understanding of Java. We also hope you will have a grasp of the basics of Java programming and can start to create your own applets to make your Web pages more fun, functional, and exciting.

Introduction to Java

CHAPTER 1

What Is Java?

Java is perhaps one of the most talked about advances in Internet technology since the World Wide Web. People in many areas of computing are discussing Java and how it will change the face of computing. Without a doubt, Java will change the way people use the Internet and networked applications. Java has introduced many ideas to the World Wide Web arena, and those ideas represent some exciting changes to the Internet and computing.

Because the hype surrounding Java has caused some confusion, this chapter explains exactly what Java is and what it is not. This chapter discusses the basics of Java in order to give you a clearer picture of the types of programs you can produce with it and how those programs function on the Internet. Because many of Java's features have been the result of a very interesting development cycle, this chapter also includes history about the development of Java. After reading this chapter, you'll know where Java has been, where it is, and where it's going.

At the heart of all the Java talk is the Java programming language. Java is an object-oriented programming (OOP) language that uses many common elements from other OOP languages, such as C++, but it adds some enhancements to make programming easier. Like any other language, Java has a particular syntax, a structure for programs, and many supporting applications.

The Java Developer's Kit (JDK) contains all of the tools necessary to create applications (or Web applets) using the Java programming language, including the following:

javac	The Java compiler
jdb	The Java debugger
javadoc	The Java documentation program
java	The Java Virtual Machine
appletviewer	The Java applet viewer

Some of these Java components might not seem so obvious, such as the Java Virtual Machine. In using Java to program, you do not directly access the Java Virtual Machine. However, other commercial Web browsers that can run Java applets use it, as does appletviewer. All these elements are related (see Figure 1.1) or are directly linked to Java and using it on the World Wide Web.

Figure 1.1.
The relationships between Java's various components.

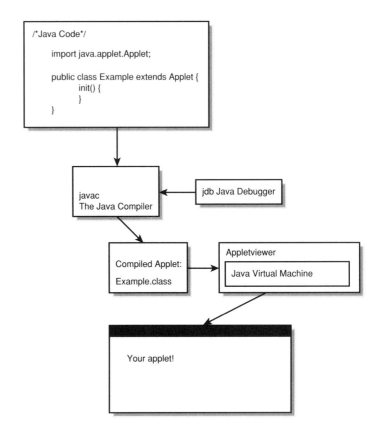

A Brief History of Java

Java began its life in 1990 as a new language called Oak. Sun Microsystems had established a project group code-named *green* to develop new products and expand Sun's markets. Oak was originally designed for a personal digital assistant called *7 that Sun intended to market with a seamless graphical user interface.

The *7 was never marketed, and eventually Sun formed a company called FirstPerson to develop the *7 in TV set-top boxes for interactive television. Due to a variety of circumstances, the promise of interactive TV soon dried up, and Oak was left without a market. However, about the time that FirstPerson and Oak were failing, the World Wide Web was exploding. Companies such as Netscape began to make software that catapulted the WWW into the Internet spotlight. Sun soon realized that Oak had possibilities with the Web, and soon Oak was released to the Internet with a new name: Java.

Java is in its first release as a development environment, and already it is beginning to influence the direction of computing and the Internet. The Java programming language is being released free of charge on the Internet (see Figure 1.2), and Sun is licensing the full implementation of Java and its components to a variety of Internet software vendors in the hope of creating a new Web programming standard.

Figure 1.2.
*The Sun Microsystems
Java Web site* (http://
java.sun.com).

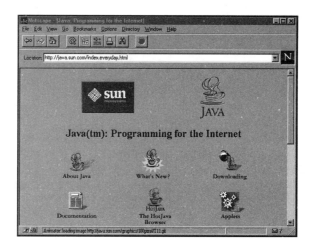

To understand Java a little better, it is quite useful to have a better understanding of some common aspects of programming environments and practices. This book doesn't go into specifics about writing Java code until much later, but it is important to understand the basics of object-oriented programming and how they have influenced Java's development. The following sections provide an overview of some of these programming issues to prepare you for the chapters ahead.

Distributed Computing

Java is revolutionary for several reasons, but one of the most important is the way Java changes the way we use our computers. Java is designed around the notion of networks and connectivity. In today's computing world, you run applications from the hard drive in your computer. You install applications, use them, and upgrade them when they become out-of-date. If you need to contact someone else with your machine, you launch an application, such as a Web browser or e-mail software, that contacts a network. But imagine instead that your applications exist on a network server and are downloaded to your machine each time you use them. In this model, your software would always be current, and your machine would constantly be in touch with the network (see Figure 1.3). *Distributed computing* is sharing program resources across networks.

Figure 1.3.
Models of distributed computing.

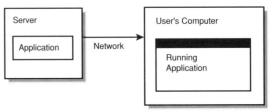

Applications can be served to local machines over a network from a server

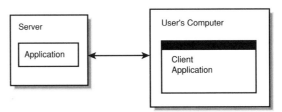

Or a client application and server application can communicate to each other over a network

The end goal for Java is to be able to produce full-blown network applications. Current bandwidth and network restrictions, however, make that reality a distant goal. Instead, Java is being used to add functionality and fun to network applications such as Web browsers. With Java, you can write mini-applications, called *applets*, that can be incorporated into Web sites and run off a home page. For example, the tickertape applet shown in Figure 1.4 scrolls text across the screen of a Web page.

Figure 1.4.
A scrolling text applet allows you to present information in an eye-catching way.

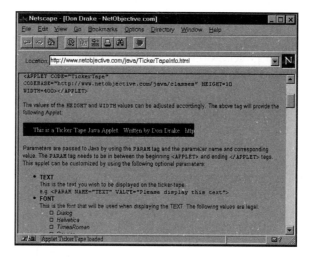

The core of distributed applications and applets is network communication. Java is designed to be integrated with networks like the Internet. Because Java has been designed to be used with the Internet and other large-scale networks, it includes a large number of networking libraries to utilize TCP/IP networking and a number of protocols commonly used on the Internet, such as HTTP and FTP. This feature means that you can easily integrate network services into your applications. The end result is a wide range of functionality on the network, and applications that lend themselves to network usage.

The idea of an applet also fits well with a distributed software model. An applet is essentially a scaled-down application. Application executables can be quite large, and often applications have a series of support files and settings files that they require in order to run. All of these files lead to large programs that are cumbersome to distribute over a network. Applet files are small and portable, which allows applets to be downloaded quickly and integrated easily into a Web page design. Applets can be added to pages to add new levels of functionality, interactivity, or just some spicy graphics and sound to make a Web site more interesting. Because applets are generally small, they don't increase the downloading time of a page significantly, and because applets are actual programs, they allow you more flexibility than traditional HTML and CGI scripts.

Security Issues and Java

Java includes security features to reinforce its use on the Internet. One potential security problem concerns the Java applets, which are executable code that runs on your local machine. Java uses code verification and limited file system access to make sure that the code won't damage anything on your local machine.

When an applet is downloaded to your local machine, the code is checked to make sure that the applet only uses valid system calls and methods. If the applet passes verification, it is allowed to run, but applets are not given access to the local machine's file system. Limiting access to the file system imposes some limits on applets, but it also prevents applets from intentionally removing files, planting viruses, or otherwise wreaking havoc with your system.

Programming for the Rest of Us

Java is largely based on the C++ programming language. C++ is one of the most popular programming languages for a variety of platforms and is a high-level, object-oriented programming language. Unfortunately, C++ is a very difficult language. It is designed for high-level commercial applications; as a result, it is very powerful and gives the programmer access to a very detailed level of machine control in order to optimize performance. The level of control that C++ provides is often unnecessary for midrange applications and can be very difficult for an inexperienced programmer to manage.

For example, C++ gives the programmer direct control over memory management for an application. This capability means that the programmer has to be very careful about allocating new memory to an application, establishing how the application uses that memory, and cleaning out unused memory when an application is finished. Memory allocation and "garbage collection" often result in very time-consuming and complicated errors in C++ programs. Fortunately, Java handles the details of memory allocation for you, which saves you many hours of complicated debugging.

This automatic memory handling is quite a blessing. Ask anyone who has programmed in C++ what the most difficult aspect of the language is and they will answer, "pointers." *Pointers* are the method C++ uses to keep track of memory locations and what is stored at those locations. Imagine having to always keep track of what data went where and how to recall that data. Sound daunting? Well, it can be. In order to make programming easier, Java is explicitly designed to eliminate pointers.

Objects, Objects, Objects

Object-oriented programming has steadily been creeping into the programming world for a number of years. The concept is not that hard to grasp—objects are small pieces of code designed to perform a specific function. A programmer can then combine these objects to create a finished program.

For example, a simple program might contain an input object, a processing object, and an output object. In a calculator applet, for example, the keypad could be thought of as the input object. It receives input from the user, and then passes it on to the processor object, which does the actual calculating. The processor object then passes the result to an output object that displays the result for the user (see Figure 1.5). Objects are designed to make programming more flexible.

Although the basic concept of object-oriented programming is simple, implementing it can be a very complex task. It involves taking a great deal of time in the planning stage of developing an applet to ensure that components are designed for portability and to work together. Well-designed objects can make programming easier in the long run, but they require considerable investment in the original planning and development. However, OOP does offer hope for the future as Java grows.

Figure 1.5.
A breakdown of a calculator applet into object components.

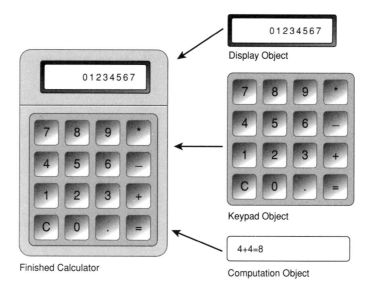

As Java begins to gain in popularity, many objects will become available as shareware and for sale as components to be used in your own applications. Someone might create a dial component that allows you to set a value with a dial, like a volume knob. The dial would need to translate its position into a value that a program would use. If this object were properly designed and documented, you could integrate it into your own applet without the headache of developing the dial from scratch; all you would need to do would be to grab the value information from the dial object. This level of program-independent functionality is the end goal and major advantage of object-oriented programming.

So now you know the truth: Java is programming. But just like any other programming language, Java can be learned with the proper documentation and time. Fortunately, Java is designed to include the functions of a high-level programming language while eliminating some of the more difficult aspects of coding in C++. Keep in mind that Java is a new language that is based on some of the more popular programming languages of today, such as C and C++. Java takes its functionality from these languages, but tries to improve on their implementation whenever possible.

Java objects are also designed to make programming easier. Everything in Java is based on the object model. Even your applets are objects that can be used in other applets. This functionality was deliberately built in Java to help speed up Java development in the long run.

The earlier calculator applet example had a keypad object. Suppose you were programming an applet that looked like a phone. Phones have keypads very similar to calculators. In fact, you could pull the keypad object out of the calculator applet and plug it into your phone applet. With only some minor modifications, you could rearrange the keys to look like a phone. This way, you can take an object that has already been developed and customize it for your applications. Objects can save an enormous amount of programming time and help you create applets even faster by enabling you to reuse components.

Java Works for You

The result of all these enhancements to Java is that Java is a programming language that works for you. However, there are some trade-offs:

■ Java's simplified memory management slows applets down. But even though Java doesn't have the raw speed of C++, Java is by no means a slow language. Although some high-end applications, such as 3-D renderers or CAD packages, are still better left to C++, you shouldn't avoid Java because it is a little slower.

■ The OOP model makes planning more critical. If you spend some time planning your applet before you start coding, OOP will work for you, not against you. As you begin to develop more applets and reuse some objects, you will find that the planning paid off and ended up saving you time in the long run.

But even with these trade-offs, Java can be a wonderful tool. Remember, Java was developed from the ground up to fix some of the problems in higher-level programming languages. The developers of Java wanted to make it as accessible as possible and fun to learn and use. Let Java and its enhancements change the way you think about programming. In the end, you will find that Java can be fun and flexible.

A Platform-Independent Solution

Java has been molded to fit many different projects since it was first created in the early 1990s. It has gone from a programming language for personal digital assistants to a programming language for interactive TV set-top boxes, and then to its final incarnation as a Web programming language. This transformation should give you some indication of Java's flexibility and portability; it is designed to be machine-independent and function within different operating systems. Portability is one of Java's principal goals. Java code is designed to be platform-independent and has several features designed to help it achieve that goal.

When you write a Java application, you are writing a program that is designed to be run on a very special computer: the Java Virtual Machine. The Java Virtual Machine is the first step towards a platform-independent solution. When you are developing software in a language like C++, you generally program for a specific platform, such as a Windows machine or a Macintosh. The programming language will use a variety of functions that are very specific to whatever processor is used by the machine you are programming for. Because the language uses machine-specific instructions, you have to modify your program for a new processor if you want to run your program on another machine. This task can be very time-consuming and resource-intensive.

Java code is not written for any type of physical computer. Instead, it is written for a special computer called the Virtual Machine, which is really another piece of software. The Virtual Machine then interprets and runs the Java program you have written. The Virtual Machine is programmed for specific machines, so there is a Windows 95 Virtual Machine, a Sun Virtual Machine, and so on. There is even a copy of the Virtual Machine built into Netscape, allowing the browser to run Java programs.

By porting the Virtual Machine from platform to platform, instead of the Java programs themselves, any Java program can be used on any machine running a version of the Virtual Machine. This feature is the reason why the same Java applet can run on UNIX workstations as well as on Windows machines. Sun has gone to great lengths to port the Virtual Machine to nearly every major type of machine on the market. By doing so, Sun ensures the portability of Java. The benefit for you is the ability to write your code once and then use it on many machines.

One Binary Fits All

The Virtual Machine requires special binary code to run Java programs. This code, called *bytecode*, does not contain any platform-specific instructions. That means if you write a program on a Sun workstation and compile it, the compiler will generate the same bytecode as a machine running Windows 95. This code is the second step towards a platform-independent development environment. Imagine the time and money that could be saved if software today could be written once and used on all computers. There would be no need for Mac or Windows versions of software and no need to hire hordes of programmers to convert some Mac program to a Windows version.

When you compile a Java program, the compiler generates the platform-independent bytecode. Any Java Virtual Machine can then run that bytecode. It can be viewed using the Java appletviewer or Netscape. It can be viewed on a Sun workstation or a Windows NT machine. The bottom line is portability. One binary fits all.

Consistent Look and Feel

The Virtual Machine also allows Java to maintain a platform-consistent look and feel. When you run a Java application on a Windows machine, the menus and toolbars in your Java application look like standard Windows components. If you were to run that same applet on a Sun system, the buttons, menus, and so on would have the look and feel of the Sun system.

Because the Virtual Machine is platform-specific, the elements used by applets retain some of the host machine's characteristics. The Abstract Window Toolkit, the standard Java interface builder, accesses windowing and interface components from the host computer. This feature allows you to create easy-to-use interfaces without much specific programming. If the person using your applet is a Mac user, he can use the applet just like he uses other Mac applications. If she is a Windows user, your applet appears to her as a normal Windows application. This feature helps avoid user confusion by allowing users to work in a familiar environment without having to learn any new user interfaces.

Interactive Web Pages

When the Web began, it was simply a means of sharing static data. Text or images were downloaded and displayed by a browser. There wasn't any interaction, and the pages didn't change unless you reloaded a new version. Eventually, with forms and CGI scripts, the Web became more interactive, but it still lacked any aspects of multimedia or real-time interaction. With Java, you can implement animation (see Figure 1.6), sound, real-time input, and data manipulation. It is even possible to use applets in conjunction with other applications, such as databases, to add new levels of functionality to Web sites.

Figure 1.6.
A simulation of Bay Area Rapid Transit trains running on schedule, developed at Lawrence Berkeley Labs, http://www-itg.lbl.gov/vbart. *The map shows trains running on various routes around the city.*

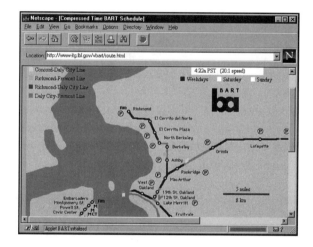

When Java was first introduced, many of the first applets showcased Java's ability to offer animation to the Web. Even today, animations tend to dominate many Java applets (see Figure 1.7). Because Java applets can easily flip through standard format images (GIF and JPEG), it is natural that this use would flourish. Previous attempts at animations on the Web had relied on network- and server-intensive methods for displaying one image at a time or server-push animation. The result was slow, clunky, and often even nonfunctional animations. Because Java applets run on your local machine, they don't tax the network while they are running, and the animations are smooth.

Figure 1.7.
A Java-animated marquee for an on-line art show. The animation draws attention and highlights the nature of the site.

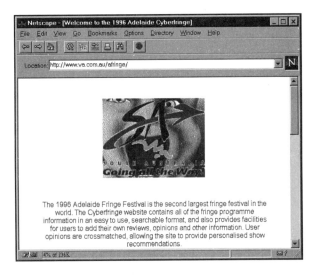

You can use animations and other types of image-based applets for more than just spicing up a Web page. Many sites are demonstrating how Java's animation functionality can be put to productive use (see Figure 1.8). Experimental Java sites are showing how applets can aid scientific, as well as artistic, visualization.

Figure 1.8.
The NASA SeaWiFS site. This site showcases a NASA project designed to monitor the Earth's oceans. Dynamically updating data is one way applets can add to a Web page.

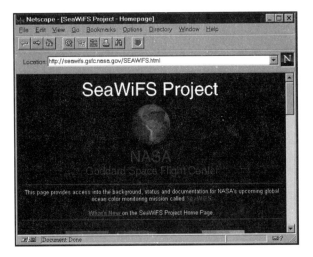

You can add any sort of animation or informational graphic to a page. Many sites are using Java applets to enhance content in an informational and entertaining way (see Figure 1.9).

Figure 1.9.
The Hotwired on-line magazine site has begun incorporating Java applets to enhance on-line articles. These applets can add a new dimension to the Web articles that distinguishes them from their print counterparts.

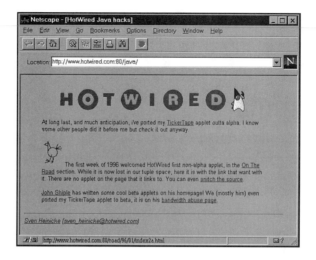

The interactive possibilities provided by Java go to the other extreme of user interactivity as well. Keep in mind that Java applets can utilize limited network connectivity. That means it is possible to join applets, and the users of applets, over the Internet. A good example of this capability is Gamelan's interactive chat (see Figure 1.10). The interactive chat featured on the Gamelan Web site (http://www.gamelan.com) is an example of how functional Java can be. This applet allows users to sign on to a chat session and write messages to each other in real time. Similar network applications have been around for some time now, but imagine adding this capability to a Web page! This applet is so flexible that it can even be converted to a standalone window, separating it from the Web page altogether.

Figure 1.10.
The Gamelan Chat applet in float mode, which allows the applet to occupy a separate window.

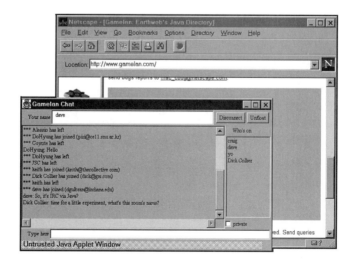

This level of interactivity was really unheard of on the Web until Java came along. Now you can imagine the types of applets that are possible, such as real-time stock quotes, interactive chats, shopping areas, and catalogs.

Summary

You've chosen a very exciting time to begin exploring Java. The World Wide Web is growing by leaps and bounds every day, and Java is helping to shape its development. You've seen some examples of what Java can do for the Web, and how it offers a promise of interactivity on the Web that was not previously available. You also have a glimpse at the programming realities that make Java possible.

The coming chapters discuss the progression of Java in more detail. They tell where to get Java and Java applets and discuss Java-ready tools. They also cover some of the design issues that are raised by Java and talk about adding Java to your own pages. Finally, you'll learn how to create your own applets. In the end, you should come away with a comprehensive look at Java from both a user and a creator's standpoint and feel confident enough to use Java to enhance your experience with the World Wide Web.

CHAPTER 2

Using Java

Java is one of the most hyped products of the last decade, with good reason. It offers capabilities that have been dreamed of but unrealized for years. However, enthusiasm for Java should be tempered with a realization of its limitations. These limitations restrict Java's usefulness to certain types of applications.

This chapter explores the capabilities and restrictions of Java. This chapter first discusses the frontiers that Java applets open up to the Web, like sound and interactivity. Next, this chapter points out the restrictions that Java places on applets. Finally, this chapter discusses the capabilities of standalone Java applications and the future of Java.

Applets: Enhancing the Web

Sun realized early on in the development of the World Wide Web that eventually people would want to expand the capabilities of Web pages beyond form-based interaction with CGI scripts. Java was a perfect fit for this type of expansion. Because Java was originally designed to work on many different types of hardware, it was platform-independent; likewise, because Java was meant to run on consumer appliances, it was relatively small, which was a major advantage on the Internet where bandwidth was relatively limited.

To exploit this market, Sun created in essence a new type of program that can be created in Java: an applet. Applets are created to run in Web pages and thus can leverage Web browsers for a great deal of functionality not available to standalone applications. In Java, applets and applications are completely different things—this point is important and often misunderstood. An applet can only run in a Web browser (or in a special program, like the appletviewer, that is meant to run applets), but a Java application can run by itself on the operating system. For example, an applet could be a small window that displays current stock data and gives a price when users enter sample amounts of the stock to buy. An application could be an entire portfolio manager that keeps personal histories of many stocks and the current value of a person's holdings.

In designing the specification for applets, Sun opened up Web pages to a great deal of the functionality normally associated with standalone applications. Except for a few restrictions that are discussed later, you can build an applet containing most of the features users expect from commercial applications.

Adding Sound to Your Web Pages

Users of the WWW have clamored for the capability to add sounds to Web pages for a long time. Many Web pages have offered sound files that users could download and then play on their local machines. Unfortunately, because a variety of sound formats are available, this process isn't always a viable method of adding sound. For example, Real Audio is a company that has begun to add sound capabilities to the Web using proprietary formats and sound players. WAV files are a popular sound format, as are AU files.

The only sound format that Java applets are currently able to use is the AU format, which was developed by Sun. This will likely change in the next major revision of Java. In the meantime, most popular sound editing applications can save files in the AU format.

Java provides a standard way to play sounds in any applet. The fact that Java applets are actual programs and not just HTML tags provides a great deal of flexibility in how sounds are played. For instance, not only can an applet play a sound when a user enters a Web page, it can also play a series of sounds associated with pictures. (Chapter 13 "The SlideShow Applet," explains how to construct such an applet.)

Adding Animation and Graphics

One of the biggest complaints about Web pages is that they just sit there until the user does something. Server-push animation is one solution to this problem, but it puts a huge strain on the server because every frame of the animation must be downloaded again and again to the browser. In addition, when the Net is running slow (as it too often does), server-push animation causes the animations to crawl along at a snail's pace. In fact, the experience of watching a server-push animation on a slow link can be approximated by staring at Figure 2.1 for 15 seconds and then blinking.

Figure 2.1.
The Netscape server-push animation: slow and not smooth.

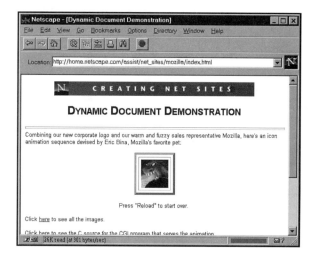

Java provides a much better solution. Instead of the server doing all the work and taxing the network when showing an animation, a Java applet can download all the frames of the animation once and then display them (see Figure 2.2). With this approach, the server only has to provide the Java applet and one copy of the frames, and then the animation applet can run for hours with no further contact with the server.

Moreover, Java has the built-in capability to draw graphics. All sorts of shapes can be drawn easily: triangles, circles, rectangles, and polygons to name a few (see Figure 2.3). By using these routines to create graphics and animations, you can include a huge amount of interesting graphics in just a few kilobytes of Java code, creating an impressive applet that doesn't require much download time.

Figure 2.2.
*The Sun Java logo
animation provides
smooth continuous
animation with no load
on the server.*

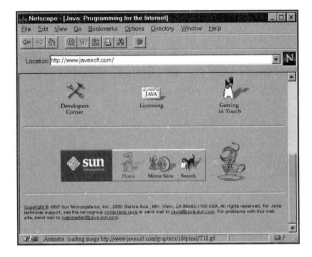

Figure 2.3.
*A sample applet with
graphics generated by
Java.*

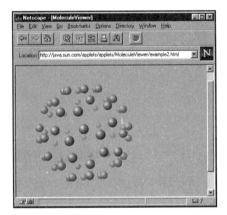

Interactivity

Adding animations and sounds to a Web page are both wonderful examples of what Java can do, but Java really shines when it comes to interacting with a user. Drawing an image is one thing, but allowing the user to click different sections of it and have the applet respond is quite another.

Java can accept both mouse and keyboard input; the decision on how to use this capability is completely up to the programmer of the applet. Suppose you were working on a calculator applet, and you had a keypad on the screen that users could click to enter numbers. Users might also want to be able to type numbers from their keyboards. No problem. Applets can accept input from the mouse and keyboard; Java applets can be as flexible as you need them to be.

The capability to take input from the user and respond to it is what makes Java so powerful. This capability opens up a whole new world of Web possibilities, from games to interactive showrooms to almost anything imaginable.

A Real User Interface

Although many simple applications won't require it, Java can create the kind of user interfaces that people are familiar with by using the Abstract Window Toolkit or AWT. All the standard components are available: buttons, checkboxes, lists, scrollbars, and so forth. The AWT will be discussed in detail in Chapter 11, "Building a User Interface."

Unfortunately, programming user interfaces is not an easy task, and the AWT reflects this fact. However, the AWT is certainly manageable for programming relatively simple interfaces, and many of the harder concepts and code can be easily transferred from program to program. Chapter 11 talks more about developing user interfaces.

Suppose you are doing a lot of Web design, and you want to look at different colors to add to your pages. Web browsers let you specify the background color of pages and the color of active and visited links so that you can have more control over a page's design. Unfortunately, you can't just say that you want something to be green. To specify a color in most browsers, you need to know the RGB values, or even the hexadecimal value, of a color. Suppose you want an applet that enables users to see how a certain RGB color appears inside their Web browser. It would make sense to use sliders to select from a range of colors and to have text fields that let the user enter the components of the color directly (see Figure 2.4).

Figure 2.4.
The ColorPicker applet.

One of the great strengths of Java is that applets written in it do not have an instantly recognizable "Java" look. Instead, all the components used in Java take on the look of the operating system the applet is currently running on. For example, look at the Spreadsheet applet supplied with the Java Developer's Kit. Figure 2.5 shows the Macintosh version, with a typical Macintosh look and feel. Figure 2.6 shows the same applet running under Windows 95. The applets function the same, but they provide the user of each operating system with a look and feel consistent with the platform the applet is running on.

Figure 2.5.
The Spreadsheet applet running on a Macintosh.

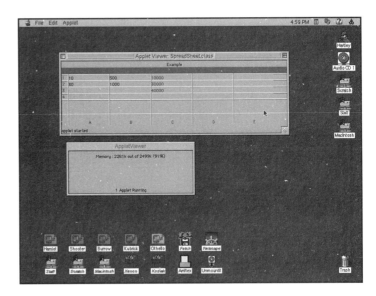

Figure 2.6.
The same Spreadsheet applet running under Windows 95.

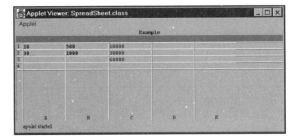

Restrictions

Java has its downsides. It is impossible to be all things to all people, and for many factors, mostly to do with security, Java applets have a few serious limitations.

No Access to Files

In version 1.0 of Java, applets don't have any access to files on the user's machine. Because of this restriction, applets cannot save any information permanently to the local machine. Although this restriction seriously limits the functionality of applets, it is quite understandable given the possibilities of what rogue applets would be capable of if they could write to hard drives.

For example, if Java applets could write file information, they could be used to spread viruses by writing the virus directly to a user's machine over the Internet, or marketers could use them to get information about what software you use. Fortunately, Java was designed to prevent these events by limiting the access provided to the file system in an effort to make Java safe for everyone.

This situation may change in the future to open up applets to a more complex area. A word processor applet is often given as an example of an eventual large Java applet. For this applet, it would be highly desirable (if not essential) to have some form of local file access in order to save and open documents.

Applets Have No Memory

Because of the lack of access to files, applets forget everything each time they are reloaded. As a result, there are no built-in ways to keep configuration information for each user of an applet; everyone gets the same applet in the same state when it's run off a Web page. Any information that needs to be kept from session to session must be stored on the server and downloaded to the applet each time it is run. This transfer of information also means that some type of user validation needs to occur between the browser and the server. Because each applet can't be configured for a different user, applets wouldn't be very useful as newsreaders, mail programs, or any other kind of program that needs to be configured for an individual user. But they could still be useful for programs that share a configuration for many users, such as a sales or inventory applet.

Although this problem isn't drastic, the lack of access to files needs to be considered early on in developing any substantial applets. Once an applet begins to have user interaction, the complexity begins to grow immediately, and concerns such as configuration and file access need to be addressed. Workarounds certainly exist, but keep in mind that they will need to be handled by the applet programmers. Chapter 10, "Applet Structure and Design," deals with configuring applets, and Chapter 11 explains user interfaces. Applets are still quite flexible in spite of these restrictions. Java can still perform a wide variety of tasks, and careful planning to work out details of configuration and access pays off in saved time in the long run.

Speed

One of Java's greatest strengths is the Java Virtual Machine (JVM), which was discussed in Chapter 1, "What Is Java?". When a Java applet is compiled, it is translated into a binary file for a generic microprocessor (which means that the code is never platform-specific). When the applet is later run in a Java-enabled browser, the JVM interprets the applet code instruction by instruction and executes it.

The price of platform independence is speed. You can expect a Java applet to run 10 to 20 times slower than many equivalent programs on any given platform. Most programs you use are specifically compiled for that particular operating system or computer. Languages such as C allow programs to be optimized for speed on a per platform basis, so although you can't run the same program on a Macintosh that you can on a Windows 95 machine, you do gain speed on the platform the software was written for. Because Java applets aren't optimized for speed on each platform, they will generally run slower than an application that was written in a language like C. As a result, Java's usefulness is limited in speed-dependent applications like intensive graphics processing, large games, or any type of serious numeric processing.

This lack of speed might seem like a major drawback at first, but Java applets can prove to be quite useful in spite of their slowness. For example, Java applets can gain perceived speed by being smaller and more focused in the tasks they perform. Users often equate efficiency with speed and might choose a Java applet that gets the job done over a large applet bloated with features.

Overall though, it makes sense when first considering an applet you may want to write to think about whether it fits well into the context of what Java offers. For instance, it might make sense to embed an applet that allows the user to enter customer information into a database. However, you would not want to write a complex customer analysis tool that assembled marketing profiles and sales statistics in Java.

Limitations of Connections

One of the important things to keep in mind about standards like Java is that not only do you need to be concerned about restrictions imposed by the standard itself, but you also need to be concerned about restrictions imposed by various implementations of that standard. For example, in the Netscape Navigator, an applet can only open up a communications connection, or socket, back to the host that the applet was downloaded from. This setup prevents malicious applets from doing all sorts of nasty things such as trying to break into machines on your network by using your machine as a gateway or sending bogus mail to people that when traced back can be proven to come from your machine.

Unfortunately, this setup also means that some communications that you may find useful are not allowed, such as an interface to a multiuser 3-D environment or an embedded terminal applet. Keep in mind that these types of applets are possible, but the Web server and the actual game/chat/whatever server must be the same machine. For example, if you wanted to write a Java applet that functioned as an interface for Internet Relay Chat (IRC) (a very popular interactive chat application available on the Internet), you would not be able to contact any IRC server on the Internet (as current IRC programs do). Instead, you would have to contact an IRC server that was running on the same machine people downloaded your applet from. As you can see, that restriction doesn't prevent you from writing such an applet, but it does limit its functionality. Keep in mind that this restriction isn't a limitation of Java per se, but it is a restriction imposed by Netscape.

Security on the Net

Most of Java's limitations center around the justifiable concern for security on the Net. The ability to run programs over the Net is an extremely attractive proposition, but if Java were to get an early reputation for being an ideal way to distribute viruses and break security on remote machines, its popularity would decrease quickly.

In this vein, Java is, if anything, a bit paranoid in what it will and won't allow. It would be reasonable, for example, to allow users to grant permission to applets to contact outside hosts. For example, if you had a chat applet, you might want to give users the option of connecting to an outside chat server. Java could just ask permission before connecting to remote hosts as a matter of protocol, which would have the same effect as limiting the hosts Java can contact. However, adding such features would weaken the security slightly, and wherever there is a way to break security, someone will try. Providing such features would also involve working out a number of different implementations of security to deal with the variety of communications protocols and Web browsers available on the Net.

There's never any guarantee that something is perfectly safe, but the general consensus is that Java strikes a pretty good balance between paranoid restrictions and total freedom by allowing the implementations to determine just how much access the applet should have to other machines.

Whenever the issue of allowing users to download executable files to their local machines is discussed, the issue of viruses comes up. In the past, viruses have spread from pre-packaged software, from bulletin boards offering software for users to download, and from users exchanging software. So the transmission of viruses is a valid concern when discussing the downloading of Java applets off the Web. As stated earlier, Java's developers decided that the best way to deal with this issue was to prevent applets from accessing the file system on users' machines. This decision means that Java applets are completely incapable of transferring a virus to your machine. Yes, this decision affects the power of applets and their flexibility, but faced with the choice of adding flexibility or releasing a product that could spread computer viruses around the world willy-nilly, the Sun engineers opted for the security, and users are thankful. Overall, Java provides robust security while still allowing for innovation—a combination that serves the user community best.

Standalone Applications

Although Java's capability to produce applets has gotten almost all the attention (and is of course the main focus of this book), Java has many more capabilities. An applet is just one type of program that Java can generate. Java can just as easily generate a standalone application that doesn't require a browser to function but is run on the machine like any other program.

The differences between applets and applications are more philosophical than physical. For example, contrast a spreadsheet with a loan calculator. A loan calculator is essentially a spreadsheet with a very specific function: to calculate the total costs of a loan and monthly payments. You can look at these two programs as an applet (the loan calculator) and an application (the full spreadsheet). From a programming standpoint, the loan calculator is significantly easier to program because it has a predefined, small number of functions, it requires less functionality, and it has a smaller user interface. The finished versions of both programs will have drastic differences in memory requirements. The spreadsheet application will require more RAM to operate because it can perform more tasks. Whereas the spreadsheet might require a megabyte (or more) of RAM, the loan calculator might only require 100K of RAM because it has a fixed number of elements and performs limited functions. Size is also important: a full spreadsheet application might take up 1M or more, and a loan calculator might take up only 350 to 500K. When you are waiting for both of these programs to download over the Web, the advantage of a smaller size program is obvious. So if you are adding a well-defined service to a Web page, applets offer many advantages over applications. Although applets might not offer the same level of flexibility, they do allow the integration of specialized functions into a very distributable medium, the World Wide Web.

Because an application runs outside of a Web browser, it has pretty much complete access to the local system. It can read and write files and connect to any desired host. If you want, you can even write a Web HTTP server in Java—Java is that general of a programming language.

When you program applications, native methods are a built-in way to get around Java being relatively slow. If you find a portion of your program is running too slowly, you can use native methods to translate it to C and then compile and access it directly from your Java program. You can expect that portion of your program to speed up by 10 to 20 times after this procedure. Because Java is considerably easier to program in than C, this feature is a tremendous advantage. You convert only the parts of the program that absolutely require the speed. Although native methods would be a great way to speed up an applet, there is not currently a way to have a browser automatically download them, mainly for security reasons (because the code would be native to the machine, it could contain viruses that Java would have no way of detecting).

The ability to produce applications may not seem to be a big deal right now, but it's nice to know that if an applet grows to be a size that you feel it would make a worthwhile application, you can convert it without having to start from scratch or rewrite it in another language.

The Future of Java

Because Java is a relatively new addition to the Internet, you may be wondering what the future of Java might have in store. Now that you have an understanding of what Java can and cannot do, the following sections provide a glimpse at what the future has in store for Java.

New Development Tools

Java is currently in the 1.0 release. Many enhancements and improvements must be made before Java can be considered a major development platform. Many programming languages begin as text-based languages. You write the programs using plain ASCII text, and the programs run in a text mode, with text-based interfaces and text output. From this point, graphical user interfaces (GUIs) are often added. GUIs allow a more natural interaction with programs, making them more user-friendly and accessible to the average computer user.

Just as you would add a GUI to make your programs more friendly, many programming languages have begun to add GUIs as well. If you have ever done any development with a package such as Delphi or Visual Basic, you have probably seen this kind of programming interface. These graphics-based programming interfaces are called Integrated Development Environments (IDEs). For any programming language, an IDE can help make programming easier. To understand how an IDE might improve Java, look at the current text-based methods for programming with Java:

1. You write a program using a text editor of your choice. Some editors are better at handling the nuances of code than others, but you manage to get your code finished.

2. You run the code through the Java compiler. If you were working in a dream world, the code would compile without problems, but in reality, the compiler spits out a list of bugs in your code. You have to either write down, print out, or otherwise keep track of the bugs, and go back into your text editor to fix them.

3. Having fixed the bugs (or so you think), you compile the code again. If everything has been corrected, you are ready to run the code. If not, repeat Step 2.

4. You run the code. There aren't any bugs, but things don't run exactly the way you had planned. Go back to Step 1.

As you can see, this process can become rather involved and quite long. With an IDE, the process might be like the following:

1. Using a Java editor you create your code, and then click a Compile button.

2. The compiler highlights possible errors in your code, and you can fix them in your editing window. Each time, you can try compiling without ever leaving the editor.

3. When the bugs are fixed, the IDE automatically runs the code for you. Now you can see how your applet is running and fix errors in the edit window.

As you can see, an IDE can provide valuable programming tools, such as an editor with features designed around the language you are using and a built-in compiler and run-time environment, so you can have all of your programming components available at once. IDEs often have many debugging features and some advanced features like automatic backups and version tracking. Two good examples of current IDEs are Symantec's Café (see Figure 2.7) and JavaWeb (see Figure 2.8).

Figure 2.7.

Symantec's Café, an Integrated Development Environment for Java, extends the existing C++ package.

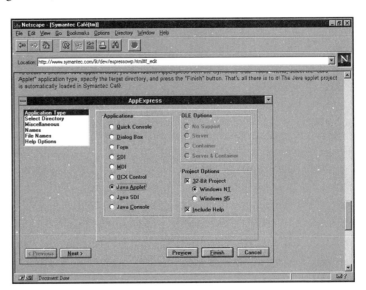

Currently Java development is all done at the command line. There is not a specialized Java editor, and the appletviewer is not a full-featured run-time environment. But several beta Java IDEs are available on the Web now, including the following:

- Symantec Café
  http://cafe.symantec.com/index.html
- JavaWeb IDE
  http://insureNetUSA.com/javaIDE.html
- Café Carouser
  http://www.coastside.net/stratum/
- JavaMaker
  http://net.info.samsung.co.kr/~hcchoi/javamaker.html
- FIDE
  http://amber.wpi.edu/~thethe/Documents/Besiex/Java/FrIJDE.html

Figure 2.8.
The JavaWeb Integrated Development Environment is based on a Web interface that allows you to interact with and code Java through your Web browser.

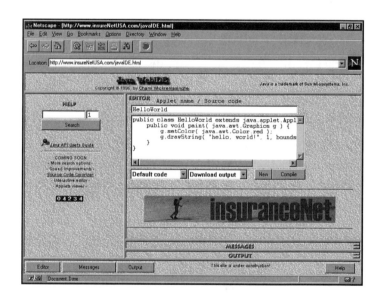

In addition to these early IDEs, many large development companies have licensed Java from Sun and are making plans to incorporate Java into their own development environments. Some of these companies, such as Borland and MetroWerks, have a great deal of experience in development tools, and some great Java products are likely to be available in the near future.

Increasing Speed

Because the bytecode for Java is not machine-specific, Java often encounters problems with speed. The code is not optimized for any specific platform, so performance suffers across the board. Consequently, Sun has already begun to plan a run-time compiler to help optimize Java's speed.

The run-time compiler, called the Just-in-Time Compiler, basically allows you to download Java code and recompile it using native code on the machine you are using to increase speed. However, the JIT Compiler does have a major drawback: compile time. Because the JIT is a compiler, it takes time to actually compile the code. For smaller applets, this amount of time might not be a big deal, but for complicated applets, the compile time might be significant. The recompiled version of the software might execute faster, but the increased time it takes to compile the program can be a significant trade-off.

The Just-in-Time Compiler is not the only new compiler in the works. Several other companies are hard at work producing compilers of their own. Some of these compilers will be geared to optimizing code like JIT, and others may even be server-side compilers that compile optimized code before downloading.

Integrating with Other Applications

Another method for gaining speed discussed earlier in this chapter is native methods. Using a C or C++ native method in conjunction with an applet can greatly increase the speed of applets. Access to native methods or cross-compilers might be available in the future to help you increase the performance of your applets even more.

You could even string together collections of applets to create larger and more detailed applets or applications. With some scripting tools such as JavaScript, you could squeeze even more mileage out of applets by using JavaScript to glue them together to produce a larger, more complete program without having to write more Java code.

Automatic Applet Updates

One of the most difficult issues facing companies that have software deployed throughout their organizations is keeping the versions of that software constant throughout the organization. This task is not easy because it requires that a new version of the software be downloaded on a regular basis. If some people forget to update their software regularly, the situation can become confusing.

Java applets circumvent this problem by being downloaded over the network automatically every time they need to be run. The applet can be updated on the server whenever needed, and when users execute the applet, they will automatically get the latest version.

JavaScript

One of the most promising advances in Java looming on the horizon is JavaScript. JavaScript had its humble beginnings at Netscape as LiveScript, a language designed to bring scripting to the World Wide Web. Today, much of JavaScript is still based on LiveScript, and the ability to script applets is still in the future. But the promise of scriptable applets is very appealing to many Web designers.

The idea behind the JavaScript scripting language is the ability to manipulate Web objects and Java objects without using a high-level programming language. JavaScript would enable users to customize applets and even control how applets function or the environment in which they execute. JavaScript could also be a powerful tool for scripting Java objects together rather than using them in code.

Well-designed objects can function as applet components, and JavaScript could allow these components to be combined without programming. This capability would be very appealing because programming in Java is by no means trivial, and JavaScript has been designed from the ground up to be programmable by the average user. Thus, an applet that allows a color to be chosen from a list could be a part of a larger script that implements an on-line store.

In its current stages, JavaScript is limited to scripting various Web and browser functions. Making applets work with JavaScript will involve development of both Java and JavaScript. JavaScript will need to have accepted methods for controlling and customizing applets. The Java language will also need to incorporate methods for passing control and communicating with JavaScript scripts. The promise of flexibility and ease of use will drive developers toward these goals, but implementation might have to wait until later versions.

Cosmo

Anyone creating or using Java applets will notice that the graphics capabilities of Java, while commendable, are somewhat limited. Java includes a number of graphics methods that allow you to create some interesting graphics, but in today's multimedia world, many potential uses for Java would be much easier to program with an expanded graphics toolkit. Cosmo is designed to be that toolkit.

In order to produce a higher level of graphics using Java, Sun has embarked on a partnership with Silicon Graphics (SGI), the industry's graphics specialists. The project has been named Cosmo and promises to include some interesting developments in Java and high-performance, 3-D graphics.

Cosmo includes special 3-D libraries, a motion engine, and media libraries designed to add video, audio, and other multimedia functions to Java applets. Unfortunately, use of Cosmo is currently limited to the SGI platform, but development in this area of Java is sure to continue. Cosmo is currently available in a beta version from `http://www.sgi.com/Products/cosmo/code/`.

The Java "Real" Machine?

All the possible advances mentioned so far have been based around software enhancements. However, Java was originally conceived to be integrated into consumer electronics, and Sun is still pursuing some of those options.

On the hardware side of Java development is JavaChips. These are a series of chips that are based on the Sparc line already produced by Sun. The JavaChips will be modified versions of Sparc chips designed to run code from the Java Virtual Machine. Sun has already begun showing demonstrations of the chips and potential products and plans a variety of hardware uses for Java.

Sun is planning to release JavaChips in three versions, each customized for a different application: a low-end chip for consumer electronics, a midrange chip for handheld devices, and a high-end chip for desktop machines. Sun has also shown prototypes of Java terminals. These mini-machines would have ethernet cards, monitors, and keyboards to enable you to interact with Java programs over a local-area network or the Internet. The advantage of using a Java terminal would be increased speed and much lower cost than traditional desktop computers. Sun is competing with other companies racing to cash in on a potential Net terminal market, so the future of Java might just include some new computing machinery.

Summary

This chapter has shown you the promises of Java. You've looked at how Java stands to change the way people use the World Wide Web. You've seen how Java applets can enhance Web pages with new interactive design and increased functionality.

You've also looked at the structure of Java applets from a user's point of view. This chapter covered the differences between applets designed for functionality and applications designed for flexibility. You've also looked at some of the security issues surrounding Java and the applets and have seen some of the things that lurk on the Java horizon.

Now it's time to get to the nitty-gritty Java world. The following chapters take you through all of the essential components you'll need to start adding applets to your Web pages. The discussion of applets and their uses continues in the next few chapters, which also talk about the methods for using applets and various Java browsers available on the Net. The following chapters also talk about some applets available on the Web and point you to some Java resources. Chapter 6 examines design issues, and Chapter 7 deals with the Java Developer's Kit. Then you'll get into Java programming. Before you know it, you'll be creating your own Java applets!

Using Java

CHAPTER 3

Java Browsers

In order to view Java applets, either a Java-capable browser or an application specifically written to run applets is required. Three programs currently fall into this category:

- HotJava, Sun's original "proof of concept" Java-capable browser
- appletviewer, the "official" way to view applets
- Netscape Navigator, the first commercial Java-capable browser

This chapter explores the capabilities and restrictions of all three of these Java environments. Java allows a great deal of latitude in deciding how much extensibility and security is necessary, and each of these programs takes a different approach.

HotJava

When Sun decided to target Java at the World Wide Web through applets, it needed a Java-capable Web browser as a prototype to work with. This prototype was necessary to prove that Sun's hope of being able to run programs in Web pages was a realistic possibility. HotJava was the result and became a surprisingly good browser (see Figure 3.1).

Figure 3.1.
The HotJava browser.

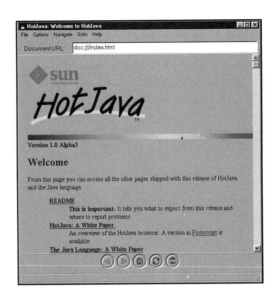

Java's Java Browser

One of the most impressive things about HotJava is the fact that it is almost entirely written in Java. Java has a somewhat undeserved reputation for being slow and limited in its capabilities. HotJava shows that Java is more than capable of producing high-quality applications that run reasonably well.

For the most part, HotJava looks and functions much like a typical Web browser. It has most of the expected features that other modern browsers have, such as hotlists, the ability to show sources, and the ability to set up proxies. For a browser originally meant solely as a showcase for Java, HotJava is surprisingly usable for general Web browsing.

HotJava is meant to display Java applets, and that area is where it really shines (see Figure 3.2). Most other Java browsers give the impression that Java was tacked on as an afterthought, but HotJava was built around Java from the beginning—and it shows. HotJava starts up quickly and runs applets more smoothly than other browsers.

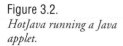

Figure 3.2.
HotJava running a Java applet.

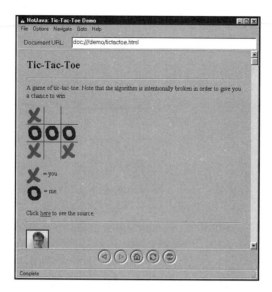

Feature-Rich and Flexible

HotJava is special because it sees Java not just as a way to run applets inside a Web browser; it aims to make the core browser much simpler by not having much built into it and having the browser download new "intelligence" when necessary. This design makes HotJava much more flexible than other browsers because it makes the browser itself very simple and open to change.

How is this flexibility achieved? In addition to applets, which HotJava refers to as Interactive Content, HotJava also contains two other innovations: dynamic content types and protocols.

Dynamic Content Types and Protocols

Most Web browsers directly support a limited number of ways to communicate over the network and file types that they understand. Moreover, most browsers' capabilities are set in stone from the beginning (see Figure 3.3), much like an all-in-one stereo system that has features you like, but no way to add new ones. Unfortunately, this means that when one browser starts supporting a new type before others, there is a period of time when other browsers do not support that type.

This kind of situation occurred when Netscape Navigator started supporting inline JPEG files before other browsers of the time (such as Mosaic). Before this time, people needed an external viewer to view a JPEG picture. Because Navigator was so popular, many people started using inline JPEGs, which would show up as broken links on browsers other than Netscape Navigator.

Figure 3.3.
*Most browsers have a
fixed amount of
functionality.*

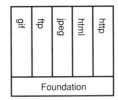

HotJava is more like a component stereo system where pieces can be attached and detached at will. HotJava aims to make sure that users never have to upgrade their browsers again just to support a new capability. When HotJava encounters a content type (picture, animation, and so on) or protocol (a way to transmit information) that it doesn't understand, it reconfigures itself to be able to work with that type (see Figure 3.4). HotJava reconfigures itself by first scanning the page it just received to find out whether the page contains anything that it cannot understand. If the page does contain something that's not understandable, HotJava then asks whether the server has the Java code to enable it to decode the content it does not understand. If the server does have the code, HotJava downloads it and integrates it to add this functionality.

When it comes to the Web (and any technology in general), predicting the future is difficult, but you can be sure of one thing: there will always be new protocols and content types. HotJava adapts itself to these changes instead of forcing users to repeatedly install new versions of the software.

Figure 3.4.
*HotJava can reconfigure
itself to handle new
functionality.*

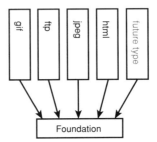

Configuration

One drawback to HotJava is that although it's very good at reconfiguring itself to respond to new and changing environments, it doesn't have a tremendous amount of configurability from the user's perspective.

The basics are available (see Figure 3.5); users can define proxies and default write and read directories on the hard drive. Most importantly, users can delay images or applets from loading if they are running HotJava over a slow network link. Unfortunately, many of the configuration options that are normally expected are missing, such as the capability to modify the appearance of the screen by changing fonts and colors and the capability to control how links are displayed.

This overall lack of configurability is a huge drawback compared to other browsers. Netscape Navigator, for instance, lets you configure almost every aspect of the way it works, even down to what colors to show Web links in. For HotJava to ever be considered a serious browser, it needs major improvements in this area.

Figure 3.5.
Configuring HotJava.

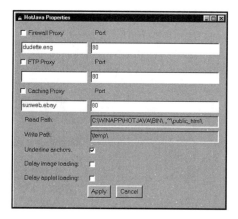

Security

One of the main issues with security in Java is what machines an applet should be able to connect to in order to transmit and receive information. Many Java applets will involve some sort of communication with other machines on the Internet. If an applet were allowed to communicate with any machine it wanted to, major security problems would result.

Still, it is often desirable to allow an applet to communicate with other machines. For instance, if you had a stock ticker applet that displayed current stock prices, it would make sense to allow it to check back for updated prices on a regular basis.

HotJava allows users to specify which machines (also called hosts) the applet can communicate with. The user can select one of four options (see Figure 3.6):

- No Access means the applet cannot connect to any host.
- Applet Host means the applet can connect only to the machine it came from.
- Firewall means the applet can connect only to hosts outside of your firewall (if one is configured).
- Unrestricted means the applet can connect to any host it wishes.

For most situations, the Applet Host option makes the most sense. However, if you have serious concerns about security, make No Access the standard choice and make exceptions when needed. For example, if you are running Java applets inside of a corporation, you might have concerns about a rogue applet somehow transmitting sensitive information outside of the company. To ensure that this situation doesn't happen, you might choose the No Access option so applets cannot contact any hosts at all.

In any circumstance, think carefully before allowing the applet Unrestricted access to any other machine on the network. This means that the entire Internet is wide open to connect to whatever the applet wishes.

Figure 3.6.
Setting security options in HotJava.

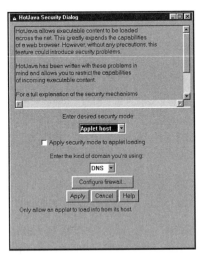

Sun's Commitment to HotJava

HotJava was the centerpiece of Sun's promotion of Java for quite a while and until early Fall 1995 was synonymous with Java. It was generally accepted that HotJava was the platform on which the majority of applets would run. Shortly after Sun moved from the Alpha version to the Beta 1 version of Java, however, Netscape released a version of their browser that supported Java as well. Unfortunately, Sun did not release another version of HotJava through the entire beta test of Java, nor had it been updated by the time of the official 1.0 release of Java. This situation is especially unfortunate because the version of HotJava available as of this writing will not execute current applets, only those written in the older Alpha version of the language.

Since Netscape has taken the lead in writing browsers that are Java-capable, Sun seems to have decided to focus its energies elsewhere. Although this change in focus is understandable, it is also unfortunate as HotJava was quite promising. Hopefully, Sun will continue developing HotJava, but for now it seems to have been relegated to obscurity.

Availability

HotJava is available via FTP at `ftp.javasoft.com` in the `/pub` directory. There are currently versions available for Windows 95, Windows NT, and Solaris 2.x.

appletviewer

The appletviewer, included in the Java Developer's Kit, is the bare-bones way to run and test applets (see Figure 3.7). It makes no pretense of trying to be a browser; all it does is run applets. That said, you may be wondering why you would ever need to use the appletviewer instead of Netscape Navigator or another Java-capable browser. There are two circumstances in which the appletviewer is a useful tool: applet development and standards testing.

Figure 3.7.
*The Java Developer's
Kit's appletviewer.*

First, when developing applets, the amount of time required to start up the appletviewer is much less than the time required to launch a full-featured browser. During development, you might want to test your applet many times, and the time saved by using the appletviewer can be substantial.

Second, it always makes sense to check your applets with the appletviewer to make sure that they are compatible with standard Java. In a perfect world, all versions of Java would be identical, but as more and more companies integrate Java into their products, there is bound to be some deviation. Using the appletviewer ensures that you are not relying on one of those deviations.

Special Capabilities

As mentioned before, the appletviewer is pretty basic. However, it does have one very nice feature. By selecting Tag in the Applet menu, you can get the correct <APPLET> tag for the running applet, even after resizing the applet (see Figure 3.8). This feature is invaluable when you're trying to figure out how large to make your applets. The <APPLET> tag is discussed in detail in Chapter 6, "Java-Enhanced Page Design."

The appletviewer also can reload an applet as if it were being loaded for the first time, whereas most Java-capable browsers only allow the applet to be started and stopped.

Figure 3.8.
*Getting the HTML tag
for an applet.*

Configuration

You can set four properties in the appletviewer: the HTTP proxy server, the firewall proxy server, the applet's ability to connect to hosts, and the applet's ability to access other areas of Java code. To change these properties, select Properties from the Applet menu (see Figure 3.9).

Figure 3.9.
*Configuring
appletviewer.*

Security

The appletviewer has a security setup very similar to HotJava, with one exception. The appletviewer omits the option that allows applets to connect only to hosts that are outside the firewall, although the appletviewer does allow configuration to work behind a firewall.

Availability

The appletviewer is included with the Java Developer's Kit (see Chapter 7, "The Java Developer's Kit").

Netscape Navigator

Although there is a bit of sorrow at Sun's apparent neglect of HotJava, the amount of credibility that Netscape's licensing of Java in August 1995 gave to Java is almost incalculable. Until then, Java had been generally seen as an interesting sideshow, but the integration of Java into Netscape Navigator placed it firmly in the Web mainstream.

Netscape Navigator 2.0 (see Figure 3.10), released in February 1996, is the first version to support Java. It went through a public beta test for several months and appears to be quite stable. It is unquestionably the most feature-rich browser currently available. In addition to providing support for Java, it integrates support for JavaScript (see Appendix B, "JavaScript and Java Language Reference"), a general standard for Plug-Ins (programs that extend the functionality of Navigator), and the addition of frames (which allow the main browser window to be split into multiple partitions).

Figure 3.10.
The Netscape Navigator browser.

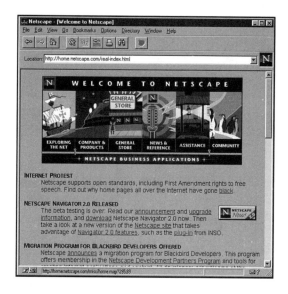

Unlike HotJava, which was designed around Java from the very beginning, Java support was integrated into Navigator after it was already a solid and shipping product. Thus, Java doesn't feel quite as integral in Navigator as it does in HotJava. (For example, Navigator lacks HotJava's ability to automatically reconfigure itself to handle new types of content.) However, this seems to be a small price to pay to have Java alongside all of Navigator's other numerous capabilities.

Also, Netscape has clearly taken a major role in the ongoing development of Java. The JavaScript scripting language was originally developed by Netscape under the name LiveScript and was later renamed and jointly released by Sun and Netscape. It seems that the leading proponent of Java outside of Sun will be Netscape for the foreseeable future, and that Navigator should stay at the forefront of Java-capable browsers.

JavaScript is a simple scripting language that allows small programs to be added within a Web page (see Figure 3.11). Although similar in purpose to Java, JavaScript is meant for smaller tasks such as validating that correct information was entered into a form (by making sure that numbers instead of characters are entered into a form that expects numbers, for example). Eventually, JavaScript will be able to directly control Java applets and make them work together, but this capability is not available in version 2.0 of Navigator.

Figure 3.11.
A JavaScript program.

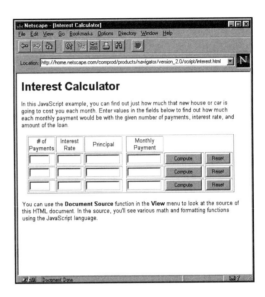

Special Capabilities

Navigator attempts to seamlessly add basic support for Java applets into Web pages and does an admirable job. While applets are loading, a light gray box indicates where the applet will appear, and a report of the applets starting and stopping appears in the status bar (see Figure 3.12).

Figure 3.12.
Netscape loading an applet.

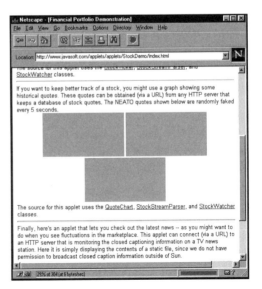

If you want to see any information that the applet may be sending to the Java Console (things like debugging data, information on the current state of the applet, and so on), choose the Show Java Console command under the Options menu. This command displays a window that shows any console output (see Figure 3.13). The Java Console allows programs to output simple text for debugging information. This capability is important because applets are by their nature graphic, and it would be difficult to relay this information any other way.

Figure 3.13.
Netscape's Java Console.

Although Navigator does not include many of the automatic integration features of HotJava, it does have support for most current protocols, and version 2.0 has added support for electronic mail and a much-improved Usenet newsreader. With the addition of all these features, the ability of a browser to reconfigure itself seems less important. Moreover, Netscape has conditioned users to upgrade their browsers to the new version on a regular basis anyway, to the point where many people see it as a normal and expected occurrence.

Netscape did not attempt to add many additional special Java-related capabilities to Navigator, and in many ways this a good thing. Java is seamlessly integrated into Navigator—you don't even know it is there until an applet appears.

However, one new capability that has been announced is enabling JavaScript to use Java applets. Because JavaScript is much simpler than Java, this capability will let people who do not have the time to learn Java use applets that have already been written by scripting them. For instance, a JavaScript script could use a Java applet that lets you pick a style of a car and then give the price of the car. This capability would be advantageous because learning to program Java is nontrivial, whereas JavaScript has been designed to be programmed by the end user. Although not available in version 2.0, the capability to script applets has been announced for the next release of Navigator.

Imposing New Standards

Even before Netscape adopted Java, it contributed a great deal to the advancement of the World Wide Web. Netscape has been on the leading edge of adding new features to its browser and has contributed extensions to HTML. For instance, Netscape was responsible for bringing both tables and frames to the Web, which are two of the most appreciated additions to HTML. Unfortunately, there is also a growing sense that Netscape feels free to do things in a proprietary manner in order to make its browser more attractive to users. This strategy has worked well for Netscape, but there is always the danger that it will go too far.

Up to this point, Netscape has remained pretty faithful to the Java standard without adding functionality that applets can access only on the Netscape browser. If this fact changes in the future, you may see Java applets that have messages next to them stating, "Works best with Netscape Navigator," as seen in many current Web pages. For better or for worse, Netscape Navigator is the standard on the Web and is the default choice for anyone who wants to browse the Web.

Configuration

Netscape Navigator is easily the most configurable of any current browser; it allows users to configure almost every aspect of the browser. For example, users can fine-tune how pages are displayed, including the language to display them in. Four distinct areas are customizable in Netscape Navigator through their respective menu items:

- The General Preferences dialog box (see Figure 3.14) lets the user choose how pages will look (by choosing fonts, colors, how images are displayed, and so on), what foreign languages the browser should recognize, and what external programs should be set up as helper applications (for new sound formats, graphics formats, and so on).

- The Mail & News Preferences dialog box (see Figure 3.15) allows the user to choose how the browser will interact with both electronic mail and Usenet news. Most importantly, the identity of the user can be configured, and the servers to use for electronic mail and news can be set up.

- A user can configure three main options through the Network Preferences dialog box (see Figure 3.16). First, the user can set the amount of cache. A *cache* is used to store images and text that have already been loaded once to keep from having to load them again. Second, the user can configure the maximum number of network connections. The more connections that are set up, the more images and text can be brought in at once, but also the slower they come in. Finally, the user can configure proxies. A *proxy* allows network connections through a firewall.

Figure 3.14.
*Netscape General
Preferences dialog box.*

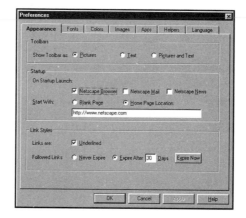

Figure 3.15.
*Netscape's Mail & News
Preferences dialog box.*

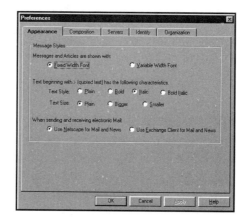

Figure 3.16.
*Netscape's Network
Preferences dialog box.*

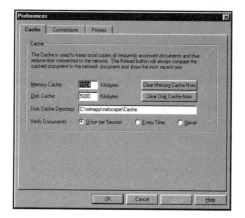

■ The Security Preferences dialog box (see Figure 3.17) is mainly concerned with whether to show alerts when loading a document that could be insecure and setting up site certificates (a *site certificate* is a way to verify that the server you are talking to is who it says it is). A user also can enable or disable Java in this dialog box. This feature is covered in the next section.

Figure 3.17.
Netscape's Security
Preferences dialog box.

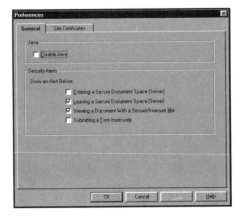

Security

Netscape has prided itself on security for quite a while. When Netscape announced Java would be integrated into Navigator, there was a great deal of concern that Java would cause security problems. Netscape has gone to great pains to make sure that doesn't happen by limiting what applets are allowed to do.

Unlike HotJava, where the user can choose a variety of Java applet security modes, Navigator 2.0 only has one option: disable or enable Java (see Figure 3.17). Note that there is no way to set what machines an applet is allowed to communicate with. Navigator allows an applet to communicate only with the server that the applet was downloaded from (the HTML server that provided the page on which the applet resides).

Unlike HotJava, you cannot set up Netscape Navigator to only connect to machines outside your firewall. More importantly, you cannot configure Navigator to not allow applets to communicate with other machines at all. With Navigator, Java is an all-or-nothing proposition. This is expected to change in later versions of Navigator, but Netscape has not outlined exactly how.

Netscape Navigator has another level of built-in security called Secure Sockets Layer (SSL). SSL is a way for Web sites to ensure that the communication that has transpired between the Web site and your machine has not been tampered with. Netscape has been a leader in this area, mainly due to the desire to facilitate electronic commerce.

Availability

Netscape Navigator is available via FTP at `ftp.netscape.com` in the `/pub/2.0` directory (the most current version can always be found in `/pub/netscape`). Java-capable versions are available for the following platforms:

Windows 95
Windows NT
Solaris 2
Dec Alpha OSF2
HP PA-Risc HPUX
Linux
386BSD
SGI Irix
IBM AIX
SunOS 4

Versions without Java are currently available for Windows 3.1 and Apple Macintosh, but Java-capable versions for these products should be available in the near future.

Summary

This chapter discussed all the currently available ways to view Java applets. HotJava holds a great deal of promise, but it seems as though Sun has lost interest in it. The appletviewer is really only useful for development in Java. Netscape Navigator currently holds the distinction of being the most useful Java-enabled Web browser. Its high level of configurability and numerous features make it the obvious choice.

This status could change, however, in the not-too-distant future. Microsoft has recently challenged Netscape's dominance of the Web browser market with the release of its Internet Explorer. In December 1995, Microsoft announced an intent to license Java, fueling speculation that they would soon be incorporating it into their browser. In addition, Spyglass, a company that provides Web browser technology for more than 45 companies who embed the technology in more than 120 products, has licensed Java. These developments should make the Java-enabled Web browser market very interesting for a long time to come.

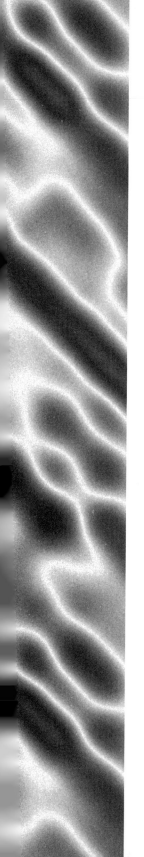

CHAPTER 4

Java's Capabilities

As discussed previously, Java is a full-featured programming language that is capable of producing full-featured standalone applications. However, the innovations that Java brings to the World Wide Web have created the most interest in Java. This chapter focuses on the ways in which applets can enhance Web pages.

Applets can add a variety of enhancements to any Web page, from a personal page to a business page. Within the restrictions placed on applets by browsers and security, you can create astounding applets. Applets can bring sound, animation, user interaction, and much more to your Web pages.

Visually Enhancing Pages (And Sound Too!)

The Web has come a long way since 1992. Now graphics are very common (and sometimes a bit annoying). With the release of Netscape, server-push animation became possible, although it was slow

and awkward. This server-push animation is not practical for animations of any significant length and has never really been used for much other than novelty purposes. But with
Java, the possibility for real-time animations is a reality.

Visual enhancements are some of the simplest applets to program and use. Often these
applets are simply variations of image viewers, but you can create surprisingly different
applets using the techniques required to make an image viewer. For example, the following applets can be created by displaying and manipulating images:

- A clock
- A applet to create an interactive demonstration
- An interactive animation
- A photo viewer

All these types of applets use image techniques: the clock moves hands to display the time,
a demonstration applet shows diagrams, an animator flips a series of images for motion,
and a photo viewer cycles through snapshots. All these applets contain a lot of similar code,
yet all accomplish different tasks. The following sections examine some of these applets
and how they enhance the appearance of Web pages.

Clock Applets

The Web is a global entity and is certainly not limited to any specific geographic area or
time zone. In fact, the global aspect of the Web is one of its most appealing factors. Java
applets can help enhance the global nature of the Web.

Many Web pages have begun to incorporate snapshots of the weather outside or other forms
of local information. Silly as it may seem, the local time is one of the most basic forms of
local information and can be a very useful navigation device. The following Java clocks
can be used to show time information on your Web page:

Clock
Written by Nils Hedström
`http://www-und.ida.liu.se/~d94nilhe/java/applets.html`

WorldClock
Written by Vijay Vaidy
`http://www.webpage.com/~vijay/java/wt/testwt.html`

The first clock uses graphic images to draw the hands of an analog clock (see Figure 4.1).
The second clock has no graphic enhancements and displays the time and date information using text (see Figure 4.2).

Figure 4.1.
*A clock is an example of
an informative applet.*

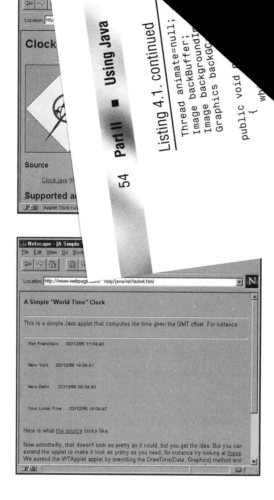

Listing 4.1. continued

```
Thread animate=null;
Image backBuffer;
Image backgroundIm
Graphics backGC

public void
    {
    wh
```

Figure 4.2.
*A simple clock applet
showing times at various
locations around the
world.*

Listing 4.1 shows some of the Java code used to produce the clock in Figure 4.1.

Listing 4.1. Partial code for the Clock applet.

```
public class Clock extends java.applet.Applet implements Runnable
{
    int width,height,num_lines,sleep,timezone,backgroundType;
    Polygon clockBackground;
    URL homepage;
    private Needle hour,minute,second;
    double pi=3.1415926535f;
    Color
clockBackground_col,clockBackgroundBorder_col,backgroundBorder_col,background_col;
```

continues

```
                   age;

            un() //Run the applet

    le (true)
       {
          updateNeedles();
          repaint();
          try {Thread.sleep(sleep);} catch (InterruptedException e){}

       }
   }
public void makeClockBackground() // Creates a polygon-background with num_lines-
corners
   {
      double add,count;
      clockBackground=new Polygon();
      add=2.*pi/num_lines;
      for(count=0;count<=2.*pi;count+=add)
         {
            clockBackground.addPoint(size().width/
2+(int)(size().width*Math.cos(count)/2.),
                         size().height/2+(int)(size().height*Math.sin(count)/2.));
         }
   }

  public void drawClockBackground(Graphics g) // Draws the background of the Clock
    {
      if(backgroundType!=1)
         {
           g.setColor(clockBackground_col);
           g.fillPolygon(clockBackground);
           g.setColor(clockBackgroundBorder_col);
           g.drawPolygon(clockBackground);
         }
      if(backgroundType!=0)
         {
           int img_width=backgroundImage.getWidth(null);
           int img_height=backgroundImage.getHeight(null);
           int x=(size().width-img_width)/2;
           int y=(size().height-img_height)/2;
           if (x<0) x=0;
           if(y<0) y=0;
           if((img_width!=-1) && (img_height!=-1))
             g.drawImage(backgroundImage,x,y,null);
         }

    }

  public void start()  // When the applet is started
    {
      if (animate == null) {
        animate = new Thread(this);
        animate.start();
```

```
      }
  }

public void stop()  // When the applet is stopped
  {
    if (animate != null) {
      animate.stop();
      animate=null;
    }
  }
```

A clock applet requires quite a bit of code. Listing 4.1 shows only a third of the code needed to produce the entire clock shown in Figure 4.1. The applet developer must also provide the images used to make up the clock face and hands and the animation that keeps the hands moving and keeping accurate time. The code shown in Listing 4.1 should give you an idea about what's involved in creating Java applets. Java applets are full-fledged programs, and as such, they require some time and planning to create.

Juggling Applet

Applets can also be used for educational purposes or to inform users about how to accomplish tasks by means of demonstration. Rather than just listing a number of steps, applets can visually demonstrate how to do something. For some topics, a visual demonstration is far more effective than a verbal explanation. The following applet is an example of how you can use graphics and animation to demonstrate concepts (see Figure 4.3):

> Juggling Applet
> Written by Christopher Sequin
> `http://www.acm.uiuc.edu/webmonkeys/juggling/`

Figure 4.3.
*The Juggling Applet is
an example of how
applets can be used for
interactive educational
purposes.*

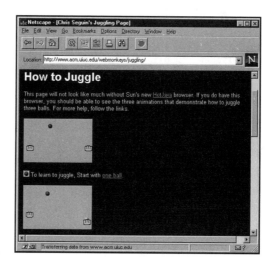

Listing 4.2 shows the code for the Juggling Applet. Keep in mind that this code does quite a bit. It lets the user configure the number of balls used in the demonstration, it animates the hands, and it animates the balls along the correct paths. Don't worry about compiling this code, the applet is included on the CD-ROM. The listing is just provided to give you an example of some real Java code.

Listing 4.2. Code for the Juggling Applet.

```
/*
 * @(#)Juggling.java                        1.0f 95/05/01 Chris Seguin
 * E-mail:  seguin@uiuc.edu
 *
 * Copyright (c) 1995 University of Illinois (UIUC)
 */

import java.io.InputStream;
import java.awt.*;
import java.net.*;

/**
 * JugglingImages class. This is a container for a list
 * of images that are animated.
 *
 * @author      Chris Seguin
 * @version     1.0f, May 1, 1995
 */
class JugglingImages {
    /**
     * The images.
     */
    Image imgs[];

    /**
     * The number of images actually loaded.
     */
    int nImagesCount = 0;

    /**
     * Load the images, from dir. The images are assumed to be
     * named T1.gif, T2.gif...
     */
    JugglingImages(URL context, String dir, Juggling parent) {

        nImagesCount = 0;
        imgs = new Image[10];
        int nWidth = 0;

        for (int i = 1; i < imgs.length; i++) {

            Image im = parent.getImage(parent.getDocumentBase(),
                                dir + "/T" + i + ".gif");

            imgs[nImagesCount++] = im;
        }
    }
}
```

```java
/**
 * BallPaths class. This is a container for a path
 * of juggling balls
 *
 * @author      Chris Seguin
 * @version     1.0f, May 1, 1995
 */
class BallPaths {

    /**
     * Arrays containing the path of the balls
     */
    int pnX[] = {0};
    int pnY[] = {0};

    int nLength = 1;

    /**
     * LookupX - looks up the appropriate value of X
     */
    public int LookupX (int nIndex)
    {
    if ((nIndex > nLength) || (nIndex < 0))
        return 0;

    return pnX[nIndex];
    }

    /**
     * LookupY - looks up the appropriate value of Y
     */
    public int LookupY (int nIndex)
    {
    if ((nIndex > nLength) || (nIndex < 0))
        return 0;

    return pnY[nIndex];
    }

    /**
     * Length - the number of data points stored in the path
     */
    public int Length ()
    {
    return nLength;
    }
}


/**
 * CascadeBallPaths class. This is a container for a path
 * of juggling balls, the balls are moving in a standard
 * cascade pattern
 *
 * @author      Chris Seguin
 * @version     1.0f, May 1, 1995
 */
class CascadeBallPaths extends BallPaths {
```

continues

Listing 4.2. continued

```java
/**
 * Arrays containing the path of the balls
 */
int pnX[] = {       20,   24,   27,   31,   35,
                    40,   45,   50,   55,   60,
                    65,   70,   75,   80,   85,
                    90,   95,  100,  105,  110,
                   115,  120,  125,  130,  135,
                   143,  144,  141,  138,  134,
                   130,  126,  123,  119,  115,
                   110,  105,  100,   95,   90,
                    85,   80,   75,   70,   65,
                    60,   55,   50,   45,   40,
                    35,   30,   25,   20,   15,
                     7,    6,    9,   12,   16
                };

int pnY[] = {       76,   78,   76,   70,   60,
                    60,   50,   42,   34,   28,
                    22,   18,   14,   12,   10,
                    10,   10,   12,   14,   18,
                    22,   28,   34,   42,   50,
                    66,   68,   70,   72,   74,
                    76,   78,   76,   70,   60,
                    60,   50,   42,   34,   28,
                    22,   18,   14,   12,   10,
                    10,   10,   12,   14,   18,
                    22,   28,   34,   42,   50,
                    66,   68,   70,   72,   74
                };

/**
 *  The length of the arrays
 */
int nLength = 60;

/**
 * LookupX - looks up the appropriate value of X
 */
public int LookupX (int nIndex)
{
if ((nIndex >= nLength) || (nIndex < 0))
    return 0;

return pnX[nIndex];
}

/**
 * LookupY - looks up the appropriate value of Y
 */
public int LookupY (int nIndex)
{
if ((nIndex >= nLength) || (nIndex < 0))
    return 0;

return pnY[nIndex];
}
```

```
    /**
     * Length - the number of data points stored in the path
     */
    public int Length ()
    {
    return nLength;
    }
}


/**
 * ReverseCascadeBallPaths class. This is a container
 * for a path of juggling balls, the balls are moving
 * in a reverse cascade pattern
 *
 * @author     Chris Seguin
 * @version    1.0f, May 1, 1995
 */
class ReverseCascadeBallPaths extends BallPaths {

    /**
     * Arrays containing the path of the balls
     */
    int pnX[] = {       12,     9,     6,     3,     0,
                         0,     5,    10,    15,    20,
                        25,    30,    35,    40,    45,
                        50,    55,    60,    65,    70,
                        75,    80,    85,    90,    95,
                       100,   103,   106,   109,   112,
                       115,   118,   121,   124,   127,
                       130,   125,   120,   115,   110,
                       105,   100,    95,    90,    85,
                        80,    75,    70,    65,    60,
                        55,    50,    45,    40,    35,
                        27,    24,    21,    18,    15  };
    int pnY[] = {       60,    60,    60,    60,    60,
                        60,    51,    42,    35,    28,
                        23,    18,    15,    12,    11,
                        10,    11,    12,    15,    18,
                        23,    28,    35,    42,    51,
                        60,    60,    60,    60,    60,
                        60,    60,    60,    60,    60,
                        60,    51,    42,    35,    28,
                        23,    18,    15,    12,    11,
                        10,    11,    12,    15,    18,
                        23,    28,    35,    42,    51,
                        60,    60,    60,    60,    60 };

    /**
     *  The length of the arrays
     */
    int nLength = 60;

    /**
     * LookupX - looks up the appropriate value of X
     */
    public int LookupX (int nIndex)
    {
```

continues

Listing 4.2. continued

```
    if ((nIndex >= nLength) || (nIndex < 0))
        return 0;

    return pnX[nIndex];
    }

    /**
     * LookupY - looks up the appropriate value of Y
     */
    public int LookupY (int nIndex)
    {
    if ((nIndex >= nLength) || (nIndex < 0))
        return 0;

    return pnY[nIndex];
    }

    /**
     * Length - the number of data points stored in the path
     */
    public int Length ()
    {
    return nLength;
    }
}

/**
 * JugglingBall class. This is a juggling ball
 *
 * @author      Chris Seguin
 * @version     1.0f, May 1, 1995
 */
class JugglingBall {

    /**
     * The location on the ball's path
     */
    int nCycleSlot;

    /**
     * The color of the ball - specified by an index into the ball array
     */
    int nBallColor;

    /**
     * The current location of the ball
     */
    int nX;
    int nY;

    /**
     * The path to follow
     */
    BallPaths ptbpPath;

    /**
     * JugglingBall - creates a juggling ball
     */
```

```java
    public JugglingBall (int nStartPos, int nStartColor, BallPaths ptbpThePath)
    {
    nCycleSlot = nStartPos;
    nBallColor = nStartColor;

    ptbpPath = ptbpThePath;

    nX = ptbpPath.LookupX(nStartPos);
    nY = ptbpPath.LookupY(nStartPos);
    }

    /**
     * Move - moves the ball to the next location
     */
    public void Move ()
    {
    nCycleSlot++;
    if ((nCycleSlot >= ptbpPath.Length ()) || (nCycleSlot <= 0)) {
        nCycleSlot = 0;
        }

    nX = ptbpPath.LookupX(nCycleSlot);
    nY = ptbpPath.LookupY(nCycleSlot);
    }

    /**
     * XLoc - returns the x location
*/
    public int XLoc ()
    {
    return nX;
    }

    /**
     * YLoc - returns the Y location
     */
    public int YLoc ()
    {
    return nY;
    }

    /**
     * Color - returns the color
     */
    public int Color ()
    {
    return nBallColor;
    }
}


/**
 * HandPath class. This is a container for the paths of the hands
 *
 * @author      Chris Seguin
 * @version     1.0f, May 3, 1995
 */
class HandPath {
```

continues

Listing 4.2. continued

```
/**
 * Arrays containing the path of the hands
 */
int pnLeftHandX[] = {
                    7,     6,     9,    12,    16,
                   20,    24,    27,    31,    35,
                   35,    31,    27,    24,    20,
                   16,    12,     9,     6,     7
                   };

int pnRightHandX[] = {
                  143,   144,   141,   138,   134,
                  130,   126,   123,   119,   115,
                  115,   119,   123,   126,   130,
                  134,   138,   141,   144,   143
                   };

int pnHandY[] = {
                   73,    75,    77,    79,    81,
                   83,    85,    83,    77,    67,
                   67,    57,    51,    49,    51,
                   53,    55,    57,    59,    61
                   };


/**
 *   The length of the arrays
 */
int nLength = 60;
int nBalls = 0;

/**
 * HandPath - creates a hand path
 */
public HandPath (int nStartBalls)
{
nBalls = nStartBalls;
}


/**
 * LookupX - looks up the appropriate value of X
 */
public int LookupX (int nIndex, boolean bLeft)
{
if ((nIndex >= nLength) ¦¦ (nIndex < 0))
    return 0;

//  Limit the lookup to the range
if (nIndex >= 20 * nBalls)
    nIndex = 19;

while (nIndex >= 20)
    nIndex -= 20;

//  Look up the value
if (bLeft)
    return pnLeftHandX[nIndex];
```

```java
    else
        return pnRightHandX[nIndex];
    }

    /**
     * LookupY - looks up the appropriate value of Y
     */
    public int LookupY (int nIndex)
    {
    if ((nIndex >= nLength) || (nIndex < 0))
        return 0;

    //  Limit the lookup to the range
    if (nIndex >= 20 * nBalls)
        nIndex = 19;

    while (nIndex >= 20)
        nIndex -= 20;

    //  Look up the value
    return pnHandY[nIndex];
    }

    /**
     * Length - the number of data points stored in the path
     */
    public int Length ()
    {
    return nLength;
    }
}


/**
 * Hand class. This is a hand
 *
 * @author      Chris Seguin
 * @version     1.0f, May 3, 1995
 */
class Hand {

    /**
     * The location on the ball's path
     */
    int nCycleSlot;

    /**
     * Whether this is the left hand
     */
    boolean bLeft;

    /**
     * The current location of the ball
     */
    int nX;
    int nY;

    /**
```

continues

Listing 4.2. continued

```
     * The path to follow
     */
    HandPath phPath;

    /**
     * Hand - creates a hand
     */
    public Hand (int nStartPos, HandPath phThePath, boolean bStartLeft)
    {
    nCycleSlot = nStartPos;
    bLeft = bStartLeft;

    phPath = phThePath;

    nX = phPath.LookupX(nStartPos, bLeft);
    nY = phPath.LookupY(nStartPos);
    }

    /**
     * Move - moves the ball to the next location
     */
    public void Move ()
    {
    nCycleSlot++;
    if ((nCycleSlot >= phPath.Length ()) || (nCycleSlot <= 0)) {
        nCycleSlot = 0;
        }

    nX = phPath.LookupX(nCycleSlot, bLeft);
    nY = phPath.LookupY(nCycleSlot);
    }

    /**
     * XLoc - returns the x location
*/
    public int XLoc ()
    {
    return nX;
    }

    /**
     * YLoc - returns the Y location
     */
    public int YLoc ()
    {
    return nY;
    }
}


/**
 * A juggling demonstration program
 *
 * @author     Chris Seguin
 * @version    1.0f, May 1, 1995
 */
public class Juggling extends java.applet.Applet implements Runnable {
```

```
/**
 * The path of the juggling balls
 */
BallPaths pjbPaths;

/**
 * The juggling balls
 */
JugglingBall pjbBalls[] = {null, null, null};

/**
 * The paths that the hands trace out
 */
HandPath phHandPaths;
/**
 * The hands
 */
Hand phLeft;
Hand phRight;

/**
 * The directory or URL from which the images are loaded
 */
String dir;

/**
 * The images used.
 */
JugglingImages jbiImages;

/**
 * The thread animating the images.
 */
Thread kicker = null;

/**
 * The delay between animation frames
 */
int nSpeed;

/**
 * Shape of the window
 */
int nHeight = 0;
int nWidth = 0;

/**
 * The number of balls in the demonstration
 */
int nBalls = 0;

/**
 * Parameter info.
 */
public String[][] getParameterInfo() {
    String[][] info = {
        {"balls", "int",  "the number of balls to animate"},
        {"speed", "int",  "the speed the balls move at"},
```

continues

Listing 4.2. continued

```java
        {"img",     "urls", "the directory where the images are located"},
    };
    return info;
}

/**
 * Initialize the applet.  Get attributes.
 */
public void init() {
    // Load the parameters from the HTML file

    String at = getParameter("img");
    dir = (at != null) ? at : "images";

    at = getParameter("speed");
    nSpeed = (at != null) ? Integer.valueOf (at).intValue() : 20;

    at = getParameter("height");
    nHeight = (at != null) ? Integer.valueOf (at).intValue() : 100;
    at = getParameter("width");
    nWidth = (at != null) ? Integer.valueOf (at).intValue() : 170;

    at = getParameter("balls");
    nBalls = (at != null) ? Integer.valueOf (at).intValue() : 3;

    // Initialize the Ball variables
    pjbPaths = new CascadeBallPaths ();
    pjbBalls[0] = new JugglingBall ( 0, 0, pjbPaths);
    pjbBalls[1] = new JugglingBall (40, 2, pjbPaths);
    pjbBalls[2] = new JugglingBall (20, 4, pjbPaths);

    // Initialize the hand variables
    phHandPaths = new HandPath (nBalls);
    phLeft = new Hand (5, phHandPaths, true);
    phRight = new Hand (35, phHandPaths, false);

    resize(nWidth, nHeight);
}

/**
 * Run the image loop. This method is called by class Thread.
 * @see java.lang.Thread
 */
public void run() {
    // Create the thread
    Thread.currentThread().setPriority(Thread.MIN_PRIORITY);

    // Load the images
    jbiImages = new JugglingImages(getDocumentBase(), dir, this);

    // Do the animation
    int ndx = 0;
    while (size().width > 0 && size().height > 0 && kicker != null) {
        for (ndx = 0; ndx < nBalls; ndx++) {
            (pjbBalls[ndx]).Move();
        }
```

```
        phLeft.Move();
        phRight.Move();

        repaint();
        try {Thread.sleep(nSpeed);} catch (InterruptedException e){}
    }
}

/**
 * Paint the current frame.
 */
public void paint(Graphics g) {
    update (g);
}
public void update(Graphics g) {
    if ((jbiImages != null) && (jbiImages.imgs != null)) {
        //  Erase the background
        g.setColor(java.awt.Color.lightGray);
        g.fillRect(0, 0, nWidth, nHeight);

        int ndx = 0;
        for (ndx = 0; ndx < nBalls; ndx++) {
            if (jbiImages.imgs[pjbBalls[ndx].Color ()] == null) {
                System.out.print ("ERROR::No Image ");
                System.out.println (ndx);
            }

            g.drawImage(jbiImages.imgs[pjbBalls[ndx].Color ()],
                (pjbBalls[ndx]).XLoc(), (pjbBalls[ndx]).YLoc(), this);
        }

        //  Draw the hands
        g.drawImage(jbiImages.imgs[7],
                phLeft.XLoc(), phLeft.YLoc(), this);
        g.drawImage(jbiImages.imgs[7],
                phRight.XLoc(), phRight.YLoc(), this);
    }
}

/**
 * Start the applet by forking an animation thread.
 */
public void start() {
    if (kicker == null) {
        kicker = new Thread(this);
        kicker.start();
    }
}

/**
 * Stop the applet. The thread will exit because kicker is set to null.
 */
public void stop() {
    kicker = null;
}
}
```

Animator Applet

This chapter has shown you some simple applets based on animating images, but suppose you wanted to spice up a Web page with something a little more dynamic, such as the capability to interact with user input. Remember that Java has a complete set of windowing tools in the Abstract Window Toolkit. These tools allow you to build interfaces into your applets and create applets that interact with user input. For example, if you wanted to have some sort of animation or display some information based on when a user clicked a mouse, Java enables you to do just that.

ClickBoard is an example of an applet that uses both animation and user input. The program can display a series of still images in sequence to create an animation, and the user activates the animation by clicking an image (see Figure 4.4 and Figure 4.5):

> ClickBoard: Interactive Animation
> Written by Steve Fu
> `http://www.intrinsa.com/personal/steve/ClickBoard/ClickBoard.html`

ClickBoard is quite flexible, and the user can configure many of the applet's attributes. For example, ClickBoard makes use of a configuration file that allows users to specify the following items:

- The background colors
- The number of images in an animation
- The image files used
- Sound files to be played during an animation
- The clickable areas
- The type and number of actions

A configuration file allows the applet to be adaptable without requiring the user to alter the actual program. When you are designing applets that incorporate a number of complex features, configuration files or applet parameters can be a great way to make your applet useful to many people or easy to change later. Implementing configuration files or applet parameters can save you the trouble of reprogramming an applet to change its functionality and also allows you to pass the applet along to other users with a user-friendly method for implementing changes.

Figure 4.4.
In the ClickBoard applet, the user activates the animation by clicking the fish.

Figure 4.5.
The ClickBoard animation plays after the user clicks the picture.

SlideShow Applet

Many personal Web pages are enhanced by putting up photographs of family or friends. With a slide show applet, you can put together a collection of images that a user can flip through like a photo album. You could even add sound to the applet to assemble a soundtrack to your slide show. Such an applet could be used for personal photos, product photos, or even presentation slides.

The following is an example of such a slide show applet:

SlideShow
Written by David Gulbransen
`http://www.fa.indiana.edu/~dgulbran/slideshow.html`

This applet allows you to specify a number of images to be loaded and a sound file to play. It also has controls to allow the user to flip through the slides or play them in a slide show and a button to turn off the soundtrack (see Figure 4.6). The SlideShow applet is a good example of a fairly simple applet that can be very flexible. Chapter 13 "The SlideShow Applet," covers the development of the SlideShow applet in detail.

Figure 4.6.
A slide show applet can add a new twist to a Web photo gallery.

Adding Functionality to Web Pages

In addition to adding more graphics and sound capabilities to Web pages, Java applets can also do a great deal to enhance the functionality of Web pages. You can use applets to provide complex information in a more intuitive way or to simplify the presentation of such information. The following sections describe some applets that show how you can add functionality to a Web page.

Curve Applet

The Curve Applet is an educational applet designed to show different types of mathematical curves and how they are manipulated (see Figure 4.7). The applet shows three types of curves and how those curves are manipulated by points on the curve. Drawing curves is a fundamental part of graphics programming, and this applet helps explain how curves function:

Curve Applet
Written by Michael Heinrichs
`http://fas.sfu.ca:80/1/cs/people/GradStudents/heinrica/personal/curve.html`

Figure 4.7.
The Curve Applet is both educational and informative, demonstrating different types of mathematical curves.

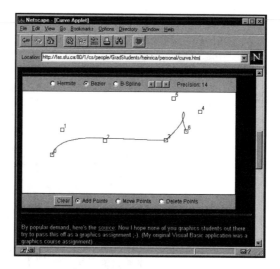

StockTrace Applet

Because Java can communicate back to a server, applets can be configured to provide data to users in real time. Stock prices, for example, are in a constant state of flux, updating from minute to minute throughout the day. An applet that could provide real-time information about stocks could be invaluable as a device for keeping track of stock prices.

The StockTrace Applet enables you to specify stocks to trace, and then fetches the price information from the server and displays current prices (see Figure 4.8). This applet also has a graphing function that enables you to plot the performance of a particular stock. Although putting server-based data onto Web pages has always been possible, updating the data in real time was not practical or easy. Updating standard HTML pages dynamically is slow and taxes both the browser and the server. But because Java applets run within the context of the Java Virtual Machine and open a separate data connection to the host machine, updating Java applets is not taxing for the browser or the Web server.

Note: The StockTrace Applet does not currently display active stock data. The data that it retrieves in its current form is for simulation only. Keep in mind that providing users with real-time data from a server requires a server that contains such data, and this applet was designed as proof of concept. The ability to provide real-time data to customers is certainly a value-added service that many companies will begin to exploit in the near future. As Java grows, so will the business opportunities that the technology presents.

StockTrace Applet
Written by Christian Dreke
`http://www.cs.virginia.edu/~cd4v/graph/StockGraph.html`

Figure 4.8.
*The StockTrace Applet
demonstrates server
communication and
updating information in
real time.*

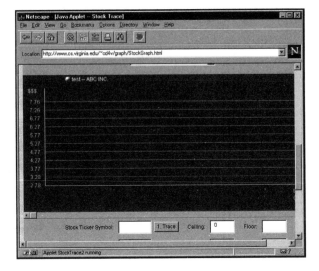

TeleRadiology Applet

Java appletscan update any kind of data in real time with the proper server connection. Another prototype applet designed to showcase this capability is the TeleRadiology applet. This applet was developed at the Los Alamos National Laboratory and is designed to show how medical information can be transmitted and viewed by using such real-time applications.

This prototype was designed to show how medical information can be transmitted to various locations, allowing consultations and diagnostics to be performed anywhere in the world. Such technology could help increase the quality of medicine in rural areas or help doctors verify opinions with colleagues around the globe.

Java TeleMed Prototype
Written by Andrew White
`http://www.acl.lanl.gov/~rdaniel/classesJDK/PickTest2.html`

Figure 4.9.
The TeleRadiology applet demonstrates how Java can communicate vital information in useful formats.

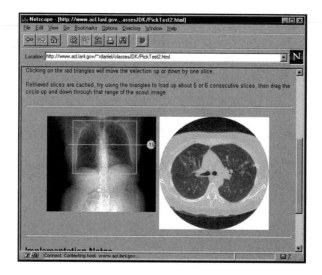

Interactive PC Scoreboard Applet

Communication with a server is not limited to updating real-time information. Java applets can be written to perform typical client/server tasks, such as functioning as database front ends. The Interactive PC Scoreboard is an example of how applets can communicate back to a database, use the database to look up information, and then redisplay the information in a useful format.

This particular applet allows users to enter information about what qualities they are looking for in a personal computer. The applet then searches a database and, based on the criteria the user has selected, displays some recommended machines. Users can then click the recommended models to get configuration and pricing information.

clnet Interactive PC Scoreboard
http://www.cnet.com/Content/Reviews/Compare/Pc100/0,30,,0200.html

Figure 4.10.
The c\net PC Scoreboard shows how Java can integrate with databases and other information sources.

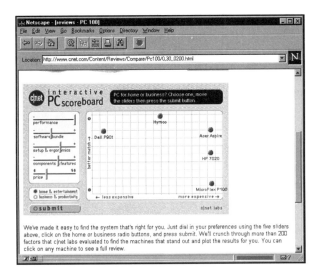

The Player Piano Applet

The lack of seamless sound has plagued the Web for many years. Downloading sounds has always been possible, but the capability to load sounds directly with a page has eluded the Web. The latest versions of Netscape and third-party applications such as Real Audio have begun to add the dimension of sound to the Web, but they still fall short of full Web integration. Java brings integrated sound to the Web. An applet can play a sound when the applet is launched, or the applet can be configured to play sounds at the click of a button.

An outstanding example of an applet that utilizes sound is the Player Piano applet. This applet simulates a player piano, displaying the roll that is used to create the sounds within the applet. Sound can enhance Web pages by adding personality and, as this applet shows, functionality.

Player Piano
Written by Mark Leather
http://reality.sgi.com/employees/mark/piano/index.html

Figure 4.11.
This applet functions like a old-fashioned player piano, integrating visuals and sound.

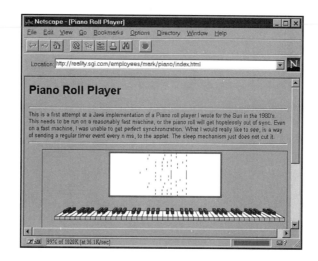

Summary

Don't be disappointed if the first applet you create doesn't allow users to select a region of the country and display real-time satellite weather photos. The applets in this chapter have been presented to show you the range of what is possible with Java, not to imply that these are beginning applets. Each of the applets shown in this chapter utilizes the basic idea of adding exciting new elements to a Web page. Some of them do so by adding animations, and others add animation and sound. They range from the functional (a clock, the TeleRadiology applet) to educational (The Juggling Applet, the PC Scoreboard) to fun (ClickBoard, the Player Piano). As you become more involved with Java, you might want to start adding some of the advanced features shown in this chapter, but every programmer still needs to start with the basics. Now that you have a handle on what Java is and what it can do, the next chapters move on to cover how you can start adding Java to your own Web pages. Chapter 5, "Finding and Using Applets," examines the issues raised in adding Java applets to your Web pages and shows you an example of how to add an applet to your page. Chapter 7, "The Java Developer's Kit," helps you to create your first applet, HelloWorld. From there, you'll move on to some more advanced programming topics, which give you the basic foundation you need to start creating your own applets.

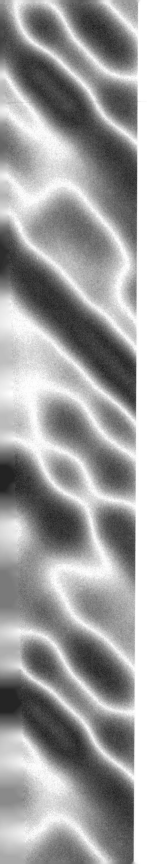

Adding Applets to Your Web Pages

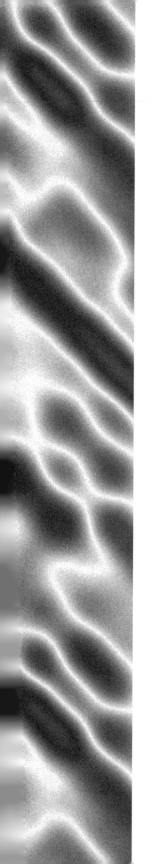

CHAPTER 5

Finding and Using Applets

You probably have some ideas now about applets that you might want to include on your Web pages. Applets are being produced by a variety of sources: individuals, institutions, and, of course, businesses. So how do you go about finding applets that you can use on your Web pages without programming them from scratch? A number of Java resources are available already and more are certainly on the way.

The best place to find applets is on the World Wide Web. Several sites are dedicated to Java and Java applets, and a number of individuals and companies offer their applets for others to use. If you are willing to spend some time looking on the Web, you will certainly come up with a wide variety of sources for applets that you can include in your own pages.

Using applets in your own pages can be a very simple process. Many sites will provide a working example of the applet that you can use to get an idea of configuration, and some sites even have step-by-step instructions for using their applets. Many sites also provide the source code for applets, enabling you to tweak applets to your specific needs or customize applets even further than parameters would allow (parameters are discussed more in Chapter 6, "Java-Enhanced Page Design"). Adding applets to your Web pages can seem more intimidating than it is. This chapter shows you step-by-step how to add the LED TickerTape applet to your Web pages. By the end of the chapter, you should have a good idea of the process involved in adding an applet to your own pages.

Where Do I Look?

Several major sites on the World Wide Web are designed to provide a wealth of information about Java and Java applets. Visiting these sites can provide you with tutorials, specifications, and sample applets. Among the major sites for finding Java information on the Net are Sun's Javasoft site, Gamelan, and the Java Applet Rating Service (JARS). Although these sites contain some of the same information, each site also has a unique twist on the Java offerings and is worth a visit on your quest for applets.

Sun

The Sun Microsystems Web site, Javasoft, is the official site for information about Java (see Figure 5.1). The site contains a wealth of information regarding Java, Java development, and future directions for Java. If you are interested in learning about Java, creating a bookmark for this site would be a good idea:

```
http://www.javasoft.com
```

Figure 5.1.
The Sun Javasoft Web site is the official site for Java material.

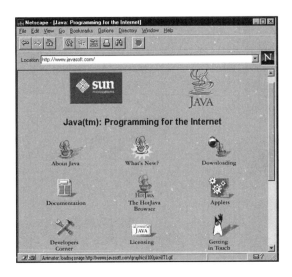

In addition to providing news and information about Java in general, the Javasoft site is also the official source for downloading the HotJava browser, the Java Developer's Kit, and all the official Java documentation. You can find the following information at the Javasoft site:

> The About Java and What's New sections include press releases and announcements relevant to Java developments. Check here for the latest developments and for a listing of Java resources.

> The Downloading section is your source for downloading the Java Developer's Kit, the HotJava browser, and the source code for the JDK.

> The Documentation section of this site is perhaps the most valuable resource. This section provides extensive documentation and tutorials for the Java language, the JDK, and the HotJava browser. This documentation includes the following:
> - The Java Language Tutorial
> - Documentation for the 1.0 Release
> - API Documentation
> - Tool Documentation
> - Java Programming Language Debugging
> - Java Language Specification
> - Using the HotJava Web Browser
> - Frequently Asked Questions (FAQs)

> These documents not only represent the official word on Java but are invaluable sources for anyone learning or seriously working with Java.

> The Applet section provides some great Java applets. The applets are broken up into sections based on the Application Programming Interface (API) they were designed with, either the Alpha API or the 1.0 release. Chapter 10, "Applet Structure and Design," covers the 1.0 release. The site also includes some great applet examples, which are accompanied by source code. Some of the applet categories include the following:
> - Applets to Spice Up a Page
> - Educational Applets
> - Utilities
> - Games and Other Diversions
> - For Programmers Only

> The Developer's Corner contains information specifically for Java developers including the documentation resources, JDK resources, and information about training sessions available directly from Sun. The Licensing area contains all of the legal fine print regarding Java, and information about licensing Java for companies that might want to include the Java Virtual Machine in products.

As you explore the possibilities of Java, you should consult the documentation on the Javasoft site quite frequently. As your Java knowledge grows, the documentation you find here can answer more advanced questions and keep your knowledge of Java as current as possible.

Gamelan

EarthWeb's Gamelan is one of the most extensive Java sites available on the Web (see Figure 5.2). It was the first non-Sun site to chronicle the course of Java and its influence on the Web:

```
http://www.gamelan.com
```

Figure 5.2.

Gamelan offers an extensive repository of Java information and sites.

The Gamelan Web site offers a wide range of Java information, including the following:

The What's New area of Gamelan provides announcements on the latest available Java information. You can specify how new (in days) you want, and the Gamelan site will return all the new resources it has available. The resources aren't just limited to applets either; they also include press releases, announcements, and other types of Java resources.

Like many other Web sites, Gamelan has a simple rating system it uses to provide you with a basic guideline to the quality of the resources it catalogs. The What's Cool index provides a listing of resources that the Gamelan administrators consider cool, for whatever reason, be it a new faster applet or a new Java innovation. This area is often a good place to check for cutting-edge applets. Keep in mind that this rating is completely subjective, and although many of the applets are cool, some are just plain goofy.

Because Java is so new, Gamelan provides an additional listing for the various types of applets available in the What's Beta category. A number of applets are designed to use the Alpha version of Java's API, some use the Beta version, and now more use the official 1.0 API. Gamelan indicates what version of Java an applet or resource uses so you will know whether it is uses the most current version of Java available.

The Who's Who category provides a listing of all the individuals, organizations, and companies that have contributed resources to Gamelan. This index can be a helpful if you have heard about an applet written by a certain person and want find that applet more directly or look at other applets that person may have written.

Gamelan also offers a search engine to search the site for specific resources (Find a Resource), and a form interface that allows you to submit your own applets for inclusion in the Gamelan site (Add a Resource).

In addition to these features, Gamelan also features a hierarchical index to allow you pursue resources based on subject groupings and a Featured Applet area designed to showcase a particularly innovative new applet. Some of the subject categories in the hierarchical index include the following:

- Animation
- Communication
- Documents
- Education
- Finance
- Special Effects
- Games
- Graphics
- JavaScript
- Network
- Java Programming
- Sites
- Sound
- Utilities

Overall, Gamelan is probably the most comprehensive Java site available and is an incredible resource for anyone working with or exploring Java.

JARS

The Java Applet Rating Service (JARS) offers a site based upon rating applets to provide you with a list of not only new applets, but also applets that are high in quality or functionality (see Figure 5.3):

```
http://www.surinam.net/java/jars/jars.html
```

Figure 5.3.
The Java Applet Rating
Service (JARS) provides
a listing of applets and
ratings.

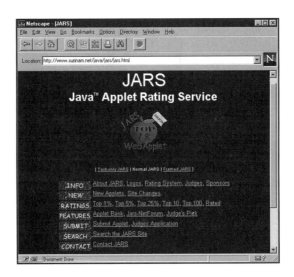

When an applet is submitted for inclusion on the JARS site, it is rated and then placed into the appropriate category. The applets are reviewed by a panel of independent judges (who are selected for their experience with Java or their knowledge of the field) and then assigned a rating based on the following criteria:

- **Presentation**. The presentation of an applet includes the User Interface design, the overall visual appeal of the applet, the quality of graphics and audio used in the applet, and so on.

- **AppletPerfect**. The AppletPerfect criteria pertains to the source code for the applet and includes the difficulty of programming the applet, the originality of the code, and other programming issues.

- **Function**. This category rates the overall functionality of the applet. Applets are ranked on usefulness, usability, and pragmatic applet issues.

- **Originality**. This category measures the uniqueness of a submitted applet. Applets that score high offer new, unique services that were not previously available or in some other way offer a twist to a feature that was not possible to offer before Java.

After the applets have been reviewed by the judges, the applets are placed into various categories that can be searched or viewed in a list. The JARS categories include the following:

The New Applets category offers a listing of applets that have recently been submitted for review. Although these applets have not yet been reviewed, this category is still a good resource for seeing what some of the newest applets are and what they have to offer.

The top percentage listings are designed to break down the applets into the top 1 percent, 5 percent, and 25 percent of all applets that have been reviewed. These listings allow you to look at the applets that ranked the highest in the JARS rating system and bypass applets that received lower rankings.

The Top 100 is simply a listing of the 100 best applets found on the JARS site. It can be worth a look if you want to see some examples of high-quality applets.

You can also use the JARS search engine to search for applets by author, type, or name, and you can use the JARS submission form to submit your own applets for review. JARS also features a "Judges' Pick" where individual judges have an opportunity to select their favorite applets.

Keep in mind that the JARS rating system is still a subjective rating system and does not represent any kind of official rating system. It is simply the JARS site's way of categorizing the applets to help you narrow your search. Many applets that might not have received an outstanding rating for one reason or another are still very useful applets. Also, many applets available on the Web have not been submitted to the JARS site to be reviewed. Consequently, JARS shouldn't be your only stop while searching the Web for new applets.

Search Engines

The Java-oriented sites are undoubtedly the best way to find a large collection of Java resources on the Net, but don't overlook traditional search engines or Web indexes in your search for Java material. Search engines can give you access to an incredible number of Java sites on the Web, and the results are not just limited to the larger Java sites. Using search engines you can uncover other Java development companies, consulting agencies, and individuals' pages. Table 5.1 tells you how to find some of the best Web search engines and indexes.

Table 5.1. Locations for Web search engines and indexes.

Name	Location
Yahoo	http://www.yahoo.com
Lycos	http://www.lycos.com
WebCrawler	http://www.webcrawler.com
Excite	http://www.excite.com
InfoSeek	http://www.infoseek.com
Alta Vista	http://altavista.digital.com

Code or Binaries?

Once you have located applets that you want to use you will need to figure out how to incorporate them into your own Web pages. There are two ways to go about adding an applet to your Web pages. One is to download the Java binary and configure the HTML code to suit your page, and the other way is to download the source code and compile the applet for yourself.

Using Binaries

Compiled Java applications are represented in binary code. A Java binary is an applet in its executable form. Downloading the binary is the simplest way to get an applet to add to your Web pages. Because the binaries for Java applets are cross-platform, one binary fits all. Authors therefore provide only one copy of their applets that everyone can use. When you find an applet you want to use and it has a binary available, then by all means use the binary. Unless you have plans to modify the code yourself for a specific purpose, downloading the binary will save you time and trouble in getting the applet up and running on your Web pages.

Depending on the configuration of your Web server, you can either download the binary to your PC and then transfer it to your Web page directories or download it straight to your Web page directories. Once you have the binary in your Web directory, adding the binary to your page is as simple as editing the HTML for your page.

Chapter 7, "The Java Developer's Kit," contains a detailed explanation of the HTML tags that are used to add Java to your Web pages. The basic tag is the <APPLET> tag, which allows you to specify an applet for any Java-capable browser. One of the best ways to learn about the HTML code for an applet is to use the View Source option in your browser to look at the HTML code for a page that already contains the applet. Because most applet authors include a working demonstration on their Web pages, it can be quite simple to look at their sources and cut and paste the relevant HTML code directly into your pages. From that point, you can begin to change any customizable code to make the applet perform best for your page, such as changing text or images that might be displayed by the applet.

When downloading a binary, be aware of the names and locations of files. Keep in mind that when you download the file, you need to make sure that you keep the same name for the applet as appears in the HTML code. For example, if an applet is referred to as `animate.class` in the HTML code, the applet must be named `animate.class`. Also, be aware that some pages might specify a location for the applet in the HTML code using the <CODEBASE> tag. If you are having trouble making an applet work, try modifying the directory listed in the <CODEBASE> tag to accurately reflect the location of the applet.

You also need to be aware of any supplementary files that the applet needs. Many applets that deal with images, animation, or sound require supplementary files that the applet must access in order to run properly. For example, if an animation applet allows you to specify pictures to be flipped in an animation, you need to be sure that the image files are present and in the proper directory in order for the applet to run properly. You will often find this type of configuration information on the page you downloaded the applet from.

> Note: Before adding applets to your pages, you should become very familiar with the applet-specific HTML code. This familiarity will help you avoid problems when customizing an applet for your Web page and will help you troubleshoot a malfunctioning applet. Chapter 7 gives a detailed explanation of the HTML code used in relation to Java applets.

To try out a Java applet, follow the process of adding the LED TickerTape applet (see Figure 5.4) to your Web page. The first step is locating the applet. A search on Gamelan for "LED TickerTape" gives you the URL for the LED TickerTape applet:

```
http://www.conveyor.com/ticker-tape.html
```

Figure 5.4.
The LED TickerTape enables you to add a scrolling message to your pages with the look of an LED sign.

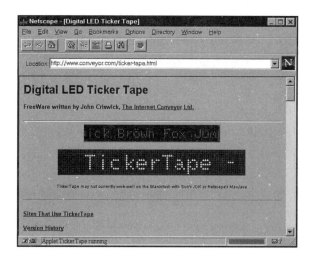

The site shows you the applet in action. The authors have even included a link to download the necessary files right from the Web page. You need the following three files to use this applet on your own Web pages:

- `TickerTape.class`
- `TickerFont.class`
- `ISO8859.class`

You must create a directory called `classes` in the directory where your home pages are stored. Place the TickerTape applet files within that `classes` directory. You can download the files one at a time, or you can download a compressed archive of the files as well. The archives are also linked on the LED TickerTape home page:

- `TickerTape.tar.Z` for UNIX
- `TickerTape.sit.hqx` for Macintosh

Once you have the files in the `classes` directory, you are halfway done. The only thing you have to do now is edit the actual HTML of the page you want the LED TickerTape applet to appear on.

Add the following code to the HTML file of the Web page to which you want to add the TickerTape applet:

```
<applet codebase="classes" code="TickerTape" width=500 height=59>
<param name=text value="Congrats! You now have a Ticker Tape applet">
<param name=backcolour value="black">
<param name=framecolour value="darkgrey">
<param name=ledcolour value="red">
<param name=ledoffcolour value="darkgray">
<param name=framethick value=3>
<param name=ledsize value=3>
<param name=ledtype value=0>
<param name=ledspacing value=1>
<param name=speed value=100>
</applet>
```

This code places the TickerTape applet on your page. You should now be able to view your new page using any Java-capable browser and see the TickerTape applet running and displaying some text (see Figure 5.5).

That's it! Now you have an applet on your page. If you are having trouble, you might want to check out the applet's install guide at `http://www.conveyor.com/ticker-tape.html#install`. This site has a listing of some common problems and their solutions.

Once you have this applet installed on your home page, you will undoubtedly want to customize it. After all, what good is a ticker tape if you can't make it say what you want? You can find the full range of customizations at `http://www.conveyor.com/ticker-tape.html#using`, but read on to get started right away.

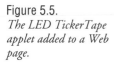

Figure 5.5.
The LED TickerTape applet added to a Web page.

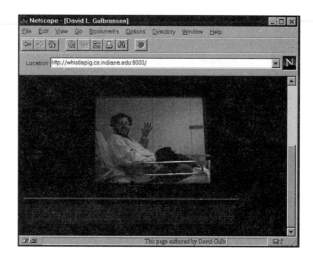

If you look at the HTML used to add this applet, you will notice the following line:

```
<param name=text value="Congrats! You now have a Ticker Tape applet">
```

This line specifies the text that appears. You can change the value to whatever text you want, and when you reload the applet, your text should appear in place of the sample text. You can also play around with the colors that are available. Each of the <PARAM> tags represents a parameter that you can configure. The applet accepts black, blue, cyan, darkgray, gray, green, lightgray, magenta, orange, pink, red, white, and yellow as color values for any of the color-related parameters. Experiment with some of these settings to customize the applet to your liking. Chapter 6 goes into more detail about adding applets to your home pages, including the details of the HTML code and some design issues.

Using Code

Many sites do not have binaries available, which means that you will have to use the raw Java code to compile your own version of the applet you want to use. Compiling your own version of an applet offers an advantage only if you are familiar with the Java programming language and want to customize an applet for specific uses on your page beyond what the original author intended. For example, many applets that use images already have a parameter to allow you to specify an image filename. But suppose you also wanted to be able to specify an extension, such as JPEG or GIF, to denote the file type. If the author had not already provided a parameter to do so, you would need to modify the source code in order to provide such capability.

Modifying an applet's source code can be a very daunting task. If the code is not well-commented, it can sometimes be difficult for even an advanced programmer to understand completely. You should avoid modifying source code if at all possible unless you have an advanced understanding of what the code does and what you need to modify. If you do attempt to modify the code, you might want to keep an original copy of the code. That way, if your modified code does not function as you anticipated, you can always revert to the original version.

Keep in mind that even if a binary is not available, you will not always have to edit source code. If source code is provided, it is most likely provided in its finished form, and all you will need to do to use it is download the code and compile it. Although modifying the code might seem like a daunting task, compiling code that is in a finished form is a pretty straightforward process once you have a basic understanding of the Java Developer's Kit and the javac compiler provided with it. Chapter 7 covers the Java Developer's Kit and explains the basics of compiling your own Java code (or someone else's). Once code has been compiled into a binary, you can use it in your pages just as you would any other applet and use the HTML code and parameters to customize the applet for your pages.

Copyright Issues

Downloading and using found elements is part of the nature of the World Wide Web. The Web is based on the open exchange of information. However, Java applets are programs that have authors, and those authors do have certain ownership rights when it comes to the use of their applets and the code they have written.

Java applets are protected by copyright law just as any other applications are, and the extent to which you may use an applet depends upon what rights the author is willing to grant you. Certainly, as Java becomes more popular and applets begin to expand their capabilities, companies will begin to sell applets or applet components. As the practice of selling Java components becomes more widespread, licensing issues will most likely be dealt with just as licensing issues for traditional software or other object-oriented components are dealt with in the market. In the meantime, Java applets are generally falling into the shareware and freeware domain.

Shareware and Freeware

Many applet authors are writing applets as learning exercises or to add specific features to their Web pages. Because they are not large companies producing software for profit, they are not out to make a specific product to sell. However, some people still might want to recover some of the expense or time that went into creating their applet, and one way to accomplish that is shareware.

Applets that are released as shareware are provided to anyone through the Net on the condition that if you use the applet past an evaluation period, you will send the author a fee. Most authors allow you to try their programs for a grace period (somewhere between a week and a month) to see whether the software performs the functions you want. However, if you continue to use the software after the trial period, you are bound to send in the shareware fee.

Shareware has some benefits over commercial software and some drawbacks. First, because you are dealing with individuals, shareware fees tend to be very reasonable (between 5 and 45 dollars). Some authors have even produced "Postcardware," with the fee being a postcard saying, "Thanks." Second, you are usually free to redistribute or modify shareware as long as you credit the original author. Shareware's major drawback can be the lack of support. Because most shareware authors don't have support lines or the time to answer all user questions, you are often on your own if you encounter problems.

In addition to shareware, some applets are released as freeware. As the name implies, freeware applets are given away for anyone to use without a registration fee. Many currently available applets are freeware, and all the author requires is that you retain a copyright statement protecting the original author's rights.

All in all, shareware can be a great way to gain access to some well-written, functional programs. Always check any applet you download to make sure that you are aware of the terms of any agreements for using the software. If you use an applet that is shareware, you are on your honor to send in the registration fee. The shareware system works because of people who register software. If people use shareware software without paying the fees, authors will discontinue to release programs as shareware, and everyone will suffer. Because the shareware fees are usually quite reasonable, it's much better to pay them than risk losing such a valuable resource.

Credit where Credit Is Due

Shareware and freeware demonstrate that not everyone is out to make money for the software they have written. However, most people want recognition in return for their time. Most applets are distributed with a copyright statement that includes information about the original author. There is no reason not to keep that information with the applet when you add it to your own page. It will not adversely effect the performance of the applet, and it is a nice way to give credit where credit is due. If someone has gone to the trouble of producing an applet that you think is great and want to use on your page, why not give them the credit for writing such a great tool? You might someday be in the position of writing applets yourself and would appreciate the same treatment.

Summary

This chapter has shown you where to look for applets and has briefly demonstrated how to include an applet on your Web page. You can begin to look for applets that you might want to include on your own home pages, but using Java applets on your home pages requires learning some new HTML and raises new design issues. Chapter 6 takes a look at the HTML used with Java applets and some of the design issues that Java raises. So read on to begin adding your own Java pages to the Web.

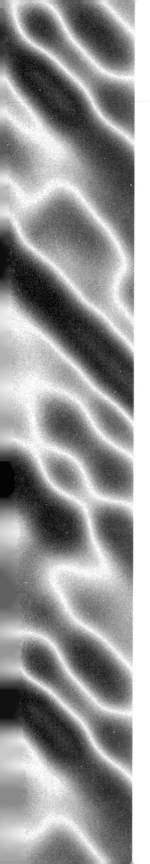

Java-Enhanced Page Design

Designing Web pages to be informational, functional, and still fun-to-view can be a challenge. Java applets only add to the challenge of designing a successful Web page. Because applets can have animated graphics, sound, or their own user interfaces, designing a page to work with applets can be difficult. It is very easy to get carried away and try to load a page with as many applets as possible. No doubt, as you explore the Web, you will find pages cluttered with applets trying to show off new capabilities.

Nonetheless, if you keep in mind the principles of good Web design, you can have great Web pages that maximize applets to create new looks and services within the context of sound judgment. When you are designing Web pages of any kind, you want to consider content, context, and courtesy. Content is obvious; a picture of a hot dog on a vegetarian page is probably not the best choice for content. Context is a little more difficult. You need to consider issues such as how the elements of a page fit together and whether the text is readable with any superimposed images. Courtesy is remembering that many people are still accessing the Web through slow modems. Taking into consideration that people might not want to wait an hour to see your applets is more than good design, it's good manners. Basically, you can use the same guidelines you would use when designing any type of publication to be viewed by a large audience. This chapter covers the HTML extensions that enable you to add applets to Web pages. This chapter also discusses some of the design issues that Java raises and how some sites deal with those issues.

HTML and Java

HTML is at the heart of Web authoring, and Java's implementation is very closely linked to HTML. Remember that Java applets are designed to be platform-independent, as is HTML. Because applets are specifically designed to be used in conjunction with the Web, there needed to be a standard way to invoke applets within a browser. To meet this need, a new set of HTML tags that specify the information needed to run an applet was created.

The HTML code that is associated with an applet provides the browser with important information about the applet. The HTML code can be used to do the following tasks:

- Specify the directory of the applet
- Specify the location of code the applet uses
- Specify the screen size of the applet
- Provide alternatives for non-Java-capable browsers
- Pass parameters on to the applet

There are really only two basic tags, <APPLET> and <PARAM>. The rest of the HTML for applets are extensions of these two tags. So by adding a few basic HTML tags and adapting some existing ones, you can specify all the necessary information needed by a browser to run your applet. The advantage of using HTML code instead of designing a new specification is compatibility. Browsers are designed to understand HTML, and even non-Java-compatible browsers can gain some information from the Applet HTML, such as an alternate image or tag to display instead of the applet.

Understanding the <APPLET> Tag

Adding an applet to your Web page is simply a matter of using the <APPLET> tag. This tag lets the browser know that you are going to provide specific information in regards to a Java applet you want to appear on your page. The <APPLET> tag also accepts a number of attributes, such as code, width, and height, that allow you to further customize the appearance of an applet on your pages. The basic <APPLET> tag format is as follows:

```
<html>
<applet code=filename.class width=n height=n>
</applet>
</html>
```

The <APPLET> tag follows HTML convention, beginning with <APPLET> and ending with </APPLET>. The <APPLET> tag has a few required attributes as well as some optional attributes.

The code attribute, which is required, specifies the name of the Java applet that you are adding to your page. Remember that Java is based on the tenets of object-oriented programming, and that all applets are themselves objects. That is why applets are named with the .class extension. Chapter 9, "Java Objects," discusses more about the nature of objects, but for now, remember that an applet is named *filename.class*:

```
code=filename.class
```

The <APPLET> tag also requires that you specify values for the width and height attributes, which control the size of the applet:

```
width=n and height=n
```

The width and height attributes are designed to enable you to specify the starting dimensions of your applet in pixels. Because the applet is a part of the Web page, you must give the applet space on the Web page to run in (see Figure 6.1).

The following guidelines are useful to keep in mind when determining the initial size of your applet:

1. If your applet contains a graphic image, use the dimensions of the graphic as your starting dimensions. If you have more than one graphic, use the dimensions of the largest graphic, if possible.

2. If your applet provides a function requiring user input, size the applet so that the input fields or user interface elements are all clearly visible.

3. Try to optimize the size of your images for a 14- or 15-inch monitor. There are a wide variety of monitors in the world, and predicting the size someone will use when viewing your page is impossible. However, 14- and 15-inch monitors are very common sizes, and those users with larger monitors will see your applet fine even if it is optimized for a smaller size.

Figure 6.1.
The width *and* height
*attributes specify an
applet's initial size in
pixels.*

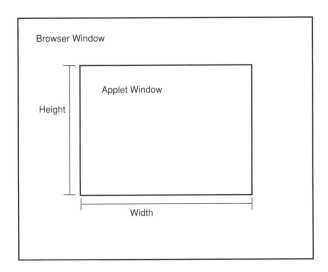

In addition to these required tags and attributes, you can use a number of other attributes to provide the details of how your applet will appear on the page. These <APPLET> attributes allow you to give very detailed information about the applet you are specifying, and they function the same as other HTML attributes. Some of them are probably familiar to you from other uses in HTML. These attributes are described in the following sections.

codebase=URL

The codebase is the base URL location of your Java applet. When you use the code=*filename*.*class* attribute, the *filename* is either relative to the current document or a specified codebase. Specifying a codebase allows you to have your code in a different directory from the page your applet appears on, which can be handy for reusing applets on different pages around your server. For example, the LED TickerTape Applet you added in Chapter 5, "Finding and Using Applets," contained the following line:

```
<applet codebase="classes" code="TickerTape" width=500 height=59>
```

In this example, the codebase attribute lets the browser know that the applet is stored in the "classes" directory. The code attribute provides the filename of the applet, and the codebase attribute can specify the location of that code.

name=name

The name attribute allows you to specify a symbolic name (like a nickname) for an applet. If you are designing your applets so that they build on each other for functionality or require another applet to process information, the applets need some way of identifying each other in order to exchange information. This attribute lets you name your applet so other applets can communicate with it by name. For example, you could add a name to the TickerTape Applet by using the following code:

```
<applet codebase="classes" code="TickerTape" name="LED" width=500 height=59>
```

If you had another applet that created text to be displayed on the LED screen, you could give that applet the name LED and it would know you were referring to TickerTape.class.

align=[center, left, right]

You have probably seen the align attribute before. With applets, the align attribute functions the same way it does for images; it enables you to align the applet on the right-hand side, left-hand side, or the center of a page. To center the TickerTape Applet, for example, you would use the following code:

```
<applet codebase="classes" code="TickerTape" width=500 height=59 align="center">
```

vspace=n and hspace=n

When you use the align attribute to position an applet, you might want to make sure that no other elements overlap or infringe on the applet's area. The vspace=n and hspace=n attributes enable you to specify a buffer space horizontally or vertically around an applet in pixels so that other elements are spaced a decent distance from the applet. For example, because the TickerTape Applet displays text, you might not want any of the page elements to bump up against it and diminish readability:

```
<applet codebase="classes" code="TickerTape" width=500 height=59 vspace=25
hspace=25>
```

This line of code ensures that no elements can be within 25 pixels of the LED display.

alt="text"

When you are designing Web pages with Java, consider the possibility that someone viewing your page is not using a Java-capable browser. The `alt` attribute allows you to specify an image, text, or URL to be viewed in place of your Java applet. That way, users of non-Java browsers are not confused by a service missing on your Web page and may even be encouraged to get a Java browser to check out your site. For example, the following line causes users without a Java-capable browser to see the "Sorry..." message:

```
<applet codebase="classes" code="TickerTape" width=500 height=59

alt"Sorry, you need a Java browser to view this applet">
```

Customizing Applets with Parameters

Many applets exist to provide customized features on a Web page, and for these applets you might actually include all the settings in the code. But for the most part, applets are most useful because they are reusable, and therefore it makes sense to make applets configurable with parameters. For example, the LED Sign Applet (see Figure 6.2) utilizes parameters to control the colors of the sign, the speed of the scrolling text, and the text that is displayed. By controlling these attributes with parameters rather than hardcoding them, the applet becomes more robust and flexible, allowing more people to add the applet to their own home pages.

Figure 6.2.
The LED Sign Applet accepts user parameters to specify the message shown.

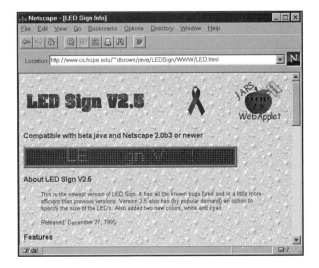

You use the <PARAM> tag to pass parameters to the applet. In fact, you must use the <PARAM> tag with the <APPLET> tag for it to have any meaning, so in a way even it is an attribute to the <APPLET> tag. The <PARAM> tag is an HTML markup tag with two attributes of its own: name and value, as shown below:

```
<param name=name value="value">
```

The name attribute enables you to specify the parameter name, and the value attribute enables you to specify the value for the named parameter. The <PARAM> tag does not require a closing tag and is used to specify the values of parameters that are passed on to your applet before it executes on the Web page. The amount of <PARAM> tags varies from applet to applet, depending on the number of parameters an applet is designed to take. An applet requires one <PARAM> tag for each parameter you want to set.

Putting It All Together

The last section covered the HTML tags and attributes you use to add a Java applet to a Web page. The following HTML code incorporates some of these tags and attributes:

```
<applet codebase="classes" code="TickerTape" width=500 height=59
alt="Sorry, this requires Java" align="center">
<param name=text value="Congrats! You now have a Ticker Tape applet">
<param name=backcolour value="black">
<param name=framecolour value="darkgrey">
<param name=ledcolour value="red">
<param name=ledoffcolour value="darkgray">
<param name=framethick value=3>
<param name=ledsize value=3>
<param name=ledtype value=0>
<param name=ledspacing value=1>
<param name=speed value=100>
<img src="sorry.gif">
</applet>
```

In this code example, the Java applets are stored in a classes directory in the Web directory, so the codebase attribute is used to specify the location. Next, the name of the applet is specified with code=TickerTape. The width and the height attributes open the applet with the dimensions of 500×59 pixels, and the applet is centered on the page, as the align attribute indicates. This applet also accepts 10 parameters, which are set with the <PARAM> tag.

Next, notice that there is an <IMG> tag before the closing <APPLET> tag. This tag specifies an alternate image for non-Java-capable browsers. The alt attribute with the <APPLET> tag enables you to specify the text displayed by text-only, non-Java browsers. A Java browser might also display this text while loading the applet.

> Note: The <APPLET> tag allows you to include any standard HTML code, such as an <IMG> tag, before closing the <APPLET> tag to be used as an alternative to the applet. The HTML tags you use here will not be displayed by a Java-compatible browser, but they will be used by other browsers to display whatever you specify. It might be a good idea here to include a screenshot of your applet along with an explanation or perhaps a sorry.gif image that lets users know they cannot view your applet.

Look at the following applet HTML file:

```
<applet codebase="calc" code="Calculator.class" width=185 height=295
alt="Yet Another RPN Calculator">
<img border=0 src="../images/calculator.gif">
</applet>
```

In this example, the applet does not accept any parameters, but it does utilize the <IMG> tag to provide an alternate image. The <APPLET> tag information is very straightforward; it provides the name of the directory containing the code, calc , the name of the applet itself, Calculator.class, and the starting size. The image specified is in the standard <IMG> tag format, but because it comes before the closing <APPLET> tag, it will only be read by non-Java-capable browsers. Figure 6.3 shows the output when this page is viewed with a non-Java-capable browser.

Figure 6.3.
The alternate image displayed by a non-Java-capable browser.

Design Issues

The HTML you need to add applets to your pages is pretty simple. If you have experience with HTML and have written your own Web pages, you should have no trouble adding Java applets to your page. But it can also be easy to go overboard on applets, and forget that too much of a good thing can lead to trouble. This section takes a look at some design issues you need to consider when using Java on the Web.

Design Aesthetics

Applets bring new aesthetic concerns to the Web just as any new visual feature does. When designing your pages, you may want to make a list of how applets can enhance your pages and also how they may detract. For example, the glowing buttons in Figure 6.4 might add a nice visual element to a page, but some people might consider them gimmicky. Once you have considered all of the implications, you will have a better sense of how to use applets you have acquired or programmed.

Figure 6.4.
The glowing buttons on the Grey Associates page (http://www.greyassoc.com) enhance the page with applets without detracting from the overall design.

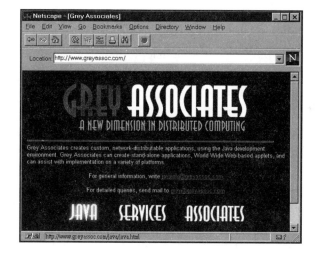

Color

Remember that applets add color to a Web page just as any other graphic element does. If you are very color-conscious, and you want to integrate a color scheme into your Web pages, try to select applets that either match your color scheme or that can be customized to fit your color scheme. Remember that an applet with a large black area might fade into the background of a black Web page (see Figure 6.5).

Figure 6.5.
The applets on this site
don't add much to the
design and fade into the
background of the page,
making them difficult
to see.

Look and Feel

Some applets have distinct looks, perhaps in the graphics and sometimes in the user interface. Try to select applets that enhance the look of your pages without going against it. For example, a scrolling LED light sign might be great for showcasing new bands for a local nightclub, but it might seem inappropriate for announcing services for a local mortuary. Applets can create distinct impressions for users, and a wrong first impression can be disastrous to a Web site.

Animation Craze

Animations can be a great way to make a Web page more lively. They can also be a great way to make a Web page more confusing. Although animations can be used in very subtle ways to make a Web page stand out, they can be overdone just like any other effect. Animation techniques and Java can be used to create anything from buttons that glow when selected to fully animated Web page mascots, and both of these uses have their place somewhere on the Web (see Figure 6.6). However, a page with a scrolling text bar, mobile buttons, a live clock, and an animated mascot might overwhelm users with too much information. Just as a boring page can keep users from coming back, so can a page that frightens them off with too many moving parts (see Figure 6.7).

Figure 6.6.
This applet shows how animation can integrate with standard elements, such as a logo, to create variation.

Figure 6.7.
This page features five separate animations: a flipping picture, rotating logos, glowing logos, and a billboard. The page is visually busy and distracting to the viewer's eye.

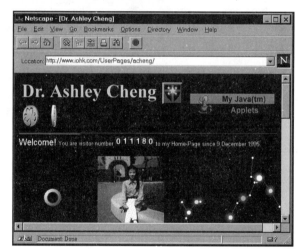

Functional Design

In addition to changing the visual design of Web pages, applets can also change the functional design. If you have an applet on your Web page that provides a specific service or performs a task for the user, you should take some functional design issues into account.

Sizing Applets

Keep in mind that you must provide the initial starting size for an applet in the HTML code that adds an applet to your page. This size could just be an arbitrary amount, but you want to select the size that maximizes an applet's features in most cases. Suppose you have an applet that asks the user to input information into various fields. If you just select an arbitrary size, input fields might get cut off. The end result is a less effective applet. The same holds true for applets that are designed to display information, be it text or images. You want to size your applets so that the prominent information is seen clearly when your applet opens, but you don't want to hog all the on-screen space. Try to strike a balance between the applet and the page content (see Figure 6.8).

Figure 6.8.
This Web page shows how you can showcase applets without forsaking overall page design.

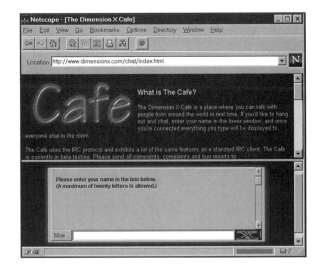

Placing Applets

Placing applets also becomes an issue when considering functionality. You might want to place the applet so it is highlighted by the text from the page, or you might want to set the applet apart from the rest of the page by using other HTML elements or standard graphics (see Figure 6.9). However you choose to integrate your applets into your Web pages, don't get carried away with applets, but instead look at the site as a whole and use applets to enhance your pages (see Figure 6.10).

Figure 6.9.
On this page, the scrolling text applet is a part of the overall design, adding functionality but not detracting from the page's look.

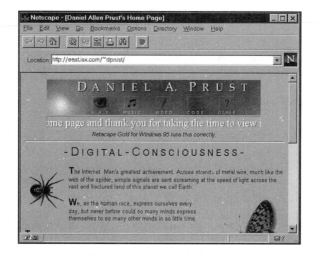

Figure 6.10.
This scrolling text applet adds confusion to the page. The text scrolls in multiple directions and speeds, making readability very difficult.

Sound

It might not seem obvious that sound is a design aspect, but until now, sound has not been obtrusive on the World Wide Web. Until Java, sounds on Web pages would require a user to click an icon to activate a sound file, so users were never surprised by sounds out of the blue. Java changes that. With Java, you can incorporate sound into a page so that a sound is played as soon as someone accesses your page. Because many people might not realize this is possible, they also might not have their machines configured to deal well with sound. They might have volumes set too loud, or they might be looking at your page from a place where extraneous sound is not appreciated, like school or work.

Sound design is not so much a matter of taste as it is a matter of manners. If sound will greatly enhance your pages, by all means use it, but try to use it wisely. The following are some tips for using sound on your pages:

- Avoid long sounds. Long sounds can cause people to panic as they wait for the sound to finish playing. People can be quite embarrassed trying to cover the speakers on a machine while waiting for a long sound to finish playing. Long sounds can also increase download time and make your pages slow.

- Avoid rude or loud sounds. Just as a long sound can cause embarrassment, so can a loud or rude sound. No one wants to click on a page to receive a loud jackhammer for an under-construction page, and certainly no one wants to have a computer swearing or making inappropriate sounds when they are viewing a page around others.

So if you need to use sound, plan it well. Some very successful sites incorporate sound in a tasteful, non-obtrusive way (see Figure 6.11). If not used with a great deal of care, sounds can actually detract from an applet (see Figure 6.12). If you use some simple common courtesy when designing your pages, they will have a far broader appeal.

Figure 6.11.
*The Dave Matthews'
Band (*http://
www.ids.net/~reddog/
dmb/*) site uses sound
well.*

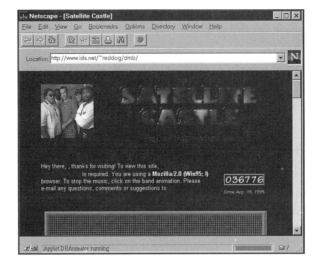

Figure 6.12.
The Jumping Frog Applet uses a very repetitive sound that annoys more than contributes to the applet.

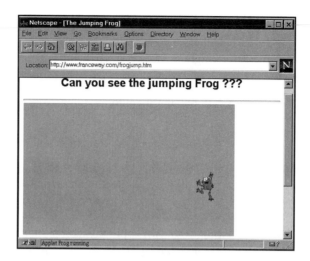

Avoiding Applet Clutter

It is very easy to go overboard on applets. Remember that not every page needs an applet, and very few pages need several. Cluttering a page with applets can decrease the number of people who will return to your pages. Applet clutter can be distracting and sometimes outright annoying. If you have been using the Web for a while, you might remember the Netscape <BLINK> tag. What was meant to be a simple device to add strong emphasis soon came to be associated with annoying Web pages. Java applets have the same potential. If used properly, they can make your site great. If they are overdone, they can make your site unpopular.

Download Time

Placing tons of applets on your Web pages might not look bad, but it might slow your pages down to the point that they are unusable. Because applets are downloaded over the Net from a host server, each applet takes a small amount of time to be downloaded before it can run. For one or two applets, this amount of time is not really significant (unless your applet is huge!) and is more like downloading a large image.

However, if your page contains several applets, it can begin to rack up download time very quickly. If users have to wait 10 minutes for all of the applets on your page to download, they might not wait at all. Many people are paying for access time, and that time is money. There is not much on the Web that people are willing to wait that long to load, so try to take into account downloading time when designing your applet pages as well.

Summary

All this information might seem a bit overwhelming, but it all boils down to a few simple design rules:

1. Design pages with the user in mind.
2. Use applets to enhance your pages, not show off.
3. Design with Java's unique features (animation and sound, for example) in mind.

If you follow these basic guidelines and produce the kinds of pages you would like to see, then other people will want to see them as well.

Chapter 7 discusses the Java Developer's Kit (JDK). The JDK is the primary tool you will need to start developing your own applets. Chapter 7 talks about the tools provided in the JDK and how to use them to create applets from scratch. Later chapters talk about the Java language.

PART IV

Learning to Program Java

The Java Developer's Kit

The Java Developer's Kit (JDK) is an assemblage of all the components you need to produce your own applets. The JDK is available on a variety of platforms, and you will need to obtain and understand the JDK in order to start producing applets. This chapter talks about the elements that make up the JDK and how you can use them to start building your own applets. Once you get started with the JDK, the chapter provides the first applet you can enter from scratch: HelloWorld.

The Components of the Java Developer's Kit

At the heart of developing applets is the Java Developer's Kit. The Java Developer's Kit combines into one package all of the tools and information that you need to program your own applets. The JDK contains a number of components designed to help you compile, debug, and view your applets on a variety of different platforms.

Currently, the JDK is available for the following platforms:

- Sun Solaris 2.3, 2.4, and 2.5 SPARC-based machines
- Microsoft Windows NT and Windows 95
- Macintosh System 7.5

In the future, the JDK may be available for more UNIX platforms, and eventually various aspects of the JDK may be assembled into commercial packages. A number of companies are already developing Integrated Development Environments (IDEs) for Java with their own compilers, which are designed to replace the Sun Java compiler. However, for the beginner, the JDK represents a good starting place and provides all the tools you need to write and compile your applets.

Each of the components provided in the JDK exists as a separate program with its own function. Unfortunately, not much integration exists among the elements in the JDK, which can make using the JDK a bit confusing at first. The following sections describe the JDK's components and how they function.

> Caution: Keep in mind that each version of the Java Developer's Kit is platform-specific. The individual commands you use to evoke each component may vary. There also might be subtle variations from platform to platform based on the interface model you are using (for example, Windows versus Macintosh). The JDK elements generally function like other programs in the operating system you choose, but you can also consult the JDK documentation to find out about specific differences in the JDK for each platform.

javac

The Java compiler is javac. The javac compiler reads in the Java code you have written and converts it to the bytecode that can be run on any platform using the Java Virtual Machine. The code you write must be contained in a file called `filename.java` in order to be compiled properly. The compiler produces a file called `filename.class`, which contains the compiled bytecode. Normally, the compiler creates the `.class` file in the same directory as the `.java` file; however, you can specify a different directory.

The compiler is invoked with the following command:

```
javac [ options ] filename.java ...
```

The compiler takes a number of options to enable you to tweak its behavior. The `-classpath` option enables you to specify a directory in which the standard Java classes are stored. The javac compiler uses a number of classes that are provided with the JDK, and generally these are all stored in a common directory, such as `C:\jdk\java\classes`. If you have stored the classes in a different directory and want to override the default installation, you can use this option to specify the path to the new directory:

```
-classpath path
```

The `-d` option enables you to specify a specific output directory for the compiler. When the compiler produces the `.class` file, it stores the file in the directory specified. The syntax for this option is as follows:

```
-d directory
```

The `-g` option enables you to turn on the compiler's debug tables. The Java debugging tools can then use the debug tables to help you debug your code. The syntax for this option is as follows:

```
-g
```

The `-nowarn` option disables warning output from the compiler. Warnings are errors in your code that do not prevent the code from executing, but might create unpredictable behavior or errors once the code is running. If you are aware of the warnings your code is producing, you might disable the warnings to concentrate on serious bugs, but remember that the warnings still apply. The `-nowarn` option can help cut down the clutter of text generated when you compile the code, but keep in mind that the warnings can be useful as well. The syntax for this option is as follows:

```
-nowarn
```

The `-O` option is designed to optimize your code to run a bit faster. Optimization generally causes your files to be a bit larger, which might be a factor when considering download time. The syntax for this option is as follows:

```
-O
```

The `-verbose` option causes the compiler to print out a variety of information about what source code is being compiled and what class libraries are being loaded. This information can be useful for optimizing and debugging your code. The syntax for this option is as follows:

```
-verbose
```

java

In the Java Developer's Kit, java is the Java interpreter, also known as the Java Virtual Machine. This program enables you to run Java bytecode by translating between the Java code and your operating system. If you are programming standalone applications with Java, you can use java to execute your application. You do not need to use java directly if you are programming applets, however, because applets are designed to be used in conjunction with a browser. If you do not have access to a Java-capable browser, you can use the appletviewer (which is also part of the JDK) instead of java to view applets.

jdb

The jdb is the Java debugger, and you use it to help you locate errors in your programs. It can be invoked in conjunction with an applet or browser and will provide you with output regarding errors in your program. Unfortunately, the debugger is only a command-line debugger. You can invoke it using a command such as the following:

```
C:\> jdb browser.hotjava
```

This command launches the debugger in conjunction with the HotJava browser. The jdb debugger also can accept the commands listed in Table 7.1.

Table 7.1. Commands for use with jdb.

Command	What it does
help	Provides help on how to use the jdb, an extremely useful command
print	Enables you to print out Java objects and view their contents
dump	Dumps all of an object's instance variables
threads	Lists all the current threads
where	Dumps the stack of the current or specified thread

For a novice programmer, the debugger can be very hard to use. As it so happens, when you use the javac compiler to compile a program that contains errors, the compiler provides you with information regarding the bug anyway. For example, the following code contains an error:

```
import java.awt.Graphics;

public class HelloWorld extends java.applet.Applet {

    public void init() {
        resize(150,25)
    }
```

```
    public void paint(Graphics g) {
        g.drawString("Hello world!", 50, 25);
    }
}
```

Suppose you don't realize that there is an error in the code and you try to compile it using the javac compiler:

```
C:\java\bin\javac> javac HelloWorld.java
```

When you invoke the compiler, it generates the following text:

```
HelloWorld.java:4: ';' expected.
                    resize(150,25)
                              ^

1 error
C:\java\bin>
```

This information is quite useful. The compiler has informed you that there is one error in the code, and it has even given you the information necessary to find the error. The :4: following the filename indicates that the error is in line 4 of your code. The compiler also points out that the error was caused because it expected a semicolon at the end of the line. Now you can go back and change the line to read as follows:

```
resize(150, 25);
```

Your code will now compile without any problems. Of course, most commercial products have compilers that automatically take you to the error in the code by launching an editor and highlighting the error, but Java still has a way to go. As Integrated Development Environments become available, debugging options will likely increase, and debugging will become much easier.

javah

As previously mentioned, Java has the capability to incorporate native methods from other programming languages, such as C. With javah, you can create C language header and source files from your Java code so that you can then compile those methods using C on your machine to create the native method. For beginning applet programming, this procedure is not necessary; in fact, because applets are designed to be platform-independent, native methods are not generally necessary.

javap

The Java Class File Disassembler that enables you to examine compiled source code is javap. You can use it to print out various methods and variables in a class in order to obtain information about the construction of a program.

javadoc

One of the more useful features of Java is javadoc. It is the Java API Documentation Generator, a program that enables you to generate documentation for your applets based on the comments contained within your code. This program makes it easy to generate an immediate guide on how to use your applet that is accurate and doesn't involve much extra work on your part.

Suppose your code were commented as follows:

```
/**
 * The text in this comment will be turned into documentation
 *
 * <pre>
 *    An example of code.
 * </pre>
 *
 * @version      1.0
 * @author       John Doe
 */

class Example extends Applet {
...
}
```

Document comments begin with /** and can contain embedded HTML tags (such as <PRE>) and special comment tags designated by the @ symbol. Chapter 8, "Speaking Java: Java Syntax" talks more about the specifics of using comments. When you then run javadoc with your source file,

```
javadoc filename.java
```

javadoc produces a formatted HTML file that contains the documentation specified in your code. You can then use that HTML file as accompanying documentation for your applet.

To understand how javadoc works, take a look at the TicTacToe sample applet provided with the JDK. First, you need to be in the same directory as the code file because javadoc reads the code and gets its information from the comments in the code. To produce the documentation for the TicTacToe applet, invoke the javadoc program with the following line:

```
C:\java\demos\TicTacToe> javadoc TicTacToe.java
```

This line should launch javadoc, which will produce output that resembles the following:

```
Generating packages.html
generating documentation for the class TicTacToe
Generating index
Sorting 5 items . . . done
Generating tree
C:\java\demos\TicTacToe>
```

That's it! Now there should be a file called `TicTacToe.html` in the directory; this file is the main page for the TicTacToe applet documentation (see Figure 7.1). This documentation includes a breakdown of the applet classes used in the applet and the comments found in the applet's code. Running this program can be an excellent way to learn more about the structure or usage of an applet.

Figure 7.1.

The javadoc application produces HTML-based documentation from the comments in the program code.

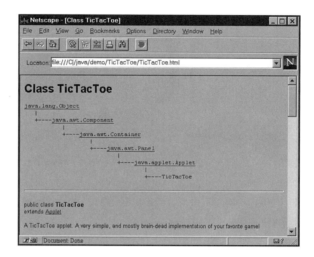

appletviewer

The appletviewer is a program that enables you to run your applets without having a Java-capable Web browser handy. The appletviewer is invoked by calling a file that contains the HTML code for your applet. The appletviewer then reads the HTML code and launches your applet in its own window on your machine.

Using the appletviewer can have several advantages over using a browser. First, the appletviewer is a relatively small program that launches very quickly. Because Web browsers do a whole lot more than just show applets, they take longer to launch and might prevent you from running an applet in the background while you tweak the code.

Second, because the appletviewer does not incorporate browser-specific features, it can be a good way to check your applet for generic compatibility issues. As discussed previously, browsers restrict applets in certain ways. The appletviewer can provide you with information about how your applet runs outside of any particular browser context. You can launch the appletviewer by typing in `appletviewer` followed by the name of the HTML file for the applet you want to view:

```
c:\java> appletviewer example.html
```

This example causes the appletviewer to display the `example.html` file, which in turn launches a sample applet. The appletviewer then opens its own window and runs the applet (see Figure 7.2).

Figure 7.2.
An applet viewed in the appletviewer.

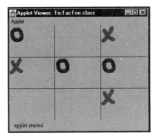

> Note: The Java Developer's Kit does not contain a Java-specific text editor. Many IDEs may contain a text editor with features geared toward writing code, but you are free to use any text editor you choose for writing code with the JDK. Keep in mind that the editor must be able to save files as plain text, but beyond that you are free to use any program you choose.

Sample Applets

In addition to these development tools, the JDK also contains a number of sample applets that are designed to showcase the abilities of Java. The sample applets are provided complete with source code and any supplementary files, so you can run them straight off your machine using the appletviewer or your Web browser. Also, because the examples include source code, you can use the code to see how specific features were implemented, which can be a very valuable learning experience.

The applets provided with the JDK 1.0 release are the following:

- The Animator applet is a simple animator that displays a series of images to create a flipbook animation effect.
- ArcTest is an applet that enables you to specify an arc and draw it on-screen. It provides a good example of advanced graphics techniques.
- BarChart is a simple bar chart example.
- Blink is an applet of text blinking out of control.
- Bouncing Heads is just what it sounds like: disembodied heads bouncing around in an area on the screen.
- Card Test is an example of various object layouts in Java.

- Dither Test is an advanced graphics test showing the results of different dithers in Java.

- Draw Test is a simple drawing applet. It enables you to draw lines or points with a selection of colors. It also is a good example of some advanced graphics techniques.

- Fractal is an applet of some fractal figures in Java.

- Graphics Test is an example of some graphics manipulations; it is designed for the advanced programmer.

- Graph Layout is an example of an interactive graph showing relationships between objects.

- Image Map is an example of an image map that provides real-time feedback rather than cryptic coordinates.

- Image Test provides examples of advanced image manipulations and transformations.

- Jumping Box is a box that jumps around based on your mouse movement.

- Molecule Viewer displays a molecule and enables the user to rotate the view of the molecule in real time.

- Nervous Text is text that hops around like jumping beans.

- Scrolling Images is an applet that scrolls a series of images across the screen.

- Simple Graph is a very simple graph example.

- Spread Sheet is an example of a spreadsheet application.

- TicTacToe is a game of tic-tac-toe played against the computer. (This applet is deliberately flawed so you can win once in a while.)

- Tumbling Duke is a variation of the Animator applet that shows a tumbling duke (the Java mascot).

- Under Construction is an animated applet featuring a construction worker duke.

- Wire Frame displays a wireframe shape that the user can manipulate with the mouse.

Where to Find the JDK

The official source for the Java Developer's Kit is Javasoft; the JDK is also on the CD-ROM accompanying this book. You can get the JDK from the CD, or you can download the JDK directly from the Web at the following URL (see Figure 7.3):

```
http://www.javasoft.com/JDK-1.0/index.html
```

Figure 7.3.
*The Javasoft site
contains a page with
links to download the
Java Developer's Kit.*

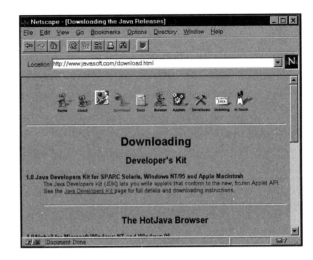

Keep in mind that this site is often very busy, and it can take up to 20 minutes to download the JDK during peak usage times. You can also obtain the files from the Javasoft FTP site:

```
ftp.javasoft.com          in the /pub directory
```

The filenames are as follows:

```
JDK-beta1-mac.sea.bin          Macintosh System 7.5 binary format
JDK-beta1-mac.sea.hqx          Macintosh System 7.5 HQX format
JDK-1_0-win32-x86.exe          Windows 95 and NT version
JDK-1_0-solaris2-sparc.tar.Z   Sun Solaris (SPARC) 2.3, 2.4, and 2.5
```

> **Caution:** Make sure that your FTP client is set to binary when downloading these files or they will not decompress properly.

Installing the JDK

After you download the archive of the JDK, you must install it on your machine. The specifics of how you complete the installation vary from platform to platform, so this section divides the steps depending on your type of machine: UNIX, Windows 95/NT, or the Macintosh.

Installing on UNIX

First, use FTP to obtain the compressed archive of the JDK, as shown in the following FTP session:

```
$ ftp ftp.javasoft.com
 Name (ftp.javasoft.com): anonymous
 331 Guest login ok, send your complete e-mail address as password.
 Password: user@machine
        << informational messages <<
 ftp> binary
 200 Type set to I.
 ftp> cd pub
        << more informational messages <<
 250 CWD command successful.
 ftp> get JDK-1_0-solaris2-sparc.tar.Z
 200 PORT command successful.
 150 Opening BINARY mode data connection for JDK-1_0-solaris2-sparc.tar.Z
(4595974 bytes).
 226 Transfer complete.
 local: JDK-1_0-solaris2-sparc.tar.Z remote: JDK-1_0-solaris2-sparc.tar.Z
 4595974 bytes received in 1.4e+02 seconds (30 Kbytes/s)
 ftp> quit
```

After you have used FTP to obtain the file JDK-1_0-solaris2-sparc.tar.Z, decompress the archive using the following command:

```
zcat JDK-1_0-solaris2-sparc.tar.Z ¦ tar xf -
```

This command creates a java directory in the current directory. The java directory will have all the tools you need to begin working with Java. Before you begin though, be sure to delete the .tar file (to clean up file space) and add the java/bin directory to your path (specified in your shell .rc file).

Caution: When you uncompress the JDK archive, **do not unzip** the file lib/ classes.zip. Doing so will adversely affect the operation of Java.

Installing on Windows (NT, 95)

The Windows versions of the JDK are self-extracting archives. Once you have downloaded the binary, you should have an executable file (with a .EXE extension) that you can run to extract the archive. Run the executable in your root directory to begin extracting the JDK. The archive creates a Java directory named c:\java that contains all the necessary files. Before running any of the applets, you need to update your environment variables for the path in your autoexec.bat file.

Caution: When you uncompress the JDK archive, **do not unzip** the file lib/ classes.zip. Doing so will adversely affect the operation of Java.

Installing on the Macintosh

The Macintosh version of the JDK is available in the binary and HQX formats. When downloading, if you choose the binary format, be sure that you have MacBinary enabled in your FTP client. If you download the HQX, make sure that you have a compression utility such as StuffIt or are using an FTP client that supports the HQX format, such as Fetch. The binary (or converted HQX document) produces a self-extracting archive that contains all the elements of the JDK. Double-click on the archive to extract it to your hard drive and begin using Java.

Where to Find Documentation

Keep in mind that Java is a full-featured programming language. Although it may seem as though this chapter has listed everything there is to know about Java, it has only scratched the surface of available information. Soon Sun will be releasing a multivolume set of complete documentation for Java, but the information will be too technical and too lengthy to be useful for most people's needs. However, a variety of documents are available at Javasoft that can help you as you learn Java and answer some more advanced questions you might have.

The Java Tool Documentation

The Java Developer's Kit tools have their own documentation that can provide you with the complete set of instructions and options available for each tool. This chapter provides you with the basic commands and options you need to get started, but you might find it useful to consult the official documentation as you progress with Java programming. You can find the JDK tools documentation at `http://java.sun.com/JDK-1.0/tools/`.

The API Documentation

The Java Application Programming Interface (API) is the specification by which all Java programs are written. Many functions that you will want to use in your applets have already been written for you by one of the Java developers, and these functions have been categorized into packages. The API packages contain a variety of classes, objects, and methods that you will need to program anything in Java. You need to be aware of what programming resources are available and how those resources are used, and this information is in the Java API. Keep in mind that the API is a fairly technical document, and you should have an understanding of the Java basics before consulting it. But once you have a solid grasp of basic Java programming, the API will prove to be an invaluable resource.

You can find the Java 1.0 API documentation at the following URL:

```
http://www.javasoft.com/JDK-1.0/api/packages.html
```

The documentation exists as a HTML document to make it easier to cross-reference sections, and is a useful document to have handy when embarking on a large programming project.

How to Compile Java Code

Now that you have the Java Developer's Kit downloaded and installed on your machine, it's time to start working with some Java code. The first applet you are going to work with is the HelloWorld applet. This applet displays the words "Hello world!" on your screen and is the simplest applet you could have that actually does something. For the time being, don't worry if you don't understand what the code for this applet means. This exercise is supposed to make you comfortable with compiling Java code and using the appletviewer before you launch into writing Java applets. You'll start with the basics of Java programming in Chapter 8 and advance from there.

First, you can either set up a directory to keep your Java code in or work straight from the Java directory. Once you start to write a lot of code, you will most likely want to keep your applets separate for organization, but for now, do things your way.

The first step in creating an applet is writing the Java code. Fire up your text editor and create a file called HelloWorld.java. The HelloWorld.java file is the source code for your first applet. Remember, this code must be in a plain text file, and it also must be named HelloWorld.java in order to compile correctly. Enter the following code into your file:

```java
import java.awt.Graphics;

public class HelloWorld extends java.applet.Applet {

    public void init() {
        resize(150,25);
    }

    public void paint(Graphics g) {
        g.drawString("Hello world!", 50, 25);
    }
}
```

In the code you just typed in, notice this line:

```java
public class HelloWorld extends java.applet.Applet {
```

This line tells the compiler that you are creating a new class called HelloWorld, which extends an existing class called java.applet.Applet. All applets are classes, which is why you use the `public class` statement. The name of your class is going to be `HelloWorld`, which also must be the name of your file. If you were to change the line to `public class MyFirstApplet`, then your source code file would have to be called `MyFirstApplet.java`.

After you have established your applet, you need to set up your applet with the following:

```
public void init() {
resize(150,25);
}
```

This code enables you to create a graphics area that is 150 by 25 pixels where you can then draw your text with the following code:

```
public void paint(Graphics g) {
g.drawString("Hello world!", 50, 25);
}
```

All this code does is use the Graphics context `drawString` to draw the specified text string at the given coordinates. Chapter 8 talks more about the syntax of Java, but for now, you have a simple, functioning applet that you are ready to compile.

> **Tip:** If you receive errors during the first time you try to compile code, don't be discouraged. The compiler is very sensitive to typographic errors in code, so double-check to make sure all of the { and } are in the correct places.

The next step is to use the javac compiler to turn your source code into a compiled Java applet that you can put on a home page. Run the Java compiler with the following command:

```
javac HelloWorld.java
```

This command should produce a file called `HelloWorld.class` in the same directory. This file is your compiled applet.

> **Note:** Macintosh users should note that the JDK components are drag-and-drop within the Macintosh OS. Instead of using a command line, you can just drag your code onto the javac icon to compile it.

As with any applet, you have to have an HTML file associated with your applet in order to view the applet with the appletviewer or a Web browser. Using your text editor, create a new file in the same directory as your code called `HelloWorld.html` that contains the following information:

```
<HTML>
<TITLE>Hello World Applet</TITLE>
<APPLET code="HelloWorld.class" width=150 height=25>
</APPLET>
</HTML>
```

Once you've saved this file, you are ready to view your applet in action. You can view it by opening the HTML file from your Java-capable Web browser or with the following appletviewer command:

```
appletviewer HelloWorld.html
```

You should then see output similar to that in Figure 7.4. Keep in mind that the way an applet looks is influenced by the method you use to view it, so if you are viewing the applet with a Web browser, it might look slightly different.

Figure 7.4.
The HelloWorld applet.

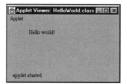

That's it! You've now created your first Web applet from scratch! You might want to get some more experience compiling applets before moving on to the following chapters. Remember, the JDK comes with a variety of sample applets, including the source code, which you can use to recompile the applets and gain some practice. When you feel comfortable compiling code, move on to Chapter 8 to learn more about the Java language.

Summary

Learning how to use the tools in the JDK is the first step in applet programming. Now you have the tools to create applets at your disposal, and you know how to use them. Keep in mind that other development environments exist; some will provide a much better programming interface, and some won't. But the JDK is the official environment from Sun and is a great way to start creating applets without investing a lot of money. You've seen how to use the JDK tools, and now you've even used those tools to create the HelloWorld applet. The next chapter moves on to discuss some more details about the Java programming language.

CHAPTER 8

Speaking Java: Java Syntax

Learning any programming language can be a daunting task. Java is no exception. It was designed to be on the cutting edge and can sometimes suffer from problems not found in more established languages. Luckily, Java also has been designed to be as simple as possible while remaining, for the most part, as powerful as any other modern programming language.

Java is, at its core, an object-oriented language. Often touted as the Holy Grail of programming, object-oriented programming is essentially a very useful way to break up large programs into smaller, more manageable pieces known as objects. Being object-oriented also means that programming isn't as straightforward as is might have been in a language like BASIC or even C.

The discussion of Java's object-oriented nature is not until the next chapter to keep things in this chapter as simple as possible so that you can better understand what can be put into objects. This chapter discusses some of the core functions in Java. If this information seems a little bit dry, it is. However, when you learn any new language (computer or human), there is a period of learning the very basics before being able to articulate interesting things. Have no fear, though; Java's syntax is not as strange as most other languages' syntax is.

Comments

Comments are the most underused syntax element in programming. A comment enables you to add notes to your code to make sure that when someone else (or you in a few years) reads your code and can't figure out what is going on, there is some guide to clear things up.

There are three ways to comment Java code:

```
/* This is a block comment */
/** This is a 'doc' comment **/

// This is a line comment
```

The block and 'doc' comments are both surrounded by beginning and end markers. They should be used when a paragraph or two needs to be said about a block of code in general. The 'doc' comments are one of Java's nicer features. This type of comment enables you to comment your code as you normally would, and they also can be read by the javadoc program to create on-the-fly HTML documentation for your applets. The line comment does not have an end marker; it marks everything to the end of the line as a comment. It is most useful to comment the program on a line-by-line basis.

The compiler ignores comments; they are there purely to help the programming. Feel free to write as much as you think is necessary, going overboard in explaining if necessary. That said, make sure that the comments you leave are pertinent. Many beginning programmers make the mistake of trying to comment every line, which is almost worse than no commenting at all. Why? First, the programmer tends to tire of all the commenting quickly and gives up on commenting entirely in the long run. Second, the important comments tend to get lost in the mass of verbiage. A good general rule on commenting is to look at a piece of code and ask yourself, "Is what this code does obvious?" If not, comment it.

Variables

Much like real life, there is a need in programming to remember things and to associate a name with those things. For instance, you refer to how old someone is by his or her age. Programming languages do the same thing. Statements in the language say things like the following line, which sets the age to be 22:

```
age = 22;
```

In this example, age is a variable because its value can be changed. You could set age to 30 at a later time. This is known as variable assignment: = assigns whatever is to the right of it to the variable to the left of it. The semicolon (;) is Java's way of indicating the end of the current statement.

In some languages, such as BASIC, variables can be created on the fly, and a statement like the preceding one could appear in the middle of a program. In Java, much like C or C++, all variables must be declared at the beginning of a program. When you declare a variable, you must specify both its name and its type. For instance, someone's age would be represented as an integer, which in Java is signified by int:

```
int age;

    age = 22;
```

The eight basic (or primitive) types available in Java fall into four categories: integer, floating-point number, character, and boolean.

Integer

Representing numbers is one of the most basic aspects of programming, and numbers can be represented as integers in most cases. An integer is a positive or negative whole number (but no fractional numbers). For example, 34 is an integer, but 34.5 is not. The following table lists the four types of integers available in Java:

Keyword	Type	Range
byte	8-bit integer	-256 to 255
short	16-bit integer	-32,768 to 32,767
int	32-bit integer	-2,147,483,648 to 2,147,483,647
long	64-bit integer	-9,223,372,036,854,775,808 to 9,223,372,036,854,775,807

The different integer types enable you to specify a larger or smaller range for the number that is stored in a variable. The int type should be sufficient for most purposes unless the value of the number that needs to be stored is huge (on the order of several billion) or if many smaller numbers need to be stored (in which case byte might make sense).

Floating-Point Numbers

Although most of the time integers are sufficient, sometimes it's necessary to store numbers with a decimal point, like 3.14132. These numbers are known as floating-point numbers. The following table lists the two types of floating-point numbers in Java.

Keyword	Type	Range
float	32-bit float	-2^24E-149 to 2^24E104
double	64-bit float	-2^53E-1045 to 2^53E1000

The following example shows how a floating-point number might be used:

```
float temperature;

temperature = 82.3;
```

The difference between the two is that the double type has more precision and can thus hold more decimal places. Most of the time it makes sense to stick with the float type, which is what most programmers do. The range for this type is quite large and needs to be indicated using scientific notation with a mantissa. A *mantissa* is the number following the E. It is the power of 10 to multiply the first part of the number by. For example, 100 would be 1.0E2, 200 would be 2.0E2, and 1,000 would be 1.0E3.

When deciding whether to use an integer or a floating-point number in an application, keep these things in mind:

■ On most machines, integers are processed much faster than floating-point numbers.

■ Floating-point numbers can hold much larger and smaller numbers than integers.

Character

A character is basically anything that can be typed on a keyboard: a letter (like *a*, *b*, or *c*), a single-digit number (1, 2, 3), or non-alphanumeric character (#, $, %).

Keyword	Type	Range
char	16-bit integer	Any Unicode character

The following is an example of how the character type could be used:

```
char letter_grade;

letter_grade = 'B';
```

Java differs slightly from other languages by including support for Unicode. Unicode is a standard that allows characters in languages other than English to be supported. Although support for this standard is not important to most people at the current time, it means that your applets can be used internationally without a complete rewrite. Think of Unicode as the new ASCII, but with the ability to handle foreign characters.

Boolean

In programming, comparisons between two things happen constantly. Decisions for what the program should do next are based upon on whether the result of a question was true or false. A variable containing a `true` or `false` value is known as a Boolean. A Boolean could be represented with an integer by using a 0 for `false` and a 1 for `true` (C programs usually use this method), but that method makes programs much harder to read. Java includes native support for Booleans.

Keyword	Type	Range
boolean	Boolean	true or false

The following is an example of the Boolean type in use:

```
boolean ready;

ready = false;
```

Booleans can only hold two values: `true` or `false`. They are not only useful for remembering what the value of a comparison was, but also to keep track of the current state of your program. For instance, you may have a slideshow applet that cycles through images automatically if the Cycle button is pressed. You could then have a Boolean called `cycle` that is changed to `true` or `false` when the button is pressed.

Expressions

An expression is the most fundamental operation in Java. Expressions are how work on and comparisons with basic data types are done. They are operations that result in a value. The following are some examples of expressions:

```
6 + (10 / 5)            // Returns the value of dividing 10 by five then adding
                        six to the result.

(37 / 10) * (82 - 3)    // Returns the value of dividing 37 by 10 and then
                        multiplying it by the result of 82 minus 3.

(value == 10)           // Returns true if value is equal to 10.

(2 < 4) && (value != 4) // Returns true if 2 is less than four and the variable
                        value does not equal 4.
```

Note that expressions are not listed with semicolons after them because by themselves they are meaningless; their result must be used for something (like a variable assignment).

Expressions are built out of operators and operands. The three main classes of operators are arithmetic, relational, and logical. An *operand* is the data that the operator does its work upon. For instance, in the expression 2 + 4, the plus sign (+) is the operator, and the numbers 2 and 4 are the operands.

Arithmetic Operators

Java uses infix notation with arithmetic operators, which means that the operators appear between the numbers (or variables). This notation should be quite familiar to you—it's the way math is usually written down, as shown in the following examples:

```
int result = 2 + 2 * 10;        // result = 22
int x = 10 / 4;                 // x = 2
int y = 10 * 10;                // y = 100
```

If you want to make sure certain operations are done first, use parentheses. For example, if you wanted to multiply 10 by the result of adding 2 plus 2 but were unsure of the rules of precedence (which operations occur before others), you could write

```
(2 + 2) * 10;
```

instead of

```
2 + 2 * 10
```

The parentheses would guarantee you that 2 would be added to 2 before it was multiplied by 10. If you are unsure of what operation takes precedence in an expression, go ahead and group parentheses around the operation you want to happen first.

Table 8.1 lists the common arithmetic operators in Java. The four major operations are obvious, but remainder, decrement, and increment need a bit more explanation.

Table 8.1. Arithmetic operators.

Operator	Action
+	Addition
-	Subtraction
*	Multiplication
/	Division
%	Remainder
--	Decrement
++	Increment

Remainder

When two numbers are divided by one another, there is often a remainder. When you use floating-point numbers, this remainder is included in the numbers that follow the decimal point. However, when you do integer division, this remainder is lost. For example, in

```
int result = 7 / 3;
```

result is equal to 2, but the information that 1 was left over is lost. The remainder operator (%) allows the remainder to be computed. Thus, in

```
int result = 7 % 3;
```

result is equal to 1 because that is what is left over when 7 is divided by 3.

Decrement and Increment

Addition and subtraction are operations that are done constantly in programming. In fact, 1 is added to or subtracted from a variable so often that this expression has its own operators: increment and decrement. The operator ++ adds (increments) 1 to its operand and -- subtracts (decrements) 1 from its operand. Therefore, the code

```
age++;
```

is equivalent to

```
age = age + 1;
```

Increment and decrement are special operators. Normally an operator couldn't appear by itself because it needs to be part of an expression. This rule is purposely broken with incrementing and decrementing, mainly in order to save typing.

Relational and Logical Operators

A relational operator is basically a way to compare two things to find out how they relate to one another. For example, you can check to see whether two things are equal to one another or whether one is greater than the other. Table 8.2 lists the available relational operators.

For example, to check to see whether age is equal to 16, you would use the == operator:

```
boolean is_sixteen == (age > 21);
```

If this expression is true, then the Boolean value true is assigned to is_sixteen, otherwise false. Note that this is very different than the assignment operator, which is a single equal sign. The assignment operator = sets the value of the variable to the left to the value of the expression on the right, whereas the equal relational operator == checks to see whether the value on the left is equivalent to the value on the right, and if it is, returns true.

Table 8.2. Relational operators.

Operator	Action
>	Greater than
<	Less than
>=	Greater than or equal
<=	Less than or equal
==	Equal
!=	Not equal

Quite often it is convenient to be able to do multiple relational tests at the same time. Logical operators (listed in Table 8.3) make this process possible.

Table 8.3. Logical operators.

Operator	Action
&&	And
||	Or
!	Negation

The And (&&) operator returns `true` only if *both* of its operands are true. Thus,

```
(2 == 2) && (3 < 4)
```

evaluates to `true` because 2 is equal to 2 and 3 is in fact less than 4. On the other hand,

```
(2 == 2) && (3 == 4)
```

evaluates to `false` because 3 is not equal to 4. In this case, one of the operands is false so the whole expression is false.

The Or operator (¦¦) is similar except that it evaluates to `true` if *either* of its operands are true. Therefore,

```
(2 == 2) && (3 == 4)
```

evaluates to `true` because (2 == 2) is true.

The Negation (!) operator is a bit strange. It takes its operand, which must be a Boolean, and gives the opposite Boolean value. Therefore, what was true is now false, and what was false is now true. For example,

```
!(2 == 2)
```

is `false` because `(2 == 2)` evaluated to true, and the opposite of true is false.

The Negation operator is powerful, but it should also be used with care because it can be very confusing to figure out what expressions that contain it mean. You should use this operator only when the meaning of the expression is clear.

Arrays

When declaring variables, it makes sense to have distinct names for them, up to a point. However, suppose you are writing a gradebook program, and you need to keep scores for 50 people in the class. You could have a variable for each: `student1`, `student2`, `student3`, and so on. This amount of variables would get quite unwieldy.

Arrays are the solution. They allow you to group what would be a large number of different variables with the same type under one name. Arrays enable you to keep things simple when you have a large number of variables that can be grouped together. An array is declared in the following manner:

```
int students[];
students = new int[50];
```

First, you specify the type of variable that will be contained in the array, which in this case is an integer. Then you name the array (in this case `students`) and follow it with `[]`, which tells the compiler that this code is an array.

At this point, you have declared that `students` will be an array, but you haven't declared how many items will be in it. The next line does that operation:

```
students = new int[50];
```

This statement creates an array of 50 integers. Then this array of integers is assigned to the variable `students`, which is functioning as an array reference in the preceding line of code. This notion of declaring a variable that is a reference and then needing to use `new` to create instances of this type is a new and important concept, which will be discussed in Chapter 9, "Java Objects."

When you first declare the array (students in the preceding example), all you are doing is saying, "This variable will at some point contain an array." That is why the number is not listed in the first declaration of students but later when the actual array is created.

The number in the square brackets ([ ]) that come after new is an index, which is the fundamental thing that separates arrays from other data types. The index of an array is an integer in the range from 0 to the size of the array minus one. For instance, the students array can be referenced by any of the following:

```
students[0]
    students[1]
    students[2]
      ...
    students[49]
```

Each indexed reference to students[ ] is called an array element and can be treated in exactly the same way as any other variable of a basic data type. The index does not necessarily have to be a constant number; it can also be a variable, as in the following:

```
students[current value]
```

When using arrays, keep in mind that you start counting with them at 0 and end at one less than the number of elements in the array. In the students array, for example, if you forgot that for a 50-element array the last valid index was 49, you might try the following,

```
......students[50]
```

which would not be a valid reference. Forgetting this counting scheme isn't quite as big a problem in Java as it is in other languages. In C, trying to reference an element of the array that does not exist can cause the program (and all too often the computer) to crash. Java is much more forgiving; it simply generates a message that an array has been referenced out of bounds.

The handling of array reference problems is a good example of how Java, although not necessarily easy to program in, is much more friendly than most other programming languages. Sun realized that programming languages tended to be far too unforgiving about handling errors and made sure Java wasn't. Errors in programming are a fact of life, but, more often than not, when your program careens out of control, Java gives you a concise and helpful message explaining why.

Statements and Blocks

In Java, each conceptual step of the program is known as a *statement*. For example, both a variable declaration and a variable assignment like the following are statements:

```
int age;
    age = 100;
```

A statement is followed by a semicolon to let the compiler know that the statement has ended.

A *block* is an arbitrary number of statements that are grouped together. The beginning and ending of the block are marked by opening and closing braces, { and } respectively. The following code shows the preceding statements contained within a block:

```
{
    int age;
    age = 100;
}
```

Blocks are used a great deal throughout the rest of the book. You have already seen them in the HelloWorld Applet example from Chapter 7, "The Java Developer's Kit," and they are also an integral part of defining object classes in Chapter 9. Most importantly for now, they are also used a great deal in controlling the flow of a program, which is discussed in the next section.

Program Flow

You now know how to represent data in Java. That's half the battle. The second half is keeping control of the program. Java statements are executed in a linear order, one after another. Flow control statements, as explained in the following sections, let you modify that order.

If...Else Statements

One of the most basic things a program needs to do is to make decisions. Test statements check the result of a boolean relational expression (discussed earlier in this chapter) and decide in which manner the program will continue based upon the result of this expression.

By far, the most important test statement is if. An if statement has the following form:

```
if (Expression) ThingsToDoIfTrue
else ThingsToDoIfFalse
```

If the expression is true, the block (or statements) contained in *ThingsToDoIfTrue* is executed. If the expression is false, the block (or statements) contained in *ThingsToDoIfFalse* that comes after the else is executed. If you just need to do something if the expression is true, the else can be left off.

Suppose you wanted to add 1 to a variable named `counter` only if the Boolean variable `add_one` is set to `true`; otherwise, you wanted to subtract 1 from the variable. The following example does this:

```
boolean add_one;
int counter;

add_one = true;
counter = 1;

if (add_one == true)
     counter = counter + 1;
else
     counter = counter - 1;
```

> **Note:** This might be a good place to use the increment and decrement operators discussed earlier in the chapter:
>
> ```
> if (add_one == true)
>     counter++;
> else
>     counter--;
> ```

In this example, `counter` ends up being equal to 2. Why? The expression in the `if` statement is evaluated first. The program checks to see whether `add_one` is equal to the boolean value `true`. In this case, the `add_one` variable is `true`, so the program evaluates the second part of the `if` statement, which adds 1 to `counter`. If the `add_one` variable were not true, the statement(s) following the `else` would have been executed.

> **Note:** If you are used to programming in C, there is one aspect of the `if` statement (and Java flow-control statements in general) that is important to remember. Unlike C, the test expression must return a Boolean value. It is an error to return a number.

Looping

Java enables you to repeat something over and over again through a construct known as iteration statements. An *iteration statement* executes a block of code based on whether an expression is true.

This process is known as *looping*. A loop occurs in a program when a single block of code is executed more than once. A loop can be set to repeat a definite number of times (a `for` loop) or a variable number of times (a `while` or `do...while` loop).

for Loops

A for loop repeats a program block a finite number of times based upon a counter. The following sample for loop repeats 10 times:

```
for (int i=0; i<10; i = i + 1) {
    // Things you want to do
}
```

The for loop has three main components:

1. Initialization sets up the variable that will be checked against in the loop to see whether the loop is executed again. In the preceding example, the initialization component is int i=0.

2. The test expression determines whether the loop is executed again. In the preceding example, the test expression is i<10, so the loop will continue if i is less than 10.

3. The increment section lets you change the value of the counter variable. This section usually consists of adding or subtracting 1 from its value, but for flexibility you can give the variable any value that you want. In the preceding example, the increment section is i = i + 1.

A semicolon is required at the end of components 1 and 2 to tell the Java compiler that this is where the component ends.

For loops make the most sense when you know ahead of time how many times the loop will need to be executed. For example, if you had a variable result that you wanted to multiply by 3 for 20 times, you could use the following:

```
for (int i=0; i<20; i = i + 1) {
    result = result * 3;
}
```

While Loops

A while loop is a much more general loop than a for loop. A while loop decides whether to evaluate the loop again based upon whether its expression is true or false. The while loop evaluates the expression again if the result is true and doesn't evaluate the expression again if its result is false. The following example only executes once because value is changed to false once the loop is entered:

```
boolean value;
value = true;

while (value == true) {
    // Do some work
    value = false;
}
```

Note that a `while` loop isn't necessarily executed even once, as the following example demonstrates:

```
boolean value;

value = false;

while (value == true) {
     // Do some work
     value = false;
}
```

In this case, the `while` expression is evaluated and is found to be false right from the beginning, so the code inside the loop is never executed.

Do...While Loops

A `do...while` loop is much like a `while` loop except that the expression to be tested is contained at the end of the loop rather than at the beginning:

```
boolean value;
value = true;

do {
     // Do some work
     value = false;
} while (value == true)
```

Note that in this case the program block is always executed at least once. There is no effect if you make the same sort of change that was made to the `while` loop:

```
boolean value;
value = false;

do {
     // Do some work
     value = false;
} while (value == true)
```

The net effect of changing `value` so it starts out as `false` is zero. It is set again to `false` at the end of the block and then the loop does not repeat. Thus the assignment inside the loop is superfluous. In general, you should decide between a `while` and a `do...while` loop based upon whether the test to see whether the loop needs to continue fits more naturally at the beginning or the end of the loop.

The Lack of Pointers

If you come from a C or C++ background, you may be wondering why pointers haven't been mentioned. That's because there are no pointers in Java. The designers of Java came to the conclusion that not only do pointers cause severe security problems in applets, but they also are generally felt to be by far the most difficult thing about programming in C and C++.

The closest thing that Java has to a pointer is a reference to an array (or, as you will see in the next chapter, an object). Like a pointer, an array reference has no value when first created, but it is then set to a value that is created later. However, there is only one way to reference variables when they are created this way, and cryptic operations like pointer arithmetic aren't supported.

If you don't know what a pointer is, count yourself lucky! Hopefully, you never will.

Summary

You are now familiar with the core syntax of Java. You can make variables, arrays, and expressions and control the flow of a program through `if` statements and `for` and `while` loops. A great deal of material in this chapter isn't very exciting, but it gives you the background to lead into the next chapter on the exciting topic of object-oriented programming.

Also, if you want to explore the concepts presented in this chapter on a deeper level, *Java Unleashed* (also available from Sams.net) would be a good place to start.

CHAPTER 9

Java Objects

Object-oriented programming is a hot topic in programming these days; it seems as though every manufacturer is jumping on the bandwagon with object-oriented products. Java is no exception. However, centering Java around objects makes sense. The function of Web applets fits well with an approach to programming that attempts to break up programs into objects. Learning object-oriented programming (or OOP) is easily one of the most difficult subjects for the beginner in Java. Have no fear though, it is also one of the most rewarding.

Programming languages and methods of programming have been evolving since the first computer program was written, and with the rapid pace of advancement in the computer industry, you would think software development would keep pace with the latest advancements. Unfortunately, this usually isn't the case. It can take a very long time before a new way of programming takes hold among the general programming population. The explosion of interest in and use of object-oriented programming recently is a testament to just how revolutionary this type of programming has been.

The Basics of Object-Oriented Programming

Object-oriented programming is an attempt to model computer programs as closely as possible on objects in the real world. Modeling in this case means trying to use real-world concepts of objects in your programs. For instance, if your program dealt with oranges, you would make orange objects.

However, for many years, the standard approach to developing all but the simplest program was what is referred to as procedural programming. With procedural programming, you would ask general questions about what you wanted the program to do. Suppose you were writing a program to control a soda-vending machine. In a procedural approach, you would split up the process of vending a can of soda into a finite number of steps. You might split it up into something similar to the following steps:

1. Wait for change to be dropped into machine.
2. If enough change has been taken, enable the soda choice buttons.
3. If soda selected is not empty, dispense soda.
4. Dispense any change.

Each of these steps would be a procedure, which is a block of code with a name attached to it. Each procedure could pass information to every other procedure. For instance, the first procedure would tell the second procedure how much money had been added, and the second procedure would call the first procedure again if there were insufficient money.

This process is a perfectly logical way to model a vending machine, and for many years, it was how things were done. Unfortunately, programmers found that the larger the program got, the more difficult it was to keep track of how procedures interacted.

For instance, each of the procedures would have to pass information back and forth to each other, so you would have to decide ahead of time what was the important information to remember. Thus, procedural programming centered around the process that needed to be programmed without much consideration of the objects involved and the relationships between them.

Also, and in some ways more importantly, it was hard to use the code that had been written for one project in another. Because procedures and design were so interwoven, it was difficult to pull out any one piece and put it into another program.

Object-oriented programming is an attempt to make things easier and more modular. It is based around the idea of looking at a problem as if it existed in the real world and trying to find the objects that would make it up.

Try this approach on the soda-vending machine example. What objects would make up the machine? The first and most obvious one would be the machine itself. What important parts of the machine would need to be modeled? There would need to be at least three objects to give basic functionality:

- A coin-intake mechanism
- A soda selection panel
- A soda dispenser

There are two main things to remember about each of these objects. First, each of these objects has variables that keep track of what is currently going on inside the object. For example, the coin-intake object would definitely know at any given time how much money had been inserted into the machine.

Second, each object has a mechanism to allow other objects to communicate with it. This process is known as messaging, and the parts of the object that enable this process are known as methods. If you are used to programming in other languages, methods are much the same as functions or procedures except that they aren't just floating around in a program, they are attached to specific objects.

Doesn't this feel like a more intuitive, and even more fun, way of programming? You take the problem and divide it up in ways that you might use in the real world. Certainly if you were to build a soda-vending machine, it would need to have a coin-intake device, and by having an equivalent in your program, the program seems to make more sense.

Moreover, dividing your program up into objects makes it much easier to reuse parts of it in other programs. For instance, after finishing the soda-vending machine, you may very well want to model a video-game machine. If the coin-intake mechanism on the soda-vending machine was designed for the general purpose of taking coins (always a good idea), you should be able to take that same object and use it in the new program with no changes to the coin-intake code.

Classes Versus Objects

Before you can start building objects, you need to understand a couple of the more confusing aspects of object-oriented programming. Remember this sentence: Classes are templates, and objects are instances.

In Java, when you want to create a new type of object, you can't just make one. You must first make a blueprint, or template, of the object you want to create. From this template, you can make as many objects as you want. Think of it as a software cookie cutter.

Objects are known as *instances* of classes. The template has been used to create an object, and the object now exists virtually inside the computer. You can think of an object as the cookie that the cookie cutter creates. If things seem confusing, don't worry. The next section gets to the process of making objects, and things should get much clearer.

Generating Your Own Classes and Objects

The basic syntax to define a class in Java is the following:

```
[ClassModifiers] class ClassName {

    // ...
    // Instance variables and Methods
    // ...

}
```

In essence, you are creating your own new data type when you create a class. Much like the data types discussed in Chapter 8, "Speaking Java: Java Syntax," this type can now be used throughout your program as many times as you want, and the instances will be independent of each other.

This distinction is important. Because classes are templates for objects and are not the objects themselves, you are creating something that can be used generally, not just a one-shot object.

The `ClassModifiers` area in the preceding code is an optional field that lets you define how restrictive you want the access to the class to be. This area is discussed in detail later in this chapter. For now, it's safe to just leave it blank.

A Basic Example: Vehicle

The rest of the chapter uses a class library that models vehicles as an example. Although meant mainly as a simple and understandable example, this library could also be used if you were writing a highway simulation or a game with vehicles, basically anywhere you need to model vehicles of any type.

Start with the most general class, a vehicle:

```
class Vehicle {

}
```

Believe it or not, that's a valid class. It doesn't do much yet, admittedly, but there it is. This code illustrates an important aspect of objects. They are completely general; you can do whatever you please with them.

Instance Variables

Objects need some way to keep track of their state. The way to allow a class to keep track of its state is to use instance variables. An instance variable can be any of the basic data types discussed in the last chapter, or it can even be another object. The variables are defined within the block (between the curly brackets) of the class.

What would be some obvious things to keep track of in the generic vehicle class? You don't want to include things like number of wheels because a generic vehicle is not necessarily a land vehicle. However, two things that every vehicle has are a weight and a speed. Add those two states as instance variables to the class:

```
class Vehicle {

    int weight;
    int speed;

}
```

Now every vehicle created must have a weight and speed. You could choose not to store anything in the created variables, but if that's the case, why include them to begin with?

Encapsulation

Some programming languages, and even Java if you insist, allow you to go ahead and address the instance variables yourself. Thus, after creating an instance of the Vehicle class, you could go in and directly change the weight and speed variables yourself. This is a straightforward way to do things, but unfortunately it has many drawbacks. One of the great things about object-oriented programming is that it allows you to reuse objects without worrying about the code that is contained within the object itself.

Suppose your program was using the Vehicle class, and the Vehicle class had been designed and implemented by someone else. It's quite possible that at some point the designer of the class came to the conclusion that maybe an integer isn't specific enough to hold the weight of many vehicles, but that a special object for weight is needed that holds the unit of measurement (pounds, tons, and so on) in addition to the number.

If you upgraded to the new version of Vehicle class and your program was going into the object and directly modifying the weight, expecting an integer, the compiler would generate an error. Encapsulation keeps this error from happening. Encapsulation is the concept that objects should, in general, not be able to change (or even look at directly) each other's instance variables. How then do you get at those variables? Through methods, that's how.

Methods

A method is much like a function or procedure in other programming languages. It lets you create a block of code that can be called from outside the object and can take arguments and optionally return a value.

The basic syntax for a method is as follows:

```
[MethodModifiers] ResultType methodName() {

    // ...
    // Method Body
    // ...

}
```

This syntax looks more complicated than it is. The `MethodModifiers` field is an optional field that enables you to state how restrictive the access to the method should be. Many options are available for this field, but there are only two essential ones to remember:

- By not putting anything in the field, you let any classes declared in the same file (actually the same package, which is discussed later) have access to the method.
- By declaring the method `public`, you allow any class to access the method, regardless of what file it is contained in.

If this method will only be used within the same file or program it is being defined in, stick with the default by leaving the field blank. If you think the object will be reused, go ahead and make the method `public`.

You then specify what type of value will be returned by the method. This type can be any of the basic types (like integer, float, and so on) or another class type. If the method does not return a value, use the `void` keyword.

The `Vehicle` class should have two methods for each instance variable: one to set the value of the variable, and one to get the value of the variable. To add these methods to the `Vehicle` class, use the following code:

```
class Vehicle {

    int weight;
    int speed;

    public void set_weight(int new_weight) {
        weight = new_weight;
    }

    public int get_weight() {
        return weight;
    }

    public void set_speed(int new_speed) {
```

```
        speed = new_speed;
    }

    public int get_speed() {
        return speed;
    }

}
```

Note that the methods that need to return a variable use the keyword return. Make sure that the value that is being returned is the same as the value specified in the method declaration.

Methods declared inside of a class have complete access to all the instance variables defined within that class and can access them as if they were defined inside the method. For example, in the set_weight method, the variable weight specified is the same as the instance variable weight declared at the start of the class with the int weight; statement.

Constructors

When an object is created from the template defined by its class, it often makes sense to have the instance variables set to default values. For instance, for the original example of a soda-vending machine, you might have a boolean flag in the coin-intake object to set whether enough money has been added to allow a soda to be dispensed. You probably would want to set this flag to false in the beginning; otherwise, whenever the machine is turned on, it might allow a soda to be dispensed for free.

For the Vehicle example, you might want to set the vehicle's weight and speed to zero by default. You set this default setting by using what is known as a constructor. A *constructor* is in essence a method that has the same name as the class, is called automatically when an instance of the class is created, and does not return a value. The following code adds a constructor to the Vehicle class:

```
Vehicle() {

        weight = 0;
        speed = 0;

}
```

Constructors can also take arguments if you want to be able to specify initial values when an instance of the object is made. In fact, this is done quite often throughout the Java class library. To enable this feature, just add parameters to the constructor:

```
Vehicle(int start_weight, int start_speed ) {

        start_weight = 0;
        start_speed = 0;

}
```

Creating Objects

Now that you know how to create basic classes, creating objects (or instances) based upon them is the logical next step. Creating a variable that contains an object takes two steps. First, like any variable, you must declare the variable name for the object and its type somewhere in your program. You perform this step by using the class name as the data type and whatever name you want for the variable. The following code is an example of this process for the `Vehicle` class:

```
Vehicle myVehicle;
```

At this point, much like an array, nothing is in the variable yet. All you have done is state that eventually `myVehicle` will contain an object. Next you need to create the object.

Creating an object is quite simple; you use the `new` keyword followed by the name of the class and any parameters that the class constructor may take. Because the `Vehicle` constructor does not take any parameters, you don't need to worry about passing it any:

```
myVehicle = new Vehicle();
```

Accessing Methods

Now that you have created the object, the next step is to be able to call the methods in the objects. This step is quite straightforward. To call the method for an object, you just put a period after the object and then the method name followed by parameters, if any. For instance, if you wanted to call the `set_weight()` method of the `myVehicle` object created in the last section and set the weight to 1000, you would use the following form:

```
myVehicle.set_weight(1000);
```

A Sample Applet

You now know how to create basic classes, add instance variables and methods to them, create instances of those classes, and access the methods of those instances. This section shows how these elements work from inside an applet.

Because the basics of applets and the Abstract Window Toolkit (the class library you use to draw on the screen) are not be covered until the next few chapters, this section already provides the essential code you need to demonstrate the `Vehicle` class. You only need to pay attention to three things inside the TestApplet definition:

1. A instance variable called `myVehicle` is declared. This variable is an instance of the `Vehicle` class.

2. The only code that should be edited is within the `init()` method of the TestApplet after the `Add Code Here` comment. This comment marks the place where your code is run.

3. A method is called `print` enables you to print things to the applet screen. You can call this method with either an integer or a string.

The code for the applet is in Listing 9.1. Other than the applet code itself, all the class definitions and object creation are identical to the code examples earlier in this chapter, with the addition of a call to the `print` method of the applet to output the weight of `myVehicle`. Figure 9.1 shows the running applet.

Listing 9.1. Code for TestApplet.

```
import java.awt.*;
import java.lang.*;

class Vehicle {

    int weight;
    int speed;

    Vehicle() {
        weight = 0;
        speed = 0;
    }

    public void set_weight(int new_weight) {
        weight = new_weight;
    }

    public int get_weight() {
        return weight;
    }

    public void set_speed(int new_speed) {
        speed = new_speed;
    }

    public int get_speed() {
        return speed;
    }

}

public class TestApplet extends java.applet.Applet {

    List output;
    Vehicle myVehicle;

    public void init() {
        setLayout(new BorderLayout() );
        output = new List();
        add("Center", output);

        // Add Code Here

        myVehicle = new Vehicle();
        myVehicle.set_weight(1000);
```

continues

Listing 9.1. continued

```
        print(myVehicle.get_weight());

        // Add No Code After This Point
    }

    public void print(int line) {
        output.addItem(String.valueOf(line));
    }

    public void print(String line) {
        output.addItem(line);
    }

}
```

The following is the HTML for the TestApplet:

```
<HTML>
<APPLET code="TestApplet.class" width=150 height=250>
</APPLET>
</HTML>
```

Figure 9.1.
*The TestApplet applet
demonstrates a simple
object.*

Inheritance

Thus far you've learned how to define basic classes and create objects, skills which add a great deal of flexibility to the types of programs you can write. The one big aspect of object-oriented programming that you're still missing is inheritance.

Inheritance lets you make new classes that are based upon and extend the functionality of old classes without having to go back and change the original class. This relationship is often called an "is-a" relationship. Thus, if you were creating a class library for representing shapes, you might have a Triangle class that is based on the Shape class. This inheritance fits because a triangle "is-a" shape. Inheriting from another class is quite easy; you just add the keyword extends after the name of the class you are defining, followed by the class you are inheriting from.

Even when you don't explicitly inherit from another class, the compiler still makes the class inherited from the generic class Object. At the top level, all objects descend from the same class.

> **Note:** You may have already noticed that the code examples from this chapter and previous chapters often contain extends java.applet.Applet. The reason for this line is that all applets are based upon the basic applet class that Sun provides, which gives basic applet functionality. This functionality is discussed in Chapter 10, "Applet Structure and Design."

Suppose you wanted to add two more specific classes that inherit from the Vehicle class, LandVehicle and AirVehicle. Defining these classes makes sense because they are two distinct types of vehicles. Figure 9.2 shows this relationship graphically. In the process, an instance variable is added to each. For LandVehicle, the variable wheels is added to store the number of wheels each vehicle has. For AirVehicle, the variable ceiling is added to store the maximum height for the vehicle. Methods to get and set each variable are also added:

```
class LandVehicle extends Vehicle {

    int wheels;

    public void set_wheels(int new_wheels) {
        wheels = new_wheels;
    }

    public int get_wheels() {
        return wheels;
    }

}

class AirVehicle extends Vehicle {

    int ceiling;

    public void set_ceiling(int new_ceiling) {
        ceiling = new_ceiling;
    }

    public int get_ceiling() {
        return ceiling;
    }

}
```

Figure 9.2.
LandVehicle and
AirVehicle inherit
from Vehicle.

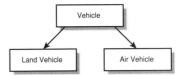

Functionality

When LandVehicle and AirVehicle were created, the only reference to Vehicle is right after the extends keyword. However, by inheriting from (or extending) Vehicle with the two new classes, you keep all the functionality of the base class. To understand the implications of this fact, look at the following code, which is perfectly legal:

```
LandVehicle myCar;

myCar = new LandVehicle();

myCar.set_weight(2000);
```

Notice that no reference is made in this code to the Vehicle class, yet a method from the Vehicle class is called. This code illustrates just how straightforward and seamless inheritance is. When inheritance is called an "is-a" relationship, that's exactly what it means. In nearly every way, an inherited class can act as if it were the base class in addition to using its new features.

Polymorphism

Often when designing classes that inherit from a base class, you encounter a situation where it would make sense to have the base class define a standard method to perform actions in subclasses. For example, if you were writing the Shape and Triangle classes mentioned earlier, you might want all shapes to have a method to draw themselves, but each shape will define that method differently.

To accomplish this task, you can define the name and return type of the method in the base class prefixed with the keyword abstract. Declaring a method abstract means that it will not be defined in this class, but that the method must be defined in any classes that inherit from this class. The class that defines the abstract method must also be declared abstract itself, so that no instances of it can be made. This rule makes sense because there would be a method with no code attached to it if you could make an instance of the abstract class.

To add a move() method to the Vehicle class, for example, you would use the following code:

```
abstract class Vehicle {

    abstract String move();

    // ... The rest of the class ...
}
```

Now every class that inherits from `Vehicle` must define the `move()` method, which must return a string. You can then define the return value to be a text description of the vehicle moving.

Next, add the `move()` method to the `LandVehicle` and `AirVehicle` classes:

```
class LandVehicle extends Vehicle {

    abstract String move() {
        return "Vrooom....";
    }

    // ... The rest of the class ...

}

class AirVehicle extends Vehicle {

    abstract String move() {
        return "Bzzzzzzz.....";
    }

    // ... The rest of the class ...

}
```

Declaring `Vehicle` to be `abstract` ensures that every class that inherits from this class has a `move()` method. This is very useful, but the true power of abstract classes comes from how they facilitate polymorphism.

Polymorphism is the capability to call a method from a class without knowing ahead of time exactly how that action will be performed. For example, no code is associated with the `move()` method in the `Vehicle` class, but you can still call that method when you have a reference to a vehicle object.

How can that be? Earlier it was stated that you cannot make an instance of an abstract class. This statement is true, but you can treat classes that inherit from that abstract class as if they were instances of that class. Remember that inherited classes retain the functionality of their parents.

This concept is pretty difficult to just imagine, so look at the example in Listing 9.2. The running applet is shown in Figure 9.3.

Listing 9.2. An example of polymorphism.

```java
import java.awt.*;
import java.lang.*;

abstract class Vehicle {
    int weight;
    int speed;

    abstract String move();

    Vehicle() {
        weight = 0;
        speed = 0;
    }

    public void set_weight(int new_weight) {
        weight = new_weight;
    }

    public int get_weight() {
        return weight;
    }

    public void set_speed(int new_speed) {
        speed = new_speed;
    }

    public int get_speed() {
        return speed;
    }

}

class LandVehicle extends Vehicle {
    int wheels;

    String move() {
        return "Vrooom....";
    }

    public void set_wheels(int new_wheels) {
        wheels = new_wheels;
    }

    public int get_wheels() {
        return wheels;
    }

}

class AirVehicle extends Vehicle {
    int ceiling;

    String move() {
        return "Bzzzzzzz.....";
    }

    public void set_ceiling(int new_ceiling) {
```

```
                ceiling = new_ceiling;
        }

        public int get_ceiling() {
            return ceiling;
        }

}

public class PolyTestApplet extends java.applet.Applet {
    List output;
    LandVehicle myCar;
    AirVehicle myPlane;
    Vehicle aVehicle;

    public void init() {
        setLayout(new BorderLayout() );
        output = new List();
        add("Center", output);

        // Add Code Here

        myCar = new LandVehicle();
        myPlane = new AirVehicle();

        aVehicle = myCar;
        print(aVehicle.move());

        aVehicle = myPlane;
        print(aVehicle.move());

        // Add No Code After This Point
    }

    public void print(int line) {
        output.addItem(String.valueOf(line));
    }

    public void print(String line) {
        output.addItem(line);
    }

}
```

The following is the HTML for the polymorphism example:

```
<HTML>
<APPLET code="PolyTestApplet.class" width=150 height=250>
</APPLET>
</HTML>
```

The most important thing to notice in this example is that aVehicle is a reference to a vehicle object, not a LandVehicle or an AirVehicle object. The myCar and myPlane objects are assigned at different times to the aVehicle reference, and then aVehicle calls the move() method.

Figure 9.3.
*An applet with
polymorphism.*

Polymorphism is a very powerful tool. Imagine you were writing a vehicle simulation program and wanted to have a loop that went through and moved all the vehicles. By using polymorphism, you could have a method go through and get references to all the vehicles in the simulation and call the move() methods of each. The important thing to remember is that because you would be getting references to each as a vehicle, not as the subclass that they were created under, you could add new vehicle types (perhaps SeaVehicle or SpaceVehicle) without changing a single line of the loop in the main program that moves the vehicles.

Summary

This chapter has moved quickly through the main topics in object-oriented programming, but if you've understood the general concepts presented here, you now can say quite truthfully that you understand object-oriented programming. In addition, the syntax and concepts that Java has for handling objects are quite similar to those of most other modern object-oriented languages like C, C++, and Delphi. Having a basic understanding of objects and object-oriented programming is essential to working with Java because it was designed from the ground up to function as an object-oriented programming language.

Don't worry if this chapter left you feeling like you only have a vague notion of objects. In terms of learning Java as a new programming language, it's a bit of a Catch-22. You need to understand objects to program Java, but you need to know Java before you can program objects in Java. This chapter tried to give you an understanding of objects, along with some real code examples to help you visualize some complex programming ideas.

The next chapter backtracks a bit to cover Java programming in more detail and to help you work your way into programming your own applets. As you read on, you will see why you have to have a basic understanding of objects when you start creating applets. Even if you are still fuzzy about objects, your knowledge of them so far will help with learning Java as a whole.

PART V

Applet
Programming

CHAPTER 10

Applet Structure and Design

Chapter 9, "Java Objects," presented an overview of object-oriented programming and discussed how it applied to Java. The applet is the best example of how object-oriented programming and Java intermix. In terms of functionality, you know that an applet is basically a small, focused application. But what is an applet in terms of programming? An applet is an object class: `class java.applet.Applet`.

The idea behind applets being objects is really quite simple. An applet as an object inherits the properties of its parent object, the applet template. If you look at the class hierarchy for Java (see Figure 10.1), you can see how inheritance works to your advantage when programming applets. OOP becomes a practical implementation rather than just theory.

Figure 10.1.
The Java class hierarchy.

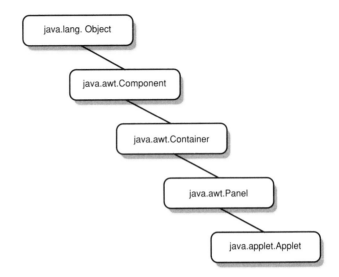

Take a look at the first line in the HelloWorld applet from Chapter 7, "The Java Developer's Kit":

```
public class HelloWorld extends java.applet.Applet {
```

This line establishes the HelloWorld applet. Notice, however, that after the class `HelloWorld` is declared, the line says `extends java.applet.Applet`. This phrase is how you specify that your applet is based on the original applet class and therefore will receive all the functionality of that class, which is quite a bit.

This chapter discusses the practical elements of building an applet. This chapter also discusses some of the more advanced programming topics, such as the methods and classes that make up the Java language. By the end of the chapter, you should have a better understanding of how applets are constructed and should finish your second applet, the Speaker applet.

The Applet Package

As you begin to program with Java, you will find that the language has a structure designed around the idea of objects. In keeping with this design strategy, many methods that perform similar functions have been grouped together in packages. For example, the Abstract Window Toolkit is a package of methods that are useful for drawing images on the screen, working with windows, and building user interfaces. The Applet Package is a package that is specifically designed for working with applets.

The Applet Package contains a number of methods that are designed to be used in the construction of applets and in the special circumstances that arise with applets. For example, applets need to be able to load images and audio clips from a server, so the methods `getImage()` and `getAudioClip()` are part of the Applet Package.

The Applet Package contains a number of useful methods. As you begin to program your own applets, you will use a number of them to control the applet and its characteristics. Table 10.1 is a summary of the most useful methods in the Applet Package. Remember that you can find the full documentation for the Applet Package on the Javasoft Web site at `http://www.javasoft.com`.

Table 10.1. A summary of methods in the Applet Package.

Method	Function
`public String getAppletInfo()`	Returns information about the applet, such as author
`public URL getDocumentBase()`	Returns the URL of the HTML document
`public String getParameter(String name)`	Returns the parameters for an applet
`public String [][] getParameterInfo()`	Returns a summary of what the parameters control
`public AudioClip getAudioClip(URL)`	Used to load an audio clip
`public Image getImage(URL)`	Used to load an image file
`public void play(URL)`	Used to play a previously loaded audio clip
`public boolean isActive()`	Lets you know whether an applet is active
`public void resize(int, int)`	Used to resize the applet
`public void showStatus(String msg)`	Displays a status string in the applet's browser
`public void init()`	Initializes the applet
`public void start()`	Starts the applet when it's finished initializing
`public void stop()`	Stops the applet when you leave the applet's page
`public void destroy()`	Destroys the applet when you leave the browser

Some of the methods in the Applet Package seem pretty self-explanatory, such as `getImage(URL)`. The `getImage()` method does just what you would think it would do: it enables you to get an image from the applet's server. The following sections describe a few of the methods in the Applet Package and how they are used.

Reading the API Documentation

As you begin to use the methods in any of the Java packages, you will find that the API documentation is invaluable for showing how those methods are used and what they do. The API does a fair job of explaining the methods, but it is a document written for programmers, so making sense of the API documentation takes some work.

You can find the API documentation at the following URL:

`http://www.javasoft.com/JDK-1.0/api/packages.html`

This documentation is a general index to all the packages that are part of the Application Programming Interface. You will find a listing of all the packages that contain Java methods, and you can go to specific package documentation. Don't worry about all the packages that you see listed. In general, the ones you will use most often are described in the following list:

- The `java.lang` package contains all the essentials of the Java language. It has the definitions for all the data types, security features, and threads that you will need in your applets. It is the foundation of the language. Fortunately, because you can't code anything without this package, it is automatically imported into all of your applets.

- The `java.net` package contains some useful methods for creating applets that communicate back to their servers. It is very useful for creating complex applets that need to use network services, but it also contains the very important URL definition. Without URL, your applets would not be able to load anything off of the server, which means that you could not use images or sound files. So although you might not use the `java.net` package to the fullest, you will almost always have the following line in your applets:

  `import java.net.URL;`

- The `java.applet` package contains all the methods that are useful in creating applets. The specifics of this package are covered in this chapter.

- The `java.awt` package, otherwise known as the Abstract Window Toolkit, contains all the graphics methods, all the windowing methods, and the components needed to create user interfaces. The AWT is one of the most complex packages and is the subject of Chapter 11, "Building a User Interface."

When you look up methods in the API documentation, they are listed in the following formats:

```
getImage(URL, String)
```

or

```
public Image getImage(URL)
```

The name of the method is `getImage()`, which is also the text you would place in your code to use this method. The terms inside the parentheses are the arguments accepted by the method. The *arguments* are the information the method needs to perform its task. In this case, `getImage()` requires both a URL and a string in order to work properly. The URL gives the location of the image files on the server, and the string is the name of the image file. In the second listing example, the words `public Image` indicate the type of information that is returned by this method. In the case of `getImage()`, the returned information is a public class, `Image`. You might also notice something like the following:

```
public void init()
```

In this case, the return type for this method is `void`, which means that the method returns no data at all, it simply performs a task.

A method that doesn't contain anything inside the parentheses, such as

```
getDocumentBase()
```

does not require any arguments, but still returns a value. The `getDocumentBase()` method, for example, returns the URL of the current applet.

The API is the best authority on what methods do and how they are used. So if you have questions about a method, the first place you should look is the API. Now that you can make a little better sense of how information there is organized, you should be able to use the API to your advantage.

getDocumentBase()

Although the `getDocumentBase()` method simply returns the URL of the document your applet is embedded in, this URL comes in very handy with other methods. For example, the methods discussed in the next two sections take a URL as one of their arguments. Instead of hard coding a URL, you can use the getDocumentBase() method to pass the URL to any methods that require a URL, such as getAudioClip() and getImage(), as in the following example:

```
graphic = getParameter("graphic");
clip = getParameter("clip");

image = getImage(getDocumentBase(), graphic);
sound = getAudioClip(getDocumentBase(), clip);
```

getAudioClip(URL, String)

The getAudioClip() method accepts a URL, which specifies the location of sound files on the server and a string to represent the name of the file. Keep in mind that you can use the getDocumentBase() method to provide the URL, so if you move your applet, you don't have to recode the getAudioClip() method. If you wanted to load an audio file called soundfile.au, you could use the following code:

```
AudioClip clip;
clip = getAudioClip(getDocumentBase(), "soundfile.au");
```

This code just defines a variable called clip for the audio file and then makes clip equal to the result of the getAudioClip() method. The getAudioClip() method uses the getDocumentBase() method to supply the URL, and then you give the getAudioClip() method the name of the sound file directly. You could also use a variable for the name of the sound file, which would make the filename a little more flexible.

Audio methods are contained with the Applet Package within the AudioClip interface. An *interface* is a specification that ensures that certain methods will be defined for a class. For example, the AudioClip interface ensures that the getAudioClip(), play(), and loop() methods will be defined. Table 10.2 summarizes the available audio methods.

Table 10.2. Audio methods.

Method	Function
getAudioClip()	Loads an audio file from the server
play()	Plays the audio file once through
loop()	Plays the audio file in a continuous loop
stop()	Stops a play() or loop() method that is in progress

getImage(URL, String)

The `getImage()` method functions identically to `getAudioClip()`, but it enables you to retrieve an image file rather than a sound file. The image files can be in GIF or JPEG format, and you must first declare an `Image` variable, with something like the following code:

```
Image picture;
```

The preceding code defines an `Image` variable called `picture` that you can then load an image file into. As with any method that takes a URL, you can use `getDocumentBase()` to pass the URL to make your applet more flexible. Because of the nature of image-processing methods, all the image methods are in the AWT except for `getImage()`.

Applet Lifecycles

The Applet Package contains a few methods that have some very special functions. These methods, called the lifecycle methods, control how an applet behaves during the course of execution.

When you load a Web page that contains an applet, the applet goes through several stages during the time you see it on-screen. During each of these stages, the applet performs very different tasks, although most of these tasks are invisible to the end-user. These stages are initialization, running, and exiting.

During the initialization stage, the applet is loading the images, sound clips, and other resources that it needs to run. Sometimes the applet displays messages such as `Loading Images…` to inform you of what might be going on behind the scenes and why you are waiting. When the applet has all the resources it needs to run, the initialization stage is over, and the applet is ready to run.

When the applet is running, it is performing whatever tasks it has been designed to perform. Conversely, when an applet is not running, it is just sitting idle, waiting for a user to re-enter the Web page. For example, a tickertape applet that scrolls text across the screen would load the text during the initialization stage, and then start scrolling the text when the applet began to run. Because applets start and stop when you enter and leave a Web page, running consists of two distinct states, starting and stopping. These states could really be thought of as two separate stages, and in fact, each has a corresponding lifecycle method. You can control what an applet does during both starting and stopping.

Because applets are loaded into your machine's memory and use CPU time, you wouldn't want the applet to remain in memory after you've left the Web browser. During the final exiting stage, the Java Virtual Machine completes some garbage collecting functions, making sure that the resources the applet used are removed from memory and that the applet is completely destroyed when you quit.

Breaking up applets into these stages has some very distinct advantages. For example, if you were writing an animator that used a large number of images, you would want to make sure the images were loaded before the applet started running. Otherwise, your animation might seem jerky or have frames missing. Manipulating these stages can come in handy, and fortunately the Applet Package contains methods to do just that.

The Applet Package has four lifecycle methods, each of which corresponds directly to the stages of an applet. Figure 10.2 shows how these cycles relate to each other and an applet.

Figure 10.2.
The applet lifecycle methods.

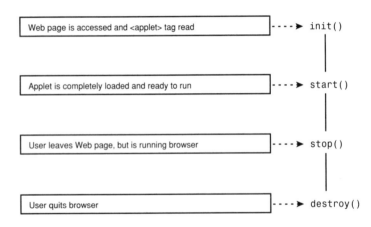

Each of these methods is automatically called as the applet loads, runs, and exits, so you might not always use each of these methods in your own applets. Also, you only need to use these methods if you need something specific to occur during a particular stage, like stopping a sound when you leave the page. Often, you will use one or two lifecycle methods, but not all of them. The decision to use a lifecycle method depends largely on what you are trying to do with your applet. You will find that init(), start(), and stop() are all used fairly commonly because these stages each have practical implications for applets. You want to make sure images and sounds load first, you want to make sure sounds stop playing, and so on. Evaluating the need to use one of these methods is a part of the planning process when writing your applets.

init()

The first method called by an applet after it has been loaded by the browser is init(). Because the applet is not running when init() is called, this method is an excellent place to take care of any groundwork that must be laid for the applet to carry out its goals. Some good tasks to take care of during init() include loading images or establishing the user interface. Take, for example, an applet that plays an audio clip at the click of a button. In such an applet, you would need to load the audio clip and set up the button before the applet began to run. You would use the following code to do these tasks:

```
public void init() {

    clip = getAudioClip(getDocumentBase(), soundfile.au);

    setLayout(new FlowLayout());
    play = new Button("Play Clip");
    add(play);

    }
```

This code defines a new audio clip, called clip, and uses another method from the Applet Package, getAudioClip(), to load the audio clip from the server. It then sets up a Play button using some methods for user interface layout in the Abstract Window Toolkit. (Chapter 11 discusses the AWT in more detail.) Now when the applet is loaded into the browser, it establishes the Play button and downloads the audio clip to prepare the applet to play the clip.

start()

After the applet has been loaded into the browser and is ready to begin, the start() method is called automatically. The start() method generally contains the meat of your applets. After all, this method is what you want the applet to do. In most applets, you will define the init() and start() methods. For example, in an applet that plays an audio clip defined as clip, you might have a start() method that looks like the following:

```
public void start() {

        clip.play();
}
```

Quite simply, this code tells the applet to play the clip sound as soon as it is loaded. You can put any kind of code in the start() method; you could draw images, play sounds, and accept user input—essentially any of the functions you might expect a program to perform.

stop()

The stop() method is the counterpart to the start() method. It is called automatically when an applet should stop execution—when you leave an applet's Web page, for example. If you use the start() method to start some functions that need to be stopped before the user moves on, you stop them with the stop() method. For example, if your applet plays a sound file, you would want to make sure the sound file didn't keep playing when someone left the page. You can use the stop() method to stop a sound file that is playing in a loop or to stop any threads that might be executing when the user moves on. A *thread* is another piece of code outside the main program that is executed simultaneously with the main program. You can think of threads as applets within an applet. The following example shows how you could use the stop() method to suspend a playing audio clip:

```
public void stop() {

        clip.stop();
}
```

You don't necessarily have to redefine the stop() method in all your applets. If an applet is simple enough, you could let the stop() method automatically terminate any methods that might be running. But if you have any sounds playing, or especially if you have any threads running, it is a good idea to invoke the stop() method on your own to keep your applet under control. For example, if you don't stop an active thread, it may interfere with other applets or cause other strange problems with your machine, such as poor performance.

destroy()

The destroy() method is essentially the death of an applet. When you leave your browser, this method is called automatically to do any cleanup that might be necessary. Just as the name would imply, the destroy() method eliminates any trace of your applet. It purges any memory that was used by your applet, and it stops any running threads or methods. Generally speaking, you do not have to do anything to use the destroy() method; a base destroy() method is predefined and automatically called, so all you have to do is sit back and let it do the dirty work.

Building an Applet

So are you ready to build an applet? You now have all the tools you need to build an applet that you can add to your home pages. This section uses a simple applet, the Speaker applet, to demonstrate the structure of applets.

The Speaker applet is a very straightforward applet that enables you to place an image on the screen and play a sound file at the same time (see Figure 10.3). This applet is a good way to see how the various components from various packages fit together and how a complete applet is constructed.

Figure 10.3.
The Speaker applet displays an image and plays a sound file.

An applet is a compiled program based on the source code that you run through the compiler, as discussed in Chapter 7. If you remember, your applet code has to be called `something.java` in order for it to be compiled correctly, and the resulting file is called `something.class`. These extensions help you distinguish between code and compiled applets, but they also contribute to class structure. This naming system is yet another result of Java's object-oriented nature. Every applet can function as an object and therefore needs to be structured so that it can be used as an object. That is why a compiled applet has a name in the form of `something.class`. The `class` extension lets the Java compiler know that the information contained in that file is a class definition. That way, if you wanted to include your applet within another applet, you could use it just as you would any other class in the Java language because the compiler would recognize it. Although this system does put some minor restrictions on naming, it is to the benefit of the entire language.

Take look at the first section of code in the Speaker applet:

```
/*  Speaker
    This Applet displays a gif or jpeg while playing a sound (.au) file.
*/

import java.awt.*;
import java.applet.*;
import java.lang.*;
import java.net.URL;

public class Speaker extends java.applet.Applet {
}
```

The code starts off with a comment that provides a name and a brief description of what the applet does. It's always a good idea to put some comments in your code so that if you pass it on to others, they can understand it better, or if you need to come back to the code at a later date, you have a refresher.

Next, notice a series of statements in the form of `import java.awt.*;`. These `import` statements enable you to use methods from various packages within your applet. Remember that different methods in Java are broken up into packages, and you need to tell the compiler what packages you will be using. By using `import` statements, you can use the entire package with a statement like `import java.awt.*;` or a single method from a package, such as `import java.net.URL;`. Generally, if you are only going to use one method from a package, as is the case with URL in the Speaker applet, you can name the method explicitly. However, if you are going to use many methods, you can use the wildcard `*` to specify the whole package, so you don't have to keep a long list of methods at the beginning of your code.

After instructing the compiler of all the packages you want to include in your applet, you need to set up the applet class itself with the following line:

```
public class Speaker extends java.applet.Applet {
}
```

This line states that you want a public class called `Speaker` that is going to be an extension of the `Applet` class. Because you've chosen the name `Speaker` for your class in this definition, the file that you store this applet in will have to be called `Speaker.java`. Now the naming conventions become a little clearer; you have an applet, class `Speaker`, in a file called `Speaker.java`. When it is compiled, the applet will be called `Speaker.class`. This name allows the compiler to keep track of the new applet as if it were just another class, and find everything by its name. If you try to change the names around, you will probably run into compiling problems. That's the basic framework for your first applet. Now everything that you want the applet to do will need to be added in between the two brackets {}.

You need to declare the variables that you will need to use in this applet. For this applet, you need three types: `Image`, `AudioClip`, and `String`. Image and AudioClip are very straightforward; these types are the image you display and the audio clip you play. The `String` type will be used so that you can set up parameters to allow the user of your applet to change the image and sound file with parameters, without editing the code:

```
public class Speaker extends java.applet.Applet {

    Image image;
    AudioClip sound;
    String graphic, clip;
}
```

So now you've told the compiler that you need an `Image` type called `image`, an `AudioClip` type called `sound`, and two `String` types, `graphic` and `clip`, which you will use for your parameters.

Parameters

Chapter 6, "Java-Enhanced Page Design," talks about the HTML <PARAM> tag that allows the user to pass parameters to an applet with the HTML file. Now you are building an applet that could use parameters to add flexibility. Because this applet shows an image and plays a sound file, you could assume that users would want to be able to change the image and the sound file. Otherwise, the applet wouldn't be useful on any pages but your own. So for this applet, you are going to allow the user to specify the graphic and clip parameters.

Applets use parameters by using some special methods to get the parameters from the HTML file, and then assigning values to the parameters based on the information the file provides. You can then use that information in your applet, say in place of an image filename, so that your applet is flexible. The following code establishes the parameters:

```
public String[][] getParameterInfo() {
    String[][] info = {
        {"graphic",    "string",    "The image file to be displayed."},
        {"clip",       "string",    "The sound file to be played."},
    };
return info;
}
```

This code is pretty standard for establishing variables. It basically establishes an array that will contain the name of each parameter, what type of parameter it is, and an information string that describes that parameter. For example, the following code defines a parameter that will be called clip, which is a string (the filename of the sound file), and a description of what that parameter controls:

```
{"clip",    "string",    "The sound file to be played."},
```

The name of this parameter is the same as the variable clip you declared as a string earlier. Keep in mind that you can use any valid data type here, such as int or float. For example, you could have used the following code to establish a volume parameter that would be an integer number:

```
{"volume",    "int",    "The volume of the sound from 1-10"},
```

Parameters can be as flexible and as detailed as you want, but remember that each parameter should perform a specific function in your applet to make it easier to use, not harder.

So now that you've established these parameters, look at how they are used in the applet code:

```
public void init() {

    graphic = getParameter("graphic");
    clip = getParameter("clip");
```

```
    image = getImage(getDocumentBase(), graphic);
    sound = getAudioClip(getDocumentBase(), clip);
}
```

You can use the init() method to put your parameters into action before your applet fires up. This amounts to a two-step process:

1. Read the parameter information into your variable.
2. Use the variable to get your support files.

In the code, you use the getParameter() function to get the value of the parameter from the HTML file:

```
graphic = getParameter("graphic");
clip = getParameter("clip");
```

Now the graphic variable is the same as the graphic parameter string. This might seem a bit confusing, but what you are doing is using the getParameter() function to read the HTML file and look for a tag in the following form:

```
<PARAM name=graphic value="image.gif">
```

The getParameter() function then returns the filename image.gif to your applet, where it is assigned to the graphic variable. Now if you use the graphic variable anywhere in your program, it will be as if you were using image.gif.

So now you have the filenames you need for the image and sound. Now you need to load the image and sound into memory so you can display and play them. Assign the information to your image and sound variables. Keep in mind that up to this point you've only been dealing with the String data type. That's because you haven't been manipulating any files, only the filenames. Now you are ready to use the Image and AudioClip data types to read in the actual files themselves, and then use them in your applet.

The following lines use two methods from the Applet Package, getImage() and getAudioClip(), to read the files into memory:

```
image = getImage(getDocumentBase(), graphic);
sound = getAudioClip(getDocumentBase(), clip);
```

If you recall these methods from before, you need to give them a URL for the file and the name of the file. So when you call these methods, substitute getDocumentBase() for the URL and your parameter variables for the filename. Now you have your files in memory and are ready to finish off your applet!

Finishing the Applet

Most of the work in this applet is in the preparation. The code used to complete the applet is pretty small, but it does quite a bit. This code can be broken down into three sections.

First, you need to refine the method for painting the applet on-screen. Then you need to display the image and play the sound. And last, you need to make sure your sound stops if the person leaves your page.

To get the image onto the screen, you need to redefine the paint() method that Java provides for you with the following code:

```
public void paint(Graphics g) {
          g.drawImage(image, 0, 0, this);
}
```

All you are doing in this code is letting the compiler know that if you use the paint() method, you want it to draw your image on the screen. You start out declaring the paint() method and setting a context (Graphics g) in which this method will perform its task.

The next line of the code uses the g. before drawImage to specify what graphics context (in this case g) you specified earlier. A *context* specifies where you want these graphics methods to perform their tasks. By providing paint() with the graphics context g, you then need to specify what graphics methods use that context when they are called. Then you let the applet know that you want it to draw image (your image variable) at the coordinates 0,0. The this at the end of the method specifies a special interface called an image observer. The *image observer* monitors the image to make sure there aren't any special problems with the image, such as an incomplete file. The keyword this refers to *this* image observer, as opposed to an image observer defined elsewhere.

Now you are ready to finish off the applet. When the applet is ready to start, you want to draw the image on-screen and play the sound file, so you define the start() method as follows:

```
public void start() {
    repaint();
    sound.play();
}
```

The method used to display the image on-screen is a bit odd. Even though you just redefined the paint() method to draw your image on-screen instead of calling the paint() method directly, the code calls the repaint() method. The repaint() method calls the new paint() method, so the end result is the same. This roundabout way of doing things is largely attributed to some quirks in the Java language.

This example also uses the play() method, in the form of sound.play(), to play the audio file. This method is similar in function to the g.drawImage line. The sound.play() method just lets the play() method know what sound file to play, just as the g. lets drawImage know what graphics context to use.

Now that you have your `start()` method, which displays your image and plays an audio file, it might be a good idea to have a `stop()` method:

```
public void stop() {
    sound.stop();
}
```

The `stop()` method just makes sure that your sound file stops playing if the user should leave your page. Obviously, if a user leaves the page, the image will vanish, so you don't need to worry about stopping its display.

Putting It All Together

Now you have all the pieces for a completed applet. Your applet fits the following structure:

1. Comment information, such as author and revision dates
2. Any `import` statements to utilize other classes
3. The `Applet` class definition, which includes the following:
   - Variable declarations
   - Parameter information
   - The `init()` method, which defines variables and loads support files
   - The redefined `paint()` method
   - The `start()` method to perform the applet's tasks
   - A `stop()` method to make sure the applet stops properly

Listing 10.1 has the complete code for the applet.

Listing 10.1. The completed Speaker applet.

```
/*    Speaker
   This Applet displays a gif or jpeg while playing a sound (.au) file.
*/

import java.awt.*;
import java.applet.*;
import java.lang.*;
import java.net.URL;

public class Speaker extends java.applet.Applet {

    Image image;
    AudioClip sound;
    String graphic, clip;

    public String[][] getParameterInfo() {
        String[][] info = {
            {"graphic",    "string",    "The image file to be displayed."},
            {"clip",       "string",    "The sound file to be played."},
```

```
        };
        return info;
    }

    public void init() {

        graphic = getParameter("graphic");
        clip = getParameter("clip");
        image = getImage(getDocumentBase(), graphic);
        sound = getAudioClip(getDocumentBase(), clip);
    }

    public void paint(Graphics g) {
            g.drawImage(image, 0, 0, this);
        }

    public void start() {
        repaint();

        // This could also be sound.loop(); to loop the sound.
        sound.play();
    }

    public void stop() {
        sound.stop();
    }
}
```

The HTML file for the Speaker applet contains the following code:

```
<HTML>
<APPLET code=Speaker.class width=100 height=150>
<PARAM name="graphic" Value="me.gif">
<PARAM name="clip" Value="hi.au">
</APPLET>
</HTML>
```

You can now compile this code by using the javac compiler to produce an applet called Speaker.java. You can view this applet using the appletviewer or add it to a Web page.

Summary

This chapter has shown the basic structure of an applet. The Speaker applet is a simple applet, but it does contain many of the basic structure elements that you will find in many applets. All applets contain import statements, variable declarations, and a class structure. Most applets also use parameters to some extent. But there are still many things that this applet doesn't do; it doesn't deal with user input, for example.

The Speaker applet is a good starting point and illustrates the basics of applet construction in the context of a working applet. As you begin to program applets, you will be surprised how common some of these elements are. For example, the parameter code used in this chapter does not usually vary much from applet to applet, and the techniques for assigning variables, using getImage(), and so forth are the same in any applet. These methods provide a solid foundation for more advanced applets, and having a firm grasp of the basics will help you as your applets become more advanced.

Now you are ready to move on to some more functional applets. Chapter 11 discusses some of the issues surrounding user interfaces and how to use the tools in the Abstract Window Toolkit to create user interfaces for your applets. Then you'll have all the tools to create fully functional applets. In Chapters 12 and 13, you will develop a TickerTape applet and a SlideShow applet to understand how some real-world applets function. These chapters also discuss issues of application development in more detail.

Building a User Interface

If you want to create an applet with anything more than bare-bones user interaction, you must create a user interface. The Abstract Window Toolkit is a Java package made specifically for this task.

This chapter covers the basic aspects of building a user interface, including the essentials of the AWT and what you need to construct the interface and make it work. This chapter also covers how to make your interface a little better-looking by manipulating colors, layout, and so on. Building user interfaces can be quite complex and is the subject of many books on its own. But this chapter should get you started in the right direction to create user-friendly interfaces for your applets right away.

Introduction to the AWT

What do you think of when you hear the term *user interface*? Most people would list some variation of the following:

■ Buttons

■ Windows

■ Checkboxes

■ Menus

■ Scrollbars

These items are what is known as *interface components*. The creators of Java realized that people would want this kind of functionality and included the capability to create applets with user interface components.

The Abstract Window Toolkit (normally referred to as the AWT) is a well-thought-out class and very portable windowing library. This standard part of the Java environment provides all the basic functionality one would expect to use in a modern windowing system: buttons, scrollbars, menus, and other standard window components.

The AWT manages to preserve the look and feel of the user's system, so AWT-based applications won't get a reputation for having a Java-specific look. This characteristic is a positive thing, because people tend to get very attached to their operating systems and resist using programs that work or look differently.

A Simple Example

The bulk of the AWT is built around the `Component` class. A component is just the representation in Java of a user interface object. A component is the base object from which all AWT visual elements are subclassed, but for now, just think of components as a set of building blocks that can be arranged as you please to do whatever you want.

One of the most basic components is a button. Listing 11.1 shows the code for a simple applet that uses the AWT to display a button.

Listing 11.1. A simple button applet.

```
import java.awt.*;
import java.applet.Applet;

public class Example1 extends Applet {
    Button hiButton;

    public void init() {
        hiButton = new Button("Click Me!");
```

```
        add(hiButton);
    }
}
```

The HTML for the applet is as follows:

```
<APPLET code=Example1.class width=250 height=100></APPLET>
```

When the code is compiled and viewed, the applet shown in Figure 11.1 is displayed. Although the applet doesn't do much at this point, the button is functional.

Figure 11.1.
A simple applet that uses the AWT.

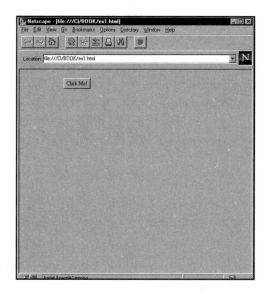

What is important at this point is not to understand exactly what every line means, but to get a general feel for what is going on:

1. A button component is created with the label "Click Me!"
2. The button is added to a container; in this case, the container is an applet.

For a windowing program that produces output, there is surprisingly little code here. Almost all the real work of handling the user interface is hidden behind the scenes. If you are using basic components, it's relatively easy to keep your code simple. However, if you want to extend the functionality of the basic components, the complexity of your code increases.

When a component is created, it is usually added to a container. A *container* is an area of the screen in which components (and even other containers) can be placed. You can keep creating containers within containers indefinitely. The calculator example at the end of this chapter demonstrates this type of flexibility.

This flexibility is one of the biggest advantages of programming the AWT. The AWT enables you to think of the user interface as objects and concentrate on the relationships between objects, a concept that fits well with Java's object-oriented programming environment.

Don't Panic: Some Practical Advice for Using the AWT

Programming any graphical interface can be a daunting task. Correspondingly, the AWT is one of the most difficult parts of Java to master. However, as long as you keep in mind a few basic tenets from the outset, the AWT is certainly manageable.

First, every viewable item in the AWT is subclassed from `Component`. Subclassing is just shorthand for "is inherited from" (inheritance is covered in detail in Chapter 9, "Java Objects"). This subclassing provides a core set of functions (things like setting color) that work across all components. Look at the API documentation to check where the class you're using is inherited from. Usually the function you are looking for is a step or two up the chain, hidden in a parent class.

Second, everything in the AWT is event-driven. Unlike many styles of programming, you construct your program to respond to user actions rather than proceed in a linear manner. Although this approach adds a level of complexity to your programs, it also makes them much more usable.

Third, components are never placed on the page in absolute positions. Java was designed from the beginning to run on many different platforms and keep the look and feel of applets consistent with the operating system's native environment. The size and precise shape of a button, for example, isn't known to an interface designer. Therefore, all components are placed inside containers that are relative to other components. Although this way of doing things seems strange at first, it is a very powerful technique that will make your applications more robust.

Note: If you've ever done Windows or Macintosh programming before, many of the underlying concepts are very similar to programming with AWT, especially if you've used a class library like OWL or MFC. The major difference is simplicity. Most concepts in the AWT are much more straightforward than other development environments.

Event Handling

An *event* is a communication from the outside world to the program that something has occurred. The following are a few basic event types:

■ **Mouse clicks.** This type of event is generated when the mouse button is clicked while positioned over a component.

■ **Mouse movement.** Whenever the mouse is moved over a component, many events are sent to the component informing it what coordinate in the component the mouse has moved to.

■ **Action events.** When the user manipulates a component that allows interaction with the user, an action event is created by default, and the owner of the component (usually the container in which the component is placed) is notified that something has happened.

One of the most important things to understand about the AWT is how events are handled. Without events, your application cannot respond to user actions.

Adding Basic Event Handling

Listing 11.2 shows the code that adds basic event handling to the example from earlier in the chapter.

Listing 11.2. The Button applet with event handling.

```
import java.awt.*;
import java.applet.Applet;

public class Example2 extends Applet {
    Button hiButton;

    public void init() {
        hiButton = new Button("Click Me!");
        add(hiButton);
    }

    public boolean action(Event evt, Object what) {
        if (evt.target == hiButton) {
            hiButton.setLabel("Clicked!");
            return true;
        }
        else
            return false;
    }
}
```

The HTML for the applet is as follows:

```
<APPLET code=Example2.class width=250 height=100></APPLET>
```

Figure 11.2 shows the output of the modified applet. All that has been changed is the addition of the action() method. When a component that has an action associated with it (for example, a button) is manipulated by the user, the action() method of that component is called.

Figure 11.2.
Adding simple event
handling.

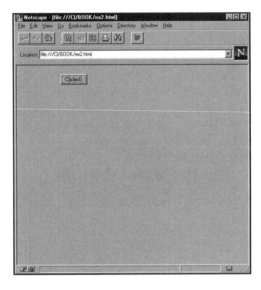

This example uses the default Button class instead of subclassing a new one. The default event handler tries to handle the action() event inside of the Button class, but cannot find a handler that will take the event. The default event handler then passes the event up the chain of components to the container that holds the component. It keeps passing the event until it finds a handler that accepts the event or hits the top of the chain.

To understand exactly what's happening, look at the first line of the action() method:

```
public boolean action(Event evt, Object what) {
```

All event handlers have a form similar to this line. They accept a parameter of type Event that provides detailed information about the event. The action() method also takes a parameter of type Object (a generic object) that lets you know what action is occurring. You can ignore this parameter in this example because there is only one possible action for a button. Lastly, event handlers return a boolean value indicating true if the event was handled or false if it was not.

The next line of the `action()` method is as follows:

```
If (evt.target == hiButton) {
```

In this line, the target of the event is being checked to see whether it is the button. Because `evt.target` and `hiButton` are both objects, you can check to see whether they are the same object.

The `action()` method then shows the following line:

```
hiButton.setLabel("Clicked!");
```

Because the button was clicked, `setLabel` is used to change the button to reflect that it was clicked.

The `action()` method ends with the following lines:

```
    return true;
}
else
    return false;
```

Finally, if the event was handled, `true` is returned. If the event wasn't handled, `false` is returned. The event handler keeps searching for a method that will accept the event. Acceptance of the event is signaled by returning `true`.

Using Event-Handling Methods

In almost all cases, you will want to use the event-handling methods that Sun has provided for you. Table 11.1 summarizes these methods. Remember that everything is relative to the component. For example, the `mouseMove()` method of a component is called when the mouse is moved inside that component.

Table 11.1. A summary of event-handling methods.

Event Type	Method
Action taken	action(*Event evt, Object what*)
Mouse button pressed	mouseDown(*Event evt, int x, int y*)
Mouse button released	mouseUp(*Event evt, int x, int y*)
Mouse moved	mouseMove(*Event evt, int x, int y*)
Mouse dragged	mouseDrag(*Event evt, int x, int y*)
Mouse enters component	mouseEnter(*Event evt, int x, int y*)

continues

Table 11.1. continued

Event Type	Method
Mouse exits component	mouseExit(*Event evt, int x, int y*)
Key pressed	keyDown(*Event evt, int key*)
Key released	keyUp(*Event evt, int key*)

When would you want to use methods other than action()? The answer is when you want to change the behavior of a component as opposed to just using it. The action() method reports only events that are essential to the function of the component, such as a mouse click on a button. Listing 11.3 shows new behaviors added to the preceding example.

Listing 11.3. The button applet with new behaviors.

```java
import java.awt.*;
import java.applet.Applet;

public class Example3 extends Applet {
    Button hiButton;

    public void init() {
        hiButton = new Button("Click Me!!!");
        add(hiButton);
    }

    public boolean mouseEnter(Event evt, int x, int y) {
        hiButton.setLabel("Go Away!");
        return true;
    }

    public boolean mouseExit(Event evt, int x, int y) {
        hiButton.setLabel("Stay Away!");
        return true;
    }


    public boolean action(Event evt, Object what) {
        if (evt.target == hiButton) {
            hiButton.setLabel("Clicked!");
            return true;
        }
        else
            return false;
    }
}
```

The HTML for the applet is as follows:

```
<APPLET code=Example3.class width=250 height=100></APPLET>
```

Figure 11.3 shows the output of the applet. Whenever the mouse moves over the applet, the user is informed that perhaps clicking the button isn't such a good idea.

Figure 11.3.
An applet with live feedback.

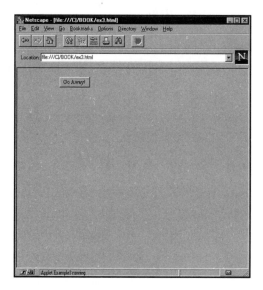

In most circumstances, you will only need to use action() to handle all the events in your applet. However, knowing how to handle things at a lower level gives you a great deal more control that can come in handy. Suppose you had an animation applet that you wanted to animate only when the mouse was over it. The mouseEnter() and mouseExit() methods would enable you to program this action.

Components

Components are the building blocks from which all programs using the AWT are built. If it's on-screen, it's a component.

All components have the following things in common:

- A screen position and size
- A foreground and background color
- Being either enabled or disabled
- A standard interface to handle events

AWT components can be broken down conceptually into three major categories:

- Interface components encompass all the standard controls normally associated with a windowing system. Examples of these include buttons, text labels, scrollbars, pick lists, and text entry fields.

- Containers encompass areas in which components can be placed. Groups of components can then be grouped together to form a more cohesive object to be manipulated. A panel is an example of this type of component. One way to think of a container is as a bookcase and components are the books that are placed there.

- Windows are a very special case of the Component class. All other components are added onto a container that already exists, whereas a window component is an actual separate window with a completely new area to create an interface upon. Dialog boxes and frames are examples of this type of component. Normally windows are not used with applet programming.

Interface Components

Interface components are components specifically designed to give information to or get information from the user. The button used in previous examples is a prototypical example of an interface component. Table 11.2 lists the components available in Java.

Table 11.2. Standard components.

Component	Explanation
Button	A clickable button
Canvas	A generic component, a blank canvas
Checkbox	A clickable box
Label	A simple text label
List	A list of things to select from
Scrollbar	A bar to scroll around a document
TextField	A one-line field to edit text
TextArea	Like a TextField, but allows multiple lines

Earlier it was mentioned that straightforwardness was one of the hallmarks of the design of the AWT. Listing 11.4 demonstrates this fact with the code for an applet that uses multiple interface components. Figure 11.4 shows what this applet looks like on-screen.

Listing 11.4. An applet to showcase multiple components.

```java
import java.awt.*;
import java.applet.Applet;

public class ManyComp extends Applet {
    Button aButton;
    Checkbox aBox;
    Label aLabel;
    TextField aTextField;

    public void init() {
        aButton = new Button("Ok");
        aBox = new Checkbox("Show");
        aLabel = new Label("Hello!");
        aTextField = new TextField("37", 5);

        add(aButton);
        add(aBox);
        add(aLabel);
        add(aTextField);
    }

}
```

The HTML for this applet is as follows:

```
<APPLET code=ManyComp.class width=250 height=600></APPLET>
```

Figure 11.4.
An applet with many components.

The variable declarations in this example are pretty straightforward. To make sure you understand exactly what's going on, this section provides a line-by-line explanation.

The following line creates a button with the caption Ok:

```
aButton = new Button("Ok");
```

The next line creates a checkbox with the caption Show. A checkbox is a labeled box that can be checked on or off.

```
aBox = new Checkbox("Show");
```

In the following line, a label containing the string Hello! is created. A label is just text that is drawn on-screen, usually to clarify things.

```
aLabel = new Label("Hello!");
```

Finally, a text field that contains 37 and allows up to five characters to display is created. A user can type in a text field, and text fields are one of the principal means of entering data into an applet.

```
aTextField = new TextField("37", 5);
```

Common Methods of All Components

The bulk of the AWT is subclassed from the Component class. Thankfully, the Component class contains a great deal of functionality that is available to all those subclassed components, as described in the following sections.

Setting Foreground and Background Color

Color in Java is abstracted into the Color class, which has a number of static variables to represent color (see Table 11.3) and the capability to specify an arbitrary color with an instance of the Color object:

```
Color aColor = new Color(int r, int g, int b)
```

In this example, the r, g, and b are the red, green, and blue components specified in a 24-bit palette. In the 24-bit color palette, each color (R, G, or B) is represented by a number from 0 to 254. By specifying the value of each color, you can create up to 16.7 million colors. However, if you want to use a fairly common color, such as red, Java provides some standard, predefined color variables, which are listed in Table 11.3.

Table 11.3. Standard color variables available in Java.

```
black

blue

cyan

darkGray

gray

green

lightGray

magenta

orange

pink

red

white

yellow
```

You can set the foreground color of a component with the `setForeground` method:

```
setForeground(Color.green)
```

This code sets the foreground color of the component to green. The foreground color is usually what is being drawn. For instance, on a label, the foreground would be the text itself and the background would be what the text is drawn upon.

You can set the background color with the `setBackground()` method:

```
void setBackground(Color.black)
```

This code sets the background color to black.

Disabling and Enabling

A component can be turned on or turned off by setting it to `enabled` or `disabled`. To enable the component, use the `enable()` method:

```
enable()
```

To disable a component, use the `disable()` method:

```
disable()
```

When a component is enabled, it has all the functionality you would expect: a button can be clicked, text can be entered into a text field, and so on. When a component is disabled, a user cannot interact with the component at all. For example, an applet that lets you calculate a loan might let you click the `Calculate` button only when all of the fields (`amount`, `interestrate`, and so forth) have been completed. Disabling the button until the applet checked the fields, and then enabling the button, is how you would program this feature.

Containers

Containers are components that can contain other components, including other containers. Think of them as a way to subdivide the user interface into plots in which components can be placed or subdivided further.

The two general types of containers are panels and windows. The major difference between them is that a panel is a defined area on a window that already exists, and a window is an entirely new window. Also, the `Applet` class is a subclass of `Panel`, so an applet can be treated just like a panel.

The example in Listing 11.5 uses the `add()` method to add components to the panel. Figure 11.5 shows the results.

Listing 11.5. A simple button applet.

```
import java.awt.*;
import java.applet.Applet;

public class Example4 extends Applet {
    Button button1, button2;

    public void init() {
        button1 = new Button("First");
        add(button1);
        button2 = new Button("Second");
        add(button2);
    }
}
```

The HTML for the applet is as follows:

```
<APPLET code=Example4.class width=250 height=100></APPLET>
```

Figure 11.5.
A simple applet displaying two buttons.

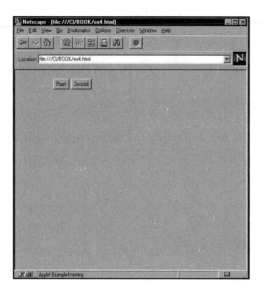

After the component is created, all that needs to be done is to call the add() method for the container with the specified component. If your interface is quite simple, adding components to a container in this manner may be enough. However, if you want to have some control over the placement of the components, you can use a layout.

Layouts

A layout can be thought of as a template that is placed over a container to define how components will be added. The most common layout is BorderLayout(), which orients components according to compass points except that the center area gets all leftover space. Table 11.4 lists all the layouts.

Table 11.4. A summary of layout methods and their features.

Method	Description
BorderLayout()	Layout according to compass points
GridLayout()	Layout on a grid
GridBagLayout()	Layout on a grid where elements can be different sizes
CardLayout()	Layout that contains a series of cards that can be flipped through
FlowLayout()	Layout that puts components left to right

The layout of a panel is established with the setLayout() method, and then new components are added using the add() method with an argument indicating placement, which can be north, south, west, east, or center. This argument comes before the component to be added. Listing 11.6 shows an applet that utilizes the BorderLayout() method. Figure 11.6 shows the resulting applet.

Listing 11.6. Using layouts to control placement of components.

```java
import java.awt.*;
import java.applet.Applet;

public class Example5 extends Applet {
    Button button1, button2;

    public void init() {
        setLayout(new BorderLayout());
        button1 = new Button("First");
        add("North", button1);
        button2 = new Button("Second");
        add("South", button2);
    }
}
```

The HTML for the applet is as follows:

```
<APPLET code=Example5.class width=250 height=100></APPLET>
```

Figure 11.6.
Demonstrating the
BorderLayout()
method.

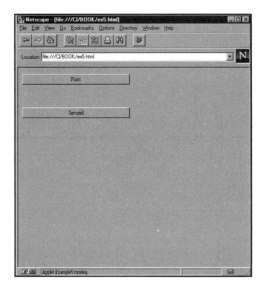

In addition to BorderLayout, the most commonly used layouts are FlowLayout and GridLayout. A FlowLayout places components onto the container one after the other, left to right, top to bottom. This layout does not allow much flexibility in designing a user interface, but it is the most straightforward.

A GridLayout allows components to be placed one after another on a rigid grid. Although this layout sounds like the FlowLayout, it differs in that a GridLayout attempts to make all of the components placed on it the same size. Therefore, this layout makes sense for things like keypads or a screen that needs to be divided into equal sections.

Designing a User Interface

Suppose you wanted to create a simple calculator applet. It would make sense to build the user interface first, and then add functionality one step at a time. A calculator would definitely require a display, so you could add that first using the code in Listing 11.7.

Listing 11.7. The calculator display.

```
import java.awt.*;
import java.applet.Applet;

public class Calculator extends Applet {
    Label display;

    public void init() {
        setLayout(new BorderLayout());
        display = new Label("0", 10);
        add("North", display);
    }
}
```

A BorderLayout makes sense in this example because the display will always be at the top of the screen. Adding the keypad is a bit trickier. The keypad needs 10 number buttons and 4 operation keys grouped together, which calls for a few more panels with the appropriate keys added. Listing 11.8 shows how to manipulate the layouts to produce the applet shown in Figure 11.7.

Listing 11.8. The calculator keypad.

```
import java.applet.Applet;
import java.AWT.*;

public class Calculator extends Applet {
    Label display;
```

continues

Listing 11.8. continued

```
Panel bottom;
Panel num_panel;
Panel func_panel;
Button number[] = new Button[10];
Button function[] = new Button[6];

public void init() {
    setLayout(new BorderLayout());
    display = new Label("0", Label.RIGHT);
    add("North", display);

    bottom = new Panel();
    bottom.setLayout(new BorderLayout());

    num_panel = new Panel();
    num_panel.setLayout(new GridLayout(4,3));

    for (int x=9; x>=0; x--) {
        number[x] = new Button((new String()).valueOf(x));
        num_panel.add(number[x]);
    }

    function[4] = new Button(".");
    num_panel.add(function[4]);

    function[5] = new Button("=");
    num_panel.add(function[5]);

    bottom.add("Center", num_panel);

    func_panel = new Panel();
    func_panel.setLayout(new GridLayout(4,1));

    function[0] = new Button("+");
    function[1] = new Button("-");
    function[2] = new Button("*");
    function[3] = new Button("/");

    for (int x=0; x<4; x++)
        func_panel.add(function[x]);

    bottom.add("East", func_panel);

    add("Center", bottom);
    }
}
```

The HTML for the applet is as follows:

```
<APPLET code=Calculator.class width=135 height=140></APPLET>
```

Figure 11.7.
A first try at a calculator
applet user interface.

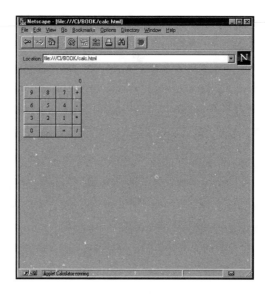

The original panel has been subdivided twice. At the top of the applet is the label for the display; below that is a panel for all the keys. However, this panel must be again subdivided to group the number and function keys separately. Thus a number panel and a function panel are added.

Because the lower panels contain keys, the GridLayout fits the purpose perfectly. This layout allows a grid to be specified and then components are added left to right, top to bottom until the grid is full. The function panel is then added to the East (right) side of the lower panel, leaving the rest of the space to the number keys. The number keys are specified to be Center and thus to use up all the space remaining in the panel.

This code provides a mock-up of how the final calculator would look and gives an idea of not just user interface considerations that will need to be considered, but also design decisions that are integral to the whole applet. For example, should all the processing be contained in the main Applet class, or should the panels become separate classes to isolate functionality and promote code reuse?

Summary

This chapter covered how to go about building a user interface in Java using the AWT. Remember these key points:

- Components are the foundation of Java user interfaces.
- Components are placed onto containers.

- A layout determines the placement of components on containers.
- Components talk to each other through events.

If you keep these basic tenets in mind, you should be able to put together simple applets with a great deal of functionality. Just keep in mind how these pieces fit together and how they function together; you might even want to keep track of these in writing while you work on your applets. Understanding how these pieces fit together and how they function with each other in your applet can keep errors in your interface to a minimum and make debugging them much easier.

Now you're ready for the big time. The following chapters take you through some real-world applets. Chapter 12, "The TickerTape Applet," covers the TickerTape applet, which scrolls user-specified text on-screen. Chapter 13, "The SlideShow Applet," covers the SlideShow applet, which allows users to set up a series of images in a slide show, complete with a soundtrack.

Programming Complete Applets

The TickerTape Applet

The preceding chapters have covered a great deal of material; now you can put that knowledge to work in a fun applet. Much of the enthusiasm surrounding Java has focused on its ability to make small, interesting applets to spice up a Web page. You'll create just such an applet in this chapter.

People are used to seeing tickertape-like signs wherever they go. You can't escape them. They're seen on major-league scoreboards, signs in front of buildings, and even some highway billboards. Even though it may seem like implementing a tickertape sign in Java would be difficult, it turns out to not be that bad.

The TickerTape applet should have the following features:

- User-specified message
- User-specified font
- Ability to change the speed at which the text moves

Over the course of the chapter, you'll go from a basic applet that just draws a word on-screen to a full-motion animated sign in three steps.

Design Issues

At its core, what does a tickertape sign do? These are a few of the basics:

1. It displays a message.
2. It waits a specified period of time.
3. It clears the screen.
4. It displays the message slightly to the left of where it was before.
5. If the message has scrolled off the left of the screen, it starts displaying the message again at the right-hand side of the screen.

Implicit in the fifth point is the fact that the message may not all be on the screen at any one time. Although this fact isn't obvious for small messages, if you have a message that is several sentences long, it probably won't fit on the screen all at once.

This point may seem minor, but as you will see later, it is important to consider as many of these issues as possible at the beginning of the design process so you can watch out for them later.

Specifying the Message

It wouldn't make much sense to have a TickerTape applet that users couldn't specify their own messages for. You can have this user-defined message retrieved in one of three ways:

1. The message could be specified in the Java applet source. This option is the simplest to implement, but it would require recompiling the applet source every time you wanted to change the message.
2. The applet could get the message through a parameter (discussed in Chapter 10, "Applet Structure and Design"). This option would allow the message to be changed by just changing the HTML source that contains the applet.
3. The applet could retrieve the message as a separate text file from the server. This option has the advantage of being the most flexible, but it is also the hardest to implement.

For this applet, the second option makes the most sense. It enables the user of the applet to easily change the message of the applet without complicating matters too much.

Specifying the Font

Having the same font for everything can get boring. Modern operating systems have a variety of fonts at your disposal. Why not go ahead and use them? Using a different font can set off the applet from other elements in your page. Specifying the font as a parameter to the applet makes the font easy to change.

Changing the Animation Speed

The TickerTape applet gives the illusion of the text moving by erasing and then redrawing the text quickly enough that the eye perceives that the text hasn't been erased and redrawn, but has actually moved. Using this fact to your advantage, you can change the speed at which the text scrolls by varying the delay between redraws of the message. Thus, the shorter the delay, the "faster" the text moves; the longer the delay, the "slower" the text moves.

Getting Started

At the core of the TickerTape applet is the drawing of the text. Applets have a set amount of screen space that they are given to work with, as specified by the <APPLET> tag. Think of this area as a blank canvas upon which anything you like can be drawn.

If you are coming from an HTML background, you might think of text and graphics as completely separate things, with areas set apart for each. In Java applets, text and graphics do not have established areas. Unless you explicitly set up areas for text with components like TextArea, the area that can be drawn upon is completely blank. You have to specify exactly where you want to put your text with x and y coordinates.

In Java, the x and y coordinates start at the upper left hand side of the applet and go down and to the right in pixels until the edge of the applet is reached. Thus, if your applet was set to be 300 by 200, the upper left hand corner of the applet would be at x=0 and y=0. The lower right corner would be at x=299 and y=199.

The area that is available for drawing is known as a *graphics context*. Although that sounds complicated, it really isn't. All this term means is that you are given an object to paint upon when it's time to paint on the canvas. That object is the graphics context, and it is represented by instances of the Graphics class.

To begin writing the applet, you start with a generic applet and add a `String` object to represent the message, as shown in the following code:

```
public class Ticker1 extends java.applet.Applet {

String message;

}
```

A string is an object that holds a sequence of characters. For example, `1234`, `hello`, and `this is a string` are all strings.

Like all objects, declaring a variable as a string type doesn't make an instance of the object, just a reference. Therefore, you need to find a place to actually make the string. Because the string only needs to be made when the applet is first created, the `init()` method would be a good place to make the string:

```
public void init() {
message = new String("Test");
    }
```

This code declares a new string with the value `Test`. Now that you have a message, you need to place it on the screen. As mentioned earlier, you need a graphics context to paint on a screen. Whenever the screen needs to be painted, the `paint()` method of the applet is called. This method is called when the applet first starts up or when something has hidden the applet and then shown it again (like when another window has been dragged over the applet).

The code for drawing the message on-screen is as follows:

```
public void paint(Graphics g) {
        g.drawString(message, 0 ,30);
    }
```

You now have the graphics context mentioned earlier, and thus a canvas to draw upon. The next line is kind of confusing:

```
g.drawString(message, 0 , 30);
```

The `Graphics` class contains the `drawString()` method, which allows strings to be drawn. This method takes three arguments:

- `String str` is the string to be drawn.
- `int x` is the x coordinate at which to draw the string.
- `int y` is the y coordinate at which to draw the string.

After you add the `drawString()` method, the string is drawn at the x and y point you specify. Listing 12.1 is the complete applet (shown in Figure 12.1).

Figure 12.1.
*Drawing text on an
applet.*

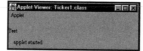

Listing 12.1. Step one, the Ticker1 applet, is a simple applet to draw text on the screen.

```
import java.awt.*;
import java.lang.*;

public class Ticker1 extends java.applet.Applet {

String message;

public void init() {
message = new String("Test");
    }

public void paint(Graphics g) {
        g.drawString(message, 0 ,30);
    }

}
```

The HTML for this applet is as follows:

```
<APPLET CODE="Ticker1.class" WIDTH=300 HEIGHT=40></APPLET>
```

Fine Control over Drawing the Text

The first step of the TickerTape applet allowed text to be drawn on- screen, but a few things in that process need to be refined:

- You need to be able to specify the font.
- The text is drawn at an arbitrary point on the screen. Because it will be moving later, you need a better handle on where to display the text and where the text is currently.

In order to make these refinements, you need to add several new variables:

- `width` and `height`: Because the text will need to be positioned finely on the applet, you will need to know the width and height of the applet.
- `fontHeight`: When text is drawn, the lower left hand corner of the text is the point specified. Because the text should appear halfway down the applet, you need to know the height of the text.
- `currentPos`: The text is drawn at different positions horizontally on the applet, and this variable keeps track of where the last text was drawn.
- `theFont`: Because different fonts can be used, this variable holds the current font.

Adding Font Control

Java has made life relatively simple when it comes to fonts by providing a Font object that can be created and then used throughout the applet. The Font object's constructor has the following format:

```
Font(String name, int style, int size)
```

The parameters for the Font object have the following meaning:

- name is the name of the font. You need to be careful which fonts you select, but most machines have standard fonts like Times, Courier, and Helvetica.
- style is the style of the text. Font.PLAIN, Font.BOLD, and Font.ITALIC create plain, bold, and italic text respectively.
- size is the size of the font desired, in points.

For this applet, the text will always be plain and 12-point (although this could easily be made configurable later). The font name will eventually be user-specified, but for now, set it to be Courier by adding the following line to the init() method:

```
theFont = new Font("Courier", Font.PLAIN, 12);
```

Next, you need to specify the height of the font. You can retrieve this information through the getSize() method:

```
fontHeight = theFont.getSize();
```

When you want to specify a font to be used for drawing, you set the font for the graphics context. This is a bit counter-intuitive because you would expect to specify a font as part of the drawString() method. At any one time, a font is selected for the current graphics context, and all text is drawn in that font.

You set the font by adding the following line to the paint() method:

```
g.setFont(theFont);
```

Tracking the Text's Location and Position

To find the height and width of the applet, call the size() method of the applet and get the width and height properties of the applet:

```
height = size().height;
width  = size().width;
```

When the text is drawn, the x and y positions of the point at which the text should be drawn need to be known. For the x position, you can start at an arbitrary place; for now, you'll start by drawing the text at 0 on the x-axis.

Finding out where to place the text on the y-axis is a bit trickier. It should appear exactly halfway down the y-axis of the applet. The obvious way to figure out this position would be to just take the height of the applet and divide it by two. Unfortunately, this way will not work. Why not? The height of the characters in the font needs to be taken into consideration as well; otherwise, the message would appear off-center.

All you need to do to correct this is to subtract half the height of the font from halfway down the y-axis. This should position the message at exactly the halfway point:

```
g.drawString(message, currentPos, height/2 - fontHeight/2);
```

The applet now has many new features that prepare it to be animated. Rather than having information for the position of the applet hardcoded into the `drawString()` method, this information has now been pulled out into variables that can be changed. Also, the font to use is no longer the default but has also been pulled out into a variable. Listing 12.2 shows the complete code for step two of the TickerTape applet.

Listing 12.2. Step two, the Ticker2 applet, adds variables.

```
import java.awt.*;
import java.lang.*;

public class Ticker2 extends java.applet.Applet {
    String message;
    int width, height;
    int fontHeight;
    int currentPos = 0;

    Font theFont;

    public void init() {
        height = size().height;
        width  = size().width;

        theFont = new Font("Courier", Font.PLAIN, 12);
        fontHeight = theFont.getSize();

        message = new String("Test");
    }

    public void paint(Graphics g) {
        g.setFont(theFont);
        g.drawString(message, currentPos, height/2 - fontHeight/2);
    }
}
```

The HTML for this applet is as follows:

```
<APPLET CODE="Ticker2.class" WIDTH=300 HEIGHT=40></APPLET>
```

Animating the Text

Next you need to get the text moving. Unfortunately, the concepts you have dealt with up to this point are not sufficient to do this because there is no method in an applet that is called on a regular basis without user interaction. Therefore, you need to have an external way to for the applet do something repeatedly. Java provides this capability through threads.

The name *thread* is derived from the concept that what is being added is an independent thread of execution. Think of it as a mini-program that runs independently alongside your applet. Adding a thread to your program is a pretty straightforward process, as long as you take it step by step. Follow these steps:

1. Add a variable of type Thread to hold the thread.
2. Add implements Runnable to the applet definition.
3. Program the thread's logic in the run() method of the applet.
4. Start the thread when the applet is started.
5. Stop the thread when the applet is stopped.

Follow this process to add a thread to animate the tickertape. First, you need a variable to hold the thread. Call it animator because that is what you need the thread to do:

```
Thread animator;
```

Second, add implements Runnable to the class definition for the applet:

```
public class Ticker3 extends java.applet.Applet implements Runnable {
```

This line lets the Java compiler know that this applet contains a thread. The compiler now expects a run() method to be included in the applet as well:

```
public void run() {
    while (animator != null) {
        try {
            Thread.sleep(100);
        } catch (InterruptedException e) {
            break;
        }

        currentPos = currentPos - 5;
        if (currentPos < -messageWidth)
            currentPos = width;
        repaint();
    }

}
```

This code looks much more complicated, so more explanation is needed. First, the thread is checked to see whether it is null:

```
while (animator != null) {
```

All this code means is that the block of code that follows this line keeps repeating until the `animator` variable contains nothing. When a thread is created, its value is set in a variable (in this case `animator`). When the thread is stopped, you set its value to `null`, and this loop ends. Changing the value to `null` is necessary to prevent the `run()` method from repeating forever.

Next, you need to make the thread delay for a period of time; otherwise, the text would move way too fast. You can create this delay by calling the `sleep()` method of the thread. Unfortunately, some methods in Java cannot just be called because they may generate an error, and `sleep()` is one of those methods.

When a method generates an error, the error is known as an exception. When you do some work after the error is generated, that is known as handling the exception. In Java, you handle the exception by trying the operation and catching the exception if something bad happened. This concept is tricky, but a real-world example might make it more understandable. Say you wanted to divide 2 by 0. You would try to divide 2 by 0, but that's not possible. What do you do then? You catch the problem with another set of things to do.

The try/catch process for this thread is as follows:

```
try {
    Thread.sleep(100);
} catch (InterruptedException e) {
    break;
}
```

What is happening in this code is that you are trying to cause the thread to go to sleep for a while (in this case, 100 milliseconds). If for some reason the operating system won't let this happen, you break out of the loop and exit the thread. Why? If the thread cannot pause itself anymore, then it is worthless to you and should stop. This shouldn't ever happen, however.

After the thread has slept for a little bit, the text needs to be moved. To do this, subtract five pixels from the `currentPos`. This amount should be enough for the user to perceive that the text has moved:

```
currentPos = currentPos - 5;
```

You can do this forever, and the text will keep scrolling to the left. Up to a point this action is good, but when the text scrolls off the edge of the left-hand side of the applet, it needs to start again at the right-hand side. One way to do this would be to check whether `currentPos` is less than 0:

```
if (currentPos < 0)
```

This code would work, but the result would be disconcerting to the eye. Why? Remember that text is drawn from left to right. When `currentPos` is equal to 0, the left edge of the message starts to scroll off the left-hand side of the applet the next time through the loop. If you move the message back to the right-hand side of the screen now, the rest of the message will not scroll off the left-hand side.

This problem can be corrected by restarting the text on the right-hand side only when the entire message has scrolled off the left-hand side of the applet. How could you do this? One way would be to find out how wide the message is, and then restart the message only when the current position is less than the negative of that. In effect, all you are doing is moving where 0 used to be the width of the message to the left. With this correction, everything will appear as it should:

```
if (currentPos < -messageWidth)
    currentPos = width;
```

First, check to see whether the current position has scrolled off too far to the left. If it has, you set the position to the width of the applet, effectively starting the process all over again. You should also have the applet start the message at the right-hand edge of the screen, so add the following line in the `init()` method:

```
currentPos = width;
```

You also need to compute the width of the message. First, add the variable `messageWidth` to the applet:

```
int messageWidth;
```

Now compute this variable in the `init()` method:

```
messageWidth = getFontMetrics(theFont).stringWidth(message);
```

You don't need to understand in detail what this line does, only that it computes how many pixels wide the message will be if drawn on the current component (in this case, the applet) with the font `theFont`.

Now that the `currentPos` has been updated to a new position to the left and all the checking that needs to be done has been done, it's time to redraw the text. In order to do this, two things need to happen:

1. The applet screen must be cleared.
2. The text must be drawn.

You can accomplish both of these steps with one line of code:

```
repaint();
```

What does repaint() do? It clears the screen, and then calls the paint() method. Because you changed the paint() method in the previous section to check currentPos for where to draw the text, you don't need to make any changes.

This is a good example of why it makes sense to keep things as general as possible when you program and avoid hardcoding in information as much as possible. By writing the drawString() method to check variables instead of relying on constant numbers, you don't have to go back and change anything.

Most of the work is done now. All that is left is to get the thread started when the applet starts up and stop the thread when the applet stops. You may remember from Chapter 10 that in addition to init(), which is called when the applet is loaded, start() and stop() are also called whenever the applet is started and stopped. You can use this fact to your advantage in this applet.

You want the tickertape to animate only while the applet is being shown, so start up the thread in the start() method:

```
public void start() {
    animator = new Thread(this);
    animator.start();
}
```

In this code, you are making a new thread each time the applet starts up. This process makes sense because the thread will be killed every time the applet stops. Making an instance of the thread creates the thread, but until you call start(), the thread just sits there. Calling start() gets things rolling.

When the applet is exited, stop() is called because you want to stop the thread when that happens:

```
public void stop() {
    if (animator != null) animator.stop();
    animator = null;
}
```

First, you check to see whether the variable animator contains a thread. The animator variable should always contain a thread because a thread should always be running before the stop() method of the applet is called. Because you will be calling a method of the animator object, it makes sense to be a little paranoid and make sure that a thread is running before stop() is called. You then call the stop() method of the animator, which stops the thread. Finally, you set the animator thread equal to null, which gets rid of the thread entirely.

The tickertape now moves along indefinitely when the applet is started. Listing 12.3 is the source code for this stage of the applet.

Listing 12.3. Step three, the Ticker3 applet, adds motion to the text.

```java
import java.awt.*;
import java.lang.*;

public class Ticker3 extends java.applet.Applet implements Runnable {
    String message;

    int width, height;
    int fontHeight;
    int messageWidth;
    int currentPos;

    Font theFont;
    Thread animator;

    public void init() {
        height = size().height;
        width  = size().width;
        currentPos = width;

        theFont = new Font("Courier", Font.PLAIN, 12);
        fontHeight = theFont.getSize();

        message = new String("Test");
        messageWidth = getFontMetrics(theFont).stringWidth(message);
    }


    public void start() {
        animator = new Thread(this);
        animator.start();
    }

    public void stop() {
        if (animator != null) animator.stop();
        animator = null;
    }

    public void run() {
        while (animator != null) {
            try {
                Thread.sleep(100);
            } catch (InterruptedException e) {
                break;
            }

            currentPos = currentPos - 5;
            if (currentPos < -messageWidth)
                currentPos = width;
            repaint();
        }

    }
```

```
    public void paint(Graphics g) {
        g.setFont(theFont);
        g.drawString(message, currentPos, height/2 - fontHeight/2);
    }

}
```

The HTML is as follows:

```
<APPLET CODE="Ticker3.class" WIDTH=300 HEIGHT=40></APPLET>
```

Adding Parameters

The TickerTape applet is almost finished. All that you need to add now is the capability to pass in parameters. This capability is covered in detail in Chapter 10, so you will just be given the basics here.

First, you need the getParameterInfo() method to expose the parameters that will be passed. You need the following three parameters:

- message is the message to display.
- font is the font the message should be displayed in.
- delay is the delay between redrawings of the message.

```
public String[][] getParameterInfo() {
    String[][] info = {
        {"message", "string", "message to display"},
        {"font", "string", "Font to use"},
        {"delay", "int", "delay in ms. between redrawing"},
    };
    return info;
}
```

First, get the parameter for the font. Add a String variable to the applet to hold the name called fontName. Then get the parameter in the init() method:

```
fontName  = getParameter("font");
theFont = new Font(fontName, Font.PLAIN, 12);
```

Once you have the parameter, you can get that font instead of having it hardcoded. To do this, change Courier in the Font() constructor to fontName.

You do a similar thing for the message and for the delay:

```
delay  = Integer.valueOf(getParameter("delay")).intValue();
message = getParameter("message");
```

All the first line does is convert the String that getParameter() returns into an integer and stores it in delay. The second line gets the message to display.

You also need to change the `sleep()` method in the `run()` method to use `delay`:

```
Thread.sleep(delay);
```

You're finished! The applet has the same functionality as in the last version, but with the added benefit of allowing parameters to be passed. Figure 12.2 shows the applet, and Listing 12.4 is the source code for the final version of the applet.

Figure 12.2.
The final version of the TickerTape applet.

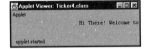

Listing 12.4. The final Ticker4 applet that provides full functionality.

```java
import java.awt.*;
import java.lang.*;

public class Ticker4 extends java.applet.Applet implements Runnable {
    String message;
    String fontName;

    int width, height;
    int fontHeight;
    int messageWidth;
    int currentPos;
    int delay;

    Font theFont;
    Thread animator;

    public String[][] getParameterInfo() {
        String[][] info = {
            {"message", "string", "message to display"},
            {"font", "string", "Font to use"},
            {"delay", "int", "delay in ms. between redrawing"},
        };
        return info;
    }

    public void init() {
        height = size().height;
        width  = size().width;
        currentPos = width;

        fontName  = getParameter("font");
        theFont = new Font(fontName, Font.PLAIN, 12);
        fontHeight = theFont.getSize();
        delay  = Integer.valueOf(getParameter("delay")).intValue();
        message = getParameter("message");
        messageWidth = getFontMetrics(theFont).stringWidth(message);

    }
```

```
public void start() {
    animator = new Thread(this);
    animator.start();
}

public void stop() {
    if (animator != null) animator.stop();
        animator = null;
}

public void run() {
    while (animator != null) {
        try {
            Thread.sleep(delay);
        } catch (InterruptedException e) {
            break;
        }

        currentPos = currentPos - 5;
        if (currentPos < -messageWidth)
            currentPos = width;
        repaint();
    }

}

public void paint(Graphics g) {
    g.setFont(theFont);
    g.drawString(message, currentPos, height/2 - fontHeight/2);
}

}
```

The HTML for this applet is as follows:

```
<APPLET CODE="Ticker4.class" WIDTH=300 HEIGHT=40>
<PARAM name="message" value="Hello, and welcome to my applet.">
<PARAM name="font" value="Courier">
<PARAM name="delay" value="175">
</APPLET>
```

Summary

This chapter went step-by-step from an applet that just displayed the word *Test* on-screen all the way to a TickerTape applet that takes parameters and animates text. Although this process wasn't trivial, it was surprisingly straightforward compared to other languages.

This applet would be a great one to modify yourself. Change it to allow the text to scroll from right to left instead of left to right. Put in a parameter to allow the text to be resized. The possibilities are endless!

CHAPTER 13

The SlideShow Applet

You started with the basics of the Java language in Chapter 7, "The Java Developer's Kit," and moved on through the basics of Java syntax, the Applet Package, and the AWT. Now with all of those tools available to use, you have everything you need to design a full-scale applet, complete with a user interface. The applet that this chapter discusses is a SlideShow applet. This SlideShow applet has the following features:

- User-specified images
- A user-specified soundtrack
- The ability to mute the soundtrack
- A user-configurable title
- An automatic slide show, with a user-specified pause between images

This chapter discusses all the issues associated with designing the applet, which are similar to those that you will face when you design your own applets. This example should help you gain a better understanding of how careful planning can help make coding your applets easier and help you in the long run.

Design Issues

Before you even start coding anything, sit down and map out the specifics of your applet, and consider some of the issues that will be involved. Time invested in the planning stage will help you save time in the coding and give you some starting points should you run into trouble when you are designing your applet. So what are some of the issues that you have to deal with in an applet like the SlideShow applet? The following is a list of questions you need to answer:

- What types of image and sound files do you support?
- What is the best way for users to specify files?
- What kinds of controls would be useful?
- How do you want the applet to start up?

Each of these broad issues raises some major issues along the way that you'll need to deal with, but now that you have some broad categories, you can start mapping out your applet.

File Support

The types of files that your applets can support are limited to the types of file support that are inherent in Java. After all, applets leverage the browser for image file support, so you have to work within that context when working with files. Currently, applets support two types of image files, GIF and JPEG. So even if you wanted to support more file types, you really couldn't without programming some very difficult image handling code in Java. Because these types also happen to be the standard image file formats on the Web, they are probably good choices anyway, so you're set for images.

As luck would have it, your sound choices are very narrow as well. Java supports only the AU sound format. So you can pretty much call this a moot issue as well. See how easy that can be! Unfortunately, not all of your decisions will be so easy.

User Parameters

Because this applet is a SlideShow, you want to allow users to be able to specify the images that they want shown in the applet. So you need to provide some mechanism for allowing users to set a parameter that specifies what image files to use. There are several ways you could do this:

1. You could have the applet take any images that are in a particular directory. This option would be easy for the user, but would involve writing some complex code, as you would need to scan all of the files in the directory, make sure they were all valid image files, and then deal with a wide variety of filenames.

2. You could have the applet read in a configuration file that was a list of the filenames to be used. This option would be similar to using a directory, and you would still have to deal with different filenames.

3. You could have a parameter for each image. This option would allow the user to specify each image file individually, but it would also mean you would have to set a fixed number of images beforehand, which would limit the applet significantly.

4. You could also have the user specify a base name for an image and then number each of his images so the filenames were sequential. That would mean a little more work for the user, but then you could allow the applet to contain the exact number of images selected by the user and have a flexible applet.

The SlideShow applet uses the fourth option. In this scheme, the user selects a base name for the image, such as `myImage`, and the images that the user wants to include in the SlideShow are named sequentially, such as `myImage0.gif`, `myImage1.gif`, `myImage2.gif`, and so on. This scheme means the user needs to rename some images, but it makes the parameters very straightforward and does not limit the total number of images.

You now know several parameters that you will need to include in the applet: the `image file` base name, the total number of images, and the image extension (GIF or JPG).

Now that you have the image parameters selected, you also need an audio parameter, the sound file name. Because the soundtrack is a background track, you only need to worry about one `soundfile`, but you should have a sound file parameter so users can specify a sound file.

Some other user parameters should be added to the applet for more functionality. For example, you want to have a specified delay interval for the automatic slide show, and you also want to allow the user to set the caption for the applet. After you add those parameters, you have a list of the parameters (see Table 13.1) you will need to specify and deal with in the applet.

Table 13.1. A summary of the SlideShow applet parameters.

Parameter	Function
imagefile	Base image file name (picture, for example)
type	Image file type (GIF, JPG, and so on)
images	Total number of image files
soundfile	Sound file name (example: audio.au)
delay	Delay in between images (in ms.)
caption	Title of the slide viewer

The parameters are a user interface of sorts; they do allow the user to have some input as to the function of the applet, but this applet has an actual user interface component as well.

User Interface

Because you want to give the SlideShow applet a fully functional user interface, you need to think about what kinds of controls you will need and how you want those controls to function. Your applet does not need too many controls, but there are some that would add functionality to the applet and make it a little more user-friendly:

- A button to move forward through the images
- A button to move backward through the images
- Some way to turn on and off the automatic cycling through images
- Some way to mute the sound

When you start to think about the user interface and adding user controls to your applets, you also need to consider how those controls should function and what would be most intuitive for the user. For example, for the Forward and Backward button you could have a toggle switch that changed the direction, or you could have a dial that you set to forward or backward. But having two distinct buttons, a forward button on the right and a backward button on the left, fits well with the image most people have of how slide projectors work. Additionally, you want users to be able to advance through the images on their own, and a button implies that level of functionality. In many cases, you will find that the simplest approach is often the best. In this case, a complex interface would have been silly and would have detracted from the value of the applet.

Checkboxes are used for the Automatic SlideShow option and the Mute option. The checkboxes are a simple way to indicate that a feature is on or off, and they provide a switching mechanism. Now you have the elements of the user interface, listed in Table 13.2, and you are ready to move on to the last stage of planning the applet.

Table 13.2. A summary of the user interface elements for the SlideShow applet.

Element	Function
Button 1	A button to move the images forward one at a time
Button 2	A button to move the images backward one at a time
Checkbox 1	A checkbox to turn off and on the Automatic SlideShow
Checkbox 2	A checkbox to mute the soundtrack

Starting the Applet

You are almost done with the planning stage of the applet. You have outlined the features you want the applet to include, the user interface for the applet, and how the user can configure different aspects of the applet. You have only a few more details to hammer out before you start coding the applet.

First, you need to decide how you want the applet to begin. Because this applet is designed to be somewhat like a photo gallery, you might decide that you want the applet to start off with sound and in the Automatic SlideShow mode. Starting the applet this way has two practical implications:

- You have to initialize the user interface components correctly so the checkboxes reflect the proper state of the application.
- You need to make sure that all of the images are downloaded to the applet before it starts to run.

Later sections explain how you deal with each of these issues as you code the actual applet, but it's a good idea to identify such issues beforehand so you can plan ahead and begin thinking about possible solutions.

Coding the Applet

Now that you have mapped out some of the issues surrounding your applet, go ahead and start to code it. The beginnings of the code can be found in Listing 13.1.

Listing 13.1. The beginnings of the SlideShow applet.

```
/*
The SlideShow Applet
*/

import java.awt.*;
import java.lang.*;
import java.applet.*;
import java.net.URL;


public class SlideShow extends Applet implements Runnable {

    MediaTracker LoadImages;
    Image slides[];
    String imagefile, soundfile, type, caption;
    Thread AutoShow;
    int images, delay;
    int index = 0;
    Button forward, backward;
```

continues

Listing 13.1. continued

```
    Checkbox auto, sound;
    Label title;
      AudioClip clip;
    Panel marquee, control;
}
```

You start off with the standard range of `import` statements so that you have all the methods you will need at our disposal. Next, you declare the class, `SlideShow`. Notice that the code has `implements Runnable` after `extends Applet`. You are going to need to incorporate threads into this applet, so in addition to having the applet be an extension to the `Applet` class, you need to say that it implements the features of `Runnable`, which allows you to start a thread.

Next, you declare the variables. Let's take a look at each one of these and what they do:

- `MediaTracker LoadImages;` declares that you are going to be using a `MediaTracker` class and that you are going to call it `LoadImages`.
- `Image slides[];` declares an array of images called `slides`. You store your image files in this array, so you can cycle through them conveniently.
- `String imagefile, soundfile, type, caption;` are the strings you will need for filenames and labels.
- `Thread AutoShow;` declares a new thread for the Automatic SlideShow.
- `int images, delay;` and `int index = 0;` are the integer variables you will need for parameters and an index variable that you can use as a base for cycling through images.
- `Button forward, backward;` are the buttons you will add to the layout.
- `Checkbox auto, sound;` are the checkboxes.
- `Label title;` is the title that is displayed in the slideshow window.
- `AudioClip clip;` is the audiofile you will be using for your soundtrack.
- `Panel marquee, control;` are the panels that you will be using to create the user interface layout.

The foundation of the applet is now built. You have declared all the variables and instances that you will be using and are ready to start reading in the parameters and loading the images.

Parsing the Parameters

The code that you are going to use to read in the parameters should look very similar to the code used to read in parameters in the Speaker applet in Chapter 10, "Applet Structure and Design," and the TickerTape applet in Chapter 12 "The TickerTape Applet." The methodology for reading in parameters doesn't vary much from applet to applet. In the SlideShow applet, you use the `getParameterInfo()` method to set up what parameters you will accept and what their function is, and then you use the `getParameter()` method to read the parameter values from the HTML file. The code used to accomplish this is in Listing 13.2.

Listing 13.2. The code for using parameters.

```
public String[][] getParameterInfo() {
    String[][] info = {
        {"caption", "string", "Title of the Slide Viewer"},
        {"imagefile", "string", "Base Image File Name (ex. picture)"},
            {"soundfile", "string", "Sound File Name (ex. audio.au)"},
            {"images", "int", "Total number of image files"},
            {"delay", "int", "Delay in between images (in ms.)"},
            {"type", "string", "Image File Type(gif, jpg, etc)"},
    };
    return info;
}

public void init() {

    LoadImages = new MediaTracker(this);

    caption = getParameter("caption");
    imagefile = getParameter("imagefile");
    soundfile = getParameter("soundfile");
    type      = getParameter("type");
    images    = Integer.valueOf(getParameter("images")).intValue();
    slides = new Image[images];
    delay     = Integer.valueOf(getParameter("delay")).intValue();
}
```

Now that you have the parameters under control, you can move on to loading the images.

MediaTracker

When you are coding an application that uses several media files, such as image files, you want to make sure that your applet has loaded all the necessary files before it begins to execute. If an animation applet, for example, requires a series of images for the animation, you would not want the animation to start until the images were all loaded. Otherwise, the animation might appear jerky, or, even worse, it might skip frames and produce an incomplete animation. So if you have to load more than one or two media files, it would be very helpful to have a way to keep track of the loading status of those files and keep the applet from executing until those files have been loaded. Fortunately, Sun has provided just such a mechanism: the `MediaTracker` class.

You can find the full documentation for the `MediaTracker` class at the following URL:

`http://www.javasoft.com/JDK1.0/api/java.awt.MediaTracker.html`

This documentation details all the functionality that is provided with the `MediaTracker` class. As the name implies, MediaTracker is designed to be used with any kind of media file, sound, or images. However, the JDK 1.0 release only supports image files. Nonetheless, the MediaTracker is a great way to make sure your files are loaded and ready to be used before your applet begins.

Some of the more useful methods from the `MediaTracker` class are described in the following paragraphs:

The `addImage()` method enables you to add an image file to the list of image files you want to keep track of.

The `checkAll()` and `checkID()` methods enable you to check whether your images have been loaded; you can either check for a specific image ID or check all the images.

The `getErrorsAny()` and `getErrorsID()` methods return any errors that have been generated during the image loading process. You can check errors for specific image IDs or all images.

The `statusAll()` and `statusID()` methods return the loading status of images being loaded. They can check the status of a particular image by image ID or all images currently in the list.

The `waitForAll()` and `waitForID()` methods start loading images that have been added using the `addImage()` method. You can invoke them to load a specific ID or all images and they will wait until the image(s) are loaded before allowing the applet to proceed.

Basically, you create an instance of the `MediaTracker` class that tracks your image files. You can then use some `MediaTracker`-specific methods to track each image as it is read into memory. `MediaTracker` notifies your applet when errors occur in loading the images and also lets your applet know when all the images are completely loaded so that the applet may execute. All in all, `MediaTracker` is a very useful class.

Loading the Images and `MediaTracker`

As mentioned before, you want to start the SlideShow applet in the Automatic SlideShow mode, so you need to make sure that the images you are going to be using have been loaded before you start running the SlideShow. To stay informed about the images, you are going to use a class called MediaTracker (see the preceding sidebar). The MediaTracker class enables you to monitor the loading status of your images and makes sure that you do not progress until all of the images have been loaded. In the code, this class looks like Listing 13.3.

Listing 13.3. An example of using MediaTracker to load the images.

```
LoadImages = new MediaTracker(this);

for (int i = 0; i < images; i++) {
    slides[i] = getImage(getDocumentBase(), imagefile + i + "." + type);
        if (i > 0)
            LoadImages.addImage(slides[i], 1);
        else
            LoadImages.addImage(slides[i], 0);
}
try {
    LoadImages.waitForID(0);
} catch (InterruptedException e) {
    System.out.println("Image Loading Failed!");
}

showStatus(imagefile + " Images Loaded");
index = 0;
repaint();
LoadImages.checkID(1,true);
```

This code starts off by declaring a new instance of the MediaTracker class called LoadImages. Then you use a for loop to add each of the user's images to the list of images to be tracked. Once all the images have been added, you use the waitForID() method to start loading the images. The try and catch terms are Java methods for handling errors. Finally, you use the checkID() method to see whether all the images are loading, and then the program can proceed.

Creating the User Interface

While you are still in the init() method, you can create the graphical user interface for this applet. When creating any graphical user interface, creating a usable layout can be quite a complex task. For example, the SlideShow applet uses three separate layouts embedded in each other to create the final GUI for the applet (see Figure 13.1).

You start out with a generic border layout, which is based on placing components at the compass points. You are going to add an element only to the South, which is displayed at the bottom of the screen. The layout you add to the South is called marquee because that's where all the applet information will be displayed. The marquee panel is also based on a border layout. This way, you can add the title to the North, and it will be unaffected by any of the user controls. Finally, you are going to create a new panel called `control` where you will place the buttons and so forth. This layout uses a simple flow layout so the elements are displayed left to right. You will then add the `control` panel to the South of the `marquee` panel and be left with the final output (see Figure 13.2). The code to produce this output can be found in Listing 13.4.

Figure 13.1.
The panels used for the SlideShow applet.

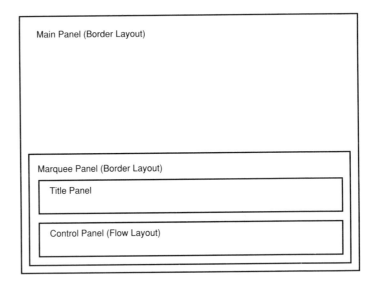

Listing 13.4. Establishing a user interface.

```
setLayout(new BorderLayout());

forward = new Button("Next");
backward = new Button("Previous");
auto = new Checkbox("AutoCycle Images");
auto.setState(true);
sound = new Checkbox("Sound On");
sound.setState(true);
title = new Label(caption);

Panel marquee = new Panel();
marquee.setLayout(new BorderLayout());

marquee.add("North", title);

Panel control = new Panel();
control.setLayout(new FlowLayout());

control.add(auto);
control.add(sound);
control.add(backward);
control.add(forward);

setFont(new Font("Helvetica", Font.BOLD, 18));
add("South", marquee);
```

```
setFont(new Font("Helvetica", Font.PLAIN, 14));
marquee.add("South", control);
}
```

Figure 13.2.
*Shows the final layout
of the SlideShow
applet elements.*

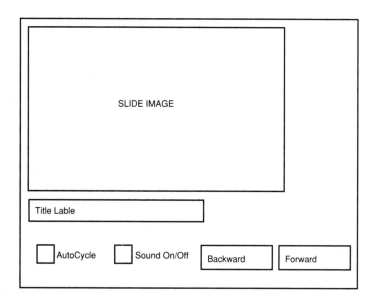

Now that you have the layout established, the last thing you need to do is to make the elements you've just laid out functional. Do this by adding the event handling code in Listing 13.5 to the `init()` method.

Listing 13.5. Event handling in the SlideShow applet.

```
public boolean action(Event evt, Object what) {
    if (evt.target == sound) {
        if (sound.getState() == true)
            clip.loop();
        else
            clip.stop();
        return true;
    } else if (evt.target == backward) {
        if (index !=0) {
            index--;
            repaint();
        }
        return true;
    } else if (evt.target == forward) {
        index++;
        repaint();
        return true;
        } else
        return false;
```

In this code, you use a series of if and else if statements to monitor any events that might be generated by the applet, and compare those events to the layout elements. The Sound checkbox starts or stops the sound. The Forward and Backward buttons repaint the screen using the repaint() method and then set the index counter forward or backward as is appropriate.

Drawing the Images

Drawing the images on-screen in the applet can be a bit confusing. There are three methods that you are going to use to accomplish this task, paint(), repaint(), and update(). They all work together in an odd way (see Figure 13.3), each one calling the other. In the start() method, you are going to use repaint() to put an image on-screen. The repaint() method calls the update() method, not the paint() method as the name might imply. The update() method then clears the screen and calls paint(), which places the new image on-screen.

Figure 13.3.
The relationship between the paint()*,* repaint()*, and* update() *methods.*

repaint()------> update() ------> paint()

Redefining all these methods may seem a bit odd, but if you didn't, there would be problems when one method called the other, and you wouldn't see the slides. The following code redefines update() to paint the slide:

```
public void update(Graphics g) {
    try {
        paint(g);
    } catch (ArrayIndexOutOfBoundsException e) {
        if(index < 0)
            index = 0;
        else if (index > images)
            index = images;
        System.out.println("No more Images!");
    }
}
```

There really is not much to the update() method. Most of that code is just there in case you have an error. The try section accomplishes the work in the method, and the catch portion only exists to deal with an error if one is generated. (In this case, an error is generated if the user tries to advance past the beginning or end of the slides.)

You are also going to subclass the paint() method. There are two reasons for doing this. First, you use the paint() method to check for error messages from the MediaTracker and replace any bad images with a black screen. That way, you don't break the applet if an image is broken. Secondly, you need to tell the paint() method what image to place on the screen. You do this by calling up an image from the array of slides, using the [index] number to call up as specific image on-screen. The end result is a paint() method that replaces any broken images and shows the slides correctly:

```
public void paint(Graphics g) {
    if (LoadImages.isErrorAny()) {
        g.setColor(Color.black);
        g.fillRect(0, 0, size().width, size().height);
        return;
    }

    g.drawImage(slides[index], 0, 0, this);

    }
```

With those methods defined, you are almost out of the woods. Now you need to set up the thread that operates the Automatic SlideShow.

The AutoShow Thread

Because you want the applet to run in two modes, AutoShow mode and user-controlled mode, you need to have two different applets running. One lets the user control what images are on-screen, and the other automatically cycles through the images. Whenever you have two distinct functions like this, you should consider using a thread.

As mentioned in the TickerTape applet in Chapter 12, threads function like an applet within an applet, but they have their own distinct qualities. Because this example (see Listing 13.6) is a standard thread, which doesn't do anything too fancy, it's defined in run():

Listing 13.6. The AutoShow thread.

```
public void run() {

    Thread running = Thread.currentThread();
    while (AutoShow==running) {
        try {
            Thread.sleep(delay);
        } catch (InterruptedException e) {
            break;
        }
        if (auto.getState() == true) {
            if (LoadImages.checkID(1,true))
                synchronized (this) {
            if (index == (slides.length - 1))
                index = 0;
            else
                index++;
            }

            repaint();
        }
    }
}
```

The code for the thread is not too extensive, but it does quite a bit. First, you need to let the applet know what thread is the current thread, and then you can refer to that thread as `running`. You actually start the thread from within the `start()` method, but this `running` label enables you to keep tabs on your thread a little better. You then use a `while` loop so that as long as the thread is running, it will carry out the rest of the instructions in the thread definition.

Inside the `while` loop, you first set the thread to `sleep` for a delay period. That delay period is the `delay` that you allowed the user to specify in the parameters as the time in between slides. The first thing the thread does is sleep for the delay whenever it is running, which is what creates the delay in between images. The thread completes its instructions, then sleeps for the delay, and then attempts to carry out its instructions again.

The instructions for the thread are contained in the `if` statements following the `try`. In these statements, the thread checks to see whether the Auto checkbox is checked. If it's not, the thread doesn't do anything. However, if it is checked, you are in the AutoShow mode, and the thread first checks to see that the images are loaded correctly, and then displays the first image. The thread also sets the index number to the next method, and then the whole loop process repeats for as long as the `Auto` checkbox is checked.

start() and stop()

Now that you have the AutoShow thread set up, you need to make sure that it starts and that the applet puts an image on-screen and begins to play the soundtrack. Use the `repaint()` method to show an image, start the clip playing, and launch the thread called AutoShow:

```
public void start() {
    images = 0;
    repaint();

    clip.loop();
    AutoShow = new Thread(this);
    AutoShow.start();

}
```

As always, the `stop()` method is just for cleanup. In particular, the `stop()` method for the SlideShow applet makes sure that the `AutoShow` thread is no longer running:

```
public void stop() {
    index = 0;
    repaint();
    if (AutoShow!= null) AutoShow.stop();
    AutoShow= null;
}
```

That's all there is to it! The code does seem like a lot when it's all broken up into sections, but the assembled final code is shown in Listing 13.7. When you see the code all together, you can see that you have a very functional robust applet with very little code.

Listing 13.7. The SlideShow applet.

```
/*
The SlideShow Applet
*/

import java.awt.*;
import java.lang.*;
import java.applet.*;
import java.net.URL;


public class SlideShow extends Applet implements Runnable {

    MediaTracker LoadImages;
    Image slides[];
    String imagefile, soundfile, type, caption;
    Thread AutoShow;
    int images, delay;
    int index = 0;
    Button forward, backward;
    Checkbox auto, sound;
    Label title;
      AudioClip clip;
    Panel marquee, control;


    public String[][] getParameterInfo() {
        String[][] info = {
            {"caption", "string", "Title of the Slide Viewer"},
            {"imagefile", "string", "Base Image File Name (ex. picture)"},
                {"soundfile", "string", "Sound File Name (ex. audio.au)"},
                  {"images", "int", "Total number of image files"},
                  {"delay", "int", "Delay in between images (in ms.)"},
                  {"type", "string", "Image File Type(gif, jpg, etc)"},
        };
        return info;
    }

    public void init() {

    //Parse the parameters from the HTML File

    LoadImages = new MediaTracker(this);

    caption = getParameter("caption");
    imagefile = getParameter("imagefile");
    soundfile = getParameter("soundfile");
    type    = getParameter("type");
    images  = Integer.valueOf(getParameter("images")).intValue();
    slides = new Image[images];
    delay   = Integer.valueOf(getParameter("delay")).intValue();
```

continues

Listing 13.7. continued

```
//Use MediaTracker to load the images

for (int i = 0; i < images; i++) {
    slides[i] = getImage(getDocumentBase(), imagefile + i + "." + type);
        if (i > 0)
            LoadImages.addImage(slides[i], 1);
        else
            LoadImages.addImage(slides[i], 0);
}

try {
    LoadImages.waitForID(0);
} catch (InterruptedException e) {
    System.out.println("Image Loading Failed!");
}

showStatus(imagefile + " Images Loaded");
index = 0;
repaint();
LoadImages.checkID(1,true);

clip = getAudioClip(getDocumentBase(), soundfile);

//Create the SlideViewer layout

setLayout(new BorderLayout());

forward = new Button("Next");
backward = new Button("Previous");
auto = new Checkbox("AutoCycle Images");
auto.setState(true);
sound = new Checkbox("Sound On");
sound.setState(true);
title = new Label(caption);

Panel marquee = new Panel();
marquee.setLayout(new BorderLayout());

marquee.add("North", title);

Panel control = new Panel();
control.setLayout(new FlowLayout());

control.add(auto);
control.add(sound);
control.add(backward);
control.add(forward);

setFont(new Font("Helvetica", Font.BOLD, 18));
add("South", marquee);
setFont(new Font("Helvetica", Font.PLAIN, 14));
marquee.add("South", control);
}

//Monitor Checkboxes and Buttons for Actions
```

```
public boolean action(Event evt, Object what) {
    if (evt.target == sound) {
        if (sound.getState() == true)
            clip.loop();
        else
            clip.stop();
        return true;
    } else if (evt.target == backward) {
        if (index !=0) {
            index--;
            repaint();
        }
        return true;
    } else if (evt.target == forward) {
        index++;
        repaint();
        return true;
      } else
        return false;


}


public void start() {
    images = 0;
    repaint();

    clip.loop();
    AutoShow = new Thread(this);
    AutoShow.start();

}

public void stop() {
    index = 0;
    repaint();
    if (AutoShow!= null) AutoShow.stop();
    AutoShow= null;
}

public void run() {

    Thread running = Thread.currentThread();
    while (AutoShow==running) {
        try {
            Thread.sleep(delay);
        } catch (InterruptedException e) {
            break;
        }
            if (auto.getState() == true) {
                if (LoadImages.checkID(1,true))
                    synchronized (this) {
                        if (index == (slides.length - 1))
                            index = 0;
                        else
                            index++;
                    }
```

continues

Listing 13.7. continued

```
                            repaint();
                        }
            }
        }


    //Update is called by repaint()

    public void update(Graphics g) {
        try {
            paint(g);
        } catch (ArrayIndexOutOfBoundsException e) {
            if(index < 0)
                index = 0;
            else if (index > images)
                index = images;
            System.out.println("No more Images!");
        }
    }

    //Paint the slide image on the screen
    //And Account for missing images

    public void paint(Graphics g) {
        if (LoadImages.isErrorAny()) {
            g.setColor(Color.black);
            g.fillRect(0, 0, size().width, size().height);
            return;
        }

        g.drawImage(slides[index], 0, 0, this);

    }

}
```

The HTML file for the SlideShow applet contains the following:

```
<HTML>
<APPLET code="SlideShow.class"  width=400 height=250>
<PARAM name="caption" value="A Sample Photo Album">
<PARAM name="imagefile" value="image">
<PARAM name="soundfile" value="song.au">
<PARAM name="images" value="5">
<PARAM name="delay" value="5000">
<PARAM name="type" value="gif">
</APPLET>
</HTML>
```

Now you have a user-configurable SlideShow applet (see Figures 13.4 through 13.6) that uses user parameters, contains a graphical user interface, and implements threads. That is no small task, and in many programming languages, you could wade though several books before being able to accomplish such a task.

Figure 13.4.
The SlideShow applet in action with the automatic show and sound enabled.

Figure 13.5.
The SlideShow applet with sound disabled.

Figure 13.6.
The SlideShow applet in user-controlled mode.

Summary

Now you have a solid background of Java from both a user's perspective and a programmer's perspective. You have a sense of Java's history and some ideas about what is possible with Java. Perhaps that's all you needed, and now you can go out and find applets to integrate with your Web pages and do so with a better understanding of what's happening behind the scenes. Maybe you've decided that you'd like to take your applets into your own hands and start working on projects of your own. Whatever direction you choose, the authors of this book hope we've provided you with the information necessary to get you excited about Java and make the best decision on how Java is going to work for you.

The applets that we've included in this book are not finished applets—there's no such thing as a finished applet. There is always room to improve them and add your own features. If you have ideas to make them even better applets, feel free to add your own code and make them function as you see fit. We hope you've enjoyed learning about Java and that you will find a place for it on your Web site. No matter what you choose to do with Java, have fun!

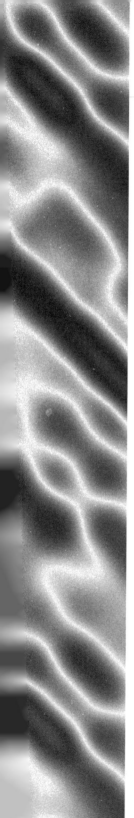

*by John December and
David Gulbransen*

Glossary of Terms

API (Application Programming Interface)   A set of packages containing various classes and methods that Java programmers use to create programs.

ASCII   American Standard Code for Information Interchange. A 7-bit character code that can represent 128 characters, some of which are control characters used for communications control that are not printable.

applet   A Java program that can be included in an HTML page with the <APPLET> HTML tag and viewed with a Java-enabled browser.

Applet Package   A collection of methods and classes provided with the Java Developer's Kit designed for use in creating applets with Java.

appletviewer   The program included in the Java Developer's Kit to view applets without a full WWW browser.

application   A standalone program that executes independently of a Java-enabled browser. You can create an application by using the java Java interpreter, which is included in the Java Developer's Kit.

attribute   A property of an HTML element, specified in the starting tag of the element. The attribute list of the <APPLET> tag is used to identify the location of applet source code (with the codebase attribute) and the name of the Java class (with the code attribute).

AWT (Abstract Window Toolkit)   A package from the Java API that enables applets and applications to use graphical user interface components such as windows, buttons, and scrollbars.

block   The code between matching curly braces, { and }.

boolean   A data type that can store the value true or false.

browser   A software program for accessing the World Wide Web; a synonym for a Web client.

bytecode   The machine-readable code created as the result of compiling a Java language source file; this is the code distributed across the network to run an applet. Bytecodes are architecture-neutral; the Java-capable browser ported to a particular platform interprets them.

child   A subclass of a class (its parent class); it inherits public (and protected) data and methods from the parent class.

class   A template for creating objects. A class defines data and methods; a class is a unit of organization in a Java program. A class can pass on its public data and methods to its subclasses.

compiler   A software program that translates human-readable source code into machine-readable code.

component   An object type in the AWT for visible user interface elements (such as a button, listbox, or scrollbar).

constructor   A method named after its class. A constructor method is invoked when an object of that class is created.

content handler   A program loaded into the user's HotJava browser that interprets files of a type defined by the Java programmer. The Java programmer provides the necessary code for the user's HotJava browser to display and interpret this special format.

CGI (Common Gateway Interface)   A standard for programs to interface with Web servers.

client   A software program that requests information or services from another software application (server) and displays this information in a form required by its hardware platform.

domain name   The alphabetic name for a computer host; this name is mapped to the computer's numeric Internet Protocol (IP) address.

firewall   A method for providing Internet security in which computers located on a common Local Area Network all use one machine (or firewall) as a gateway to the

Internet. Firewalls restrict the type of traffic flowing in and out from the local network to the Internet.

FTP (File Transfer Protocol)   A means to exchange files across a network.

garbage collection   The process by which memory allocated for objects in a program is reclaimed. Java automatically performs this process.

GIF (Graphic Interchange Format)   A type of graphic file format developed by CompuServe. GIF files use a data compression technique to create smaller graphic files with little loss in image quality.

HTML (Hypertext Markup Language)   The mechanism used to create Web pages; Web browsers display these pages according to a browser-defined rendering scheme.

HTTP (Hypertext Transfer Protocol)   The native protocol of the Web, used to transfer hypertext documents.

HotJava   A Web browser designed to execute applets written in the Java programming language.

hypertext   Text that is not constrained to a single linear sequence. Hypertext documents contain special embedded "links" that enable users to connect to other documents on a similar topic.

imagemap   A graphic inline image on an HTML page that potentially connects each pixel or region of an image to a Web resource; users retrieve the resources by clicking the image.

infinite loop   See *infinite loop.*

inheritance   The ability to define a child class that has all of the functionality of its parent class.

instance   An object.

interface   A set of methods that Java classes can implement.

Internet   The cooperatively run, globally distributed collection of computer networks that exchange information through the TCP/IP protocol suite.

Java   An object-oriented programming language for creating distributed, executable applications.

javac   The Java compiler provided with the Java Developer's Kit.

Java-enabled browser   A World Wide Web browser that can display Java applets.

JDK (Java Developer's Kit)   A collection of tools, documentation, and examples designed to provide Java programmers with the resources needed to complete applets and applications. It includes the Java compiler, the Java debugger, and the appletviewer.

Java Virtual Machine   The software "machine" that actually executes all Java programs. The Java Virtual Machine is built into the appletviewer, and any Java-capable Web browsers.

method   A function that can perform operations on data.

MIME (Multipurpose Internet Mail Extensions)   A specification for multimedia document formats.

native methods   Class methods that are declared in a Java class but implemented in C.

Net, the   A slang term for the Internet. (Also a bad movie starring Sandra Bullock.)

OOP (object-oriented programming)   A new programming paradigm based on the idea that programs can be broken down into component parts.

object   An instance of a class.

overload   To use the same name for several items in the same scope; Java methods can be overloaded.

package   A set of classes with a common high-level function declared with the `package` keyword.

parameter (HTML)   A name and value pair identified by the `Name` and `Value` attributes of the `<PARAM>` tag used inside an `<APPLET>` tag.

parent class   The originating class of a given subclass.

protocol handler   A program that is loaded into the user's HotJava browser and that interprets a protocol. These protocols include standard protocols, such as HTTP, and programmer-defined protocols.

proxy   An intermediary between a client software (such as a browser) and server software (such as a Web site). Proxy servers provide an added level of security.

scope   The program segment in which a reference to a variable is valid.

server   A software application that provides information or services based on requests from client programs.

server-push animation   An animation technique in which a series of images are "pushed" to the Web browser by the Web server. Server-push animation is dependent on network speed, and is a significant performance hit on the Web server.

site   File section of a computer on which Web documents (or other documents served in another protocol) reside, for example, a Web site, a Gopher site, or an FTP site.

Solaris   Sun Microsystems' software platform for networked applications. Solaris includes an operating system, SunOS.

SPARC (Scalable Processor ARChitecture)   Based on a reduced instruction set computer (RISC) concept in which a microprocessor is designed for very efficient handling of a small set of instructions. (See `http://www.sparc.com/`.)

subclass   See *child*.

tag   The code used to make up part of an HTML element; for example, the TITLE element has a starting tag, <TITLE>, and an ending tag, </TITLE>.

TCP/IP (Transmission Control Protocol/Internet Protocol)   The set of protocols used for network communication on the Internet.

thread   A subset of code in a Java application that runs in conjunction with the rest of the program. Threads can be thought of as a program within a program and are often necessary to deal with complex user interfaces.

Unicode   A character set that supports many world languages.

URL (Uniform Resource Locator)   The scheme for addressing on the Web; a URL identifies a resource on the Web.

Usenet   A system for disseminating asynchronous text discussion among cooperating computer hosts. The Usenet discussion space is divided into newsgroups, each on a particular topic or subtopic.

Web   See *WWW*.

WWW (World Wide Web)   A hypertext information and communication system popularly used on the Internet computer network with data communications operating according to a client/server model. Web clients (browsers) can access multiprotocol and hypermedia information using an addressing scheme.

Web server   Software that provides services to Web clients.

APPENDIX A

Java Resources on the World Wide Web

One of the best places to find information about Java is on the World Wide Web. Several sites deal specifically in Java resources from the official Sun Java Site to independent developers. This appendix lists the major Java resources on the Web. There are certainly more pages out there then can listed here, so please keep in mind that these resources are only starting points.

Java Sites

There are many sites on the Internet dedicated to showcasing Java applets. They range from large commercial sites to smaller individual sites. You should always go ahead and perform searches to find the most complete information regarding Java sites, but a few standard sites that are dedicated to providing Java info are large enough and well-established enough to be worth mentioning here. These are the same sites that were discussed in detail in Chapter 5, "Finding and Using Applets," listed here with the major site URLs. These three major Java sites (Javasoft, Gamelan, and JARS) are described in the following sections.

Sun's Java Site: Javasoft

The Sun Javasoft site is the official Java site on the World Wide Web. Here you can find developers' information, examples, tutorials, and other types of official release information. This is an invaluable Java site:

```
http://www.javasoft.com
```

The resources include the following:

About Java:	`http://www.javasoft.com/about.html`
What's New:	`http://www.javasoft.com/new.html`
Downloading:	`http://www.javasoft.com/download.html`
Documentation:	`http://www.javasoft.com/doc.html`
HotJava:	`http://www.javasoft.com/HotJava/index.html`
Applets:	`http://www.javasoft.com/applets/index.html`
Developers:	`http://www.javasoft.com/devcorner.html`
Licensing:	`http://www.javasoft.com/license.html`

Gamelan: The Directory and Registry of Java Resources

EarthWeb's Gamelan is one of the most extensive unofficial Java Web sites. This site is a compendium of Java applets and resources organized by category:

```
http://www.gamelan.com
```

Gamelan's resources include the following:

What's New:	`http://www.gamelan.com/frame/New.html`
What's Cool:	`http://www.gamelan.com/frame/Cool.html`
Gamelan News:	`http://www.gamelan.com/frame/news.html`
Find a Resource:	`http://www.gamelan.com/find.cgi`
Add a Resource:	`http://www.gamelan.com/add/add.shtml`
Who's Who:	`http://www.gamelan.com/whoswho.shtml`
Community:	`http://www.gamelan.com/frame/community.html`

JARS: The Java Applet Rating Service

JARS provides a listing of Java applets and a rating system for the applets based on the input of a panel of judges. You can find JARS at the following URL:

```
http://www.jars.com
```

JARS features include the following:

Info:	`http://www.jars.com/info.html`
New:	`http://www.jars.com/new.html`
Ratings:	`http://www.jars.com/ratings.html`
Features:	`http://www.jars.com/features.html`
Submissions:	`http://www.jars.com/submit.html`
Search:	`http://paradise.littleblue.com/Architext/AT-javaquery.html`

Search Engines

In addition to the Java-specific sites, you can use a number of available Internet search engines and indexes to find Java resources. The following list gives the URLs to many of the major search engines and index sites:

Yahoo	`http://www.yahoo.com`
Lycos	`http://www.lycos.com`
WebCrawler	`http://www.webcrawler.com`
Excite	`http://www.excite.com`
InfoSeek	`http://www.infoseek.com`
Alta Vista	`http://altavista.digital.com`

Resources from the Text

Integrated Development Environments:

Café Carouser	`http://www.coastside.net/stratum/`
FIDE	`http://amber.wpi.edu/~thethe/Documents/Besiex/Java/FrIJDE.html`
JavaMaker	`http://net.info.samsung.co.kr/~hcchoi/javamaker.html`
JavaWeb IDE	`http://insureNetUSA.com/javaIDE.html`
Symantec Café	`http://cafe.symantec.com/index.html`

Browsers:

appletviewer	`http://www.javasoft.com`
HotJava	`http://www.javasoft.com`
Netscape	`http://www.netscape.com`

Sites:

Adelaide Fringe Show	`http://www.va.com.au/afringe`
Dave Matthews Band Site	`http://www.ids.net/~reddog/dmb/`
Grey Associates	`http://www.greyassoc.com`
HotWired	`http://www.hotwired.com`

Applets:

ClickBoard

`http://www.intrinsa.com/personal/steve/ClickBoard/ClickBoard.html`

Clock

`http://www-und.ida.liu.se/~d94nilhe/java/applets.html`

clnet PC Scoreboard

`http://www.cnet.com/Content/Reviews/Compare/Pc100/0,30,,0200.html`

Color Picker Applet

`http://www.greyasscoc.com`

Curve Applet

`http://fas.sfu.ca:80/1/cs/people/GradStudents/heinrica/personal/curve.html`

Java TeleMed Prototype

`http://www.acl.lanl.gov/~rdaniel/classesJDK/PickTest2.html`

Juggling Applet

`http://www.acm.uiuc.edu/webmonkeys/juggling/`

LED Sign

`http://www.conveyor.com/ticker-tape.html`

Player Piano

`http://reality.sgi.com/employees/mark/piano/index.html`

SlideShow

`http://www.fa.indiana.edu/~dgulbran/slideshow.html`

StockTrace Applet

`http://www.cs.virginia.edu/~cd4v/graph/StockGraph.html`

WorldClock

`http://www.webpage.com/~vijay/java/wt/testwt.html`

by John J. Kottler

JavaScript and Java Language Reference

This appendix contains a summary or quick reference for the Java language.

> Note: This is not a grammar, nor is it a technical overview of the language itself. It's a quick reference to be used after you already know the basics of how the language works. If you need a technical description of the language, your best bet is to visit the Java Web site (`http://java.sun.com`) and download the specification, which includes a full BNF grammar.

Language keywords and symbols are shown in a monospace font. Arguments and other parts to be substituted are in italic monospace.

Optional parts are indicated by brackets (except in the array syntax section). If there are several options that are mutually exclusive, they are shown separated by pipes (¦¦) like this:

```
[ public ¦ private ¦ protected ] type varname
```

Reserved Words

The following words are reserved for use by the Java language itself (some of them are reserved but not currently used). You cannot use these terms to refer to classes, methods, or variable names:

abstract	do	implements	package	throw
boolean	double	import	private	throws
break	else	inner	protected	transient
byte	extends	instanceof	public	try
case	final	int	rest	var
cast	finally	interface	return	void
catch	float	long	short	volatile
char	for	native	static	while
class	future	new	sure	
const	generic	null	switch	
continue	goto	operator	synchronized	
default	if	outer	this	

Comments

```
/* this is a multiline comment */
// this is a single-line comment
/** Javadoc comment */
```

Literals

number	Type int
number[l ¦¦ L]	Type long
0xhex	Hex integer
0Xhex	Hex integer

`0octal`	Octal integer
`[ number ].number`	Type `double`
`number[ f ¦¦ f]`	Type `float`
`number[ d ¦¦ D]`	Type `double`
`[ + ¦¦ - ] number`	Signed
`numberenumber`	Exponent
`numberEnumber`	Exponent
`'character'`	Single character
`"characters"`	String
`""`	Empty string
`\b`	Backspace
`\t`	Tab
`\n`	Line feed
`\f`	Form feed
`\r`	Carriage return
`\"`	Double quote
`\'`	Single quote
`\\`	Backslash
`\uNNNN`	Unicode escape (NNNN is hex)
`true`	Boolean
`false`	Boolean

Variable Declaration

`[ byte ¦¦ short ¦¦ int ¦¦ long ] varname`	Integers (pick one type)
`[ float ¦¦ double ] varname`	Floats (pick one type)
`char varname;`	Characters
`boolean varname`	Boolean
`classname varname;`	Class types
`type varname, varname, varname;`	Multiple variables

The following options are available only for class and instance variables. Any of these options can be used with a variable declaration:

`[ static ] variableDeclaration`	Class variable
`[ final ] variableDeclaration`	Constants
`[ public ¦¦ private ¦¦ protected ] variableDeclaration`	Access control

Variable Assignment

`variable = value`	Assignment
`variable++`	Postfix Increment
`++variable`	Prefix Increment
`variable--`	Postfix Decrement
`--variable`	Prefix Decrement
`variable += value`	Add and assign
`variable -= value`	Subtract and assign
`variable *= value`	Multiply and assign
`variable ¦¦= value`	Divide and assign
`variable %= value`	Modulus and assign
`variable &= value`	AND and assign
`variable ¦¦= value`	OR and assign
`variable ^= value`	XOR and assign
`variable <<= value`	Left-shift and assign
`variable >>= value`	Right-shift and assign
`variable <<<= value`	Zero-fill right-shift and assign

Operators

`arg + arg`	Addition
`arg - arg`	Subtraction
`arg * arg`	Multiplication
`arg ¦¦ arg`	Division
`arg % arg`	Modulus
`arg < arg`	Less than
`arg > arg`	Greater than
`arg <= arg`	Less than or equal to
`arg >= arg`	Greater than or equal to
`arg == arg`	Equal
`arg   arg`	Not equal
`arg && arg`	Logical AND
`arg ¦¦¦¦ arg`	Logical OR
`! arg`	Logical NOT

`arg & arg`	AND
`arg ¦¦ arg`	OR
`arg ^ arg`	XOR
`arg << arg`	Left-shift
`arg >> arg`	Right-shift
`arg >>> arg`	Zero-fill right-shift
`~ arg`	Complement
`(type)thing`	Casting
`arg instanceof class`	Instance of
`test ? trueOp : falseOp`	Tenary (`if`) operator

Objects

`new class();`	Create new instance
`new class(arg,arg,arg...)`	New instance with parameters
`object.variable`	Instance variable
`object.classvar`	Class variable
`Class.classvar`	Class variable
`object.method()`	Instance method (no args)
`object.method(arg,arg,arg...)`	Instance method
`object.classmethod()`	Class method (no args)
`object.classmethod(arg,arg,arg...)`	Class method
`Class.classmethod()`	Class method (no args)
`Class.classmethod(arg,arg,arg...)`	Class method

Arrays

Note: The brackets in this section are parts of the array creation or access statements. They do not denote optional parts as they do in other parts of this appendix.

`type varname[]`	Array variable
`type[] varname`	Array variable

```
new type[numElements]
```
New array object

```
array[index]
```
Element access

```
array.length
```
Length of array

Loops and Conditionals

```
if ( test) block
```
Conditional

```
if ( test ) block
else block
```
Conditional with `else`

```
switch (test) {
    case value : block
    ...
    default : block
}
```
`switch` (only with integer or char types)

```
for (initializer, test, change ) block
```
`for` loop

```
while ( test ) block
```
`while` loop

```
do block
while (test)
```
`do` loop

```
break [ label ]
continue [ label ]
```
`break` from loop or switch

`continue` loops

```
label:
```
Labeled loops

Class Definitions

```
class classname block
```
Simple class definition

Any of the following optional modifiers can be added to the class definition:

```
[ final ] class classname block
```
No subclasses

```
[ abstract ] class classname block
```
Cannot be instantiated

`[ public ] class classname block`	Accessible outside package
`class classname [ extends Superclass ] block`	Define superclass
`class classname [ implements interfaces ] block`	Implement one or more interfaces

Method and Constructor Definitions

The basic method looks like this, where `returnType` is a type name, a class name, or `void`.

`returnType methodName() block`	Basic method
`returnType methodName(parameter, parameter, block ...)`	Method with parameters

Method parameters look like this:

`type parameter`	Name

Method variations can include any of the following optional keywords:

`[ abstract ] returnType methodName() block`	Abstract method
`[ static ] returnType methodName() block`	Class method
`[ native ] returnType methodName() block`	Native method
`[ final ] returnType methodName() block`	Final method
`[ synchronized ] returnType methodName() block`	Thread lock before executing
`[ public ¦¦ private ¦¦ protected ] returnType methodName()`	Block access control

Constructors look like this:

`classname() block`	Basic constructor
`classname(parameter, parameter, parameter...) block`	Constructor with parameters
`[ public ¦¦ private ¦¦ protected] classname()block`	Access control

In the method/constructor body you can use these references and methods:

`this`	Refers to current object
`super`	Refers to superclass
`super.methodName()`	Call a superclass's method
`this(...)`	Calls class's constructor
`super(...)`	Calls superclass's constructor
`return [ value ]`	Returns a value

Packages, Interfaces, and Importing

```
import package.className    Imports specific class name
import package.*            Imports all classes in package
package packagename         Classes in this file belong to this package
```

```
interface interfaceName [ extends anotherInterface ] block
[ public ] interface interfaceName block
[ abstract ] interface interfaceName block
```

Exceptions and Guarding

```
synchronized ( object ) block    Waits for lock on object
```

```
try block               Guarded statements
catch ( exception ) block   Executed if exception is thrown
[ finally block ]       Always executed
```

```
try block                           Same as previous example (can use optional
[ catch ( exception ) block ]       catch or finally, but not both)
finally block
```

APPENDIX C

by Lay Wah Ooi and Billy Barron

50
Useful Java
Applets

This appendix contains 50 useful Java applets that are available over the Internet. You can download any of these applets over the Internet and use them on your own pages. Some of them do not have links so that you can easily download the applet. In these cases, you can look at the HTML source and discover the name of the Java class file to download. However, whenever you download any applet code, please make sure you do not violate any copyright restrictions when you do so.

Adam Minu's Calculator

`http://www.hk.super.net/~caminu/Calculator.html`

This simple calculator applet is fairly good but can be slow to load.

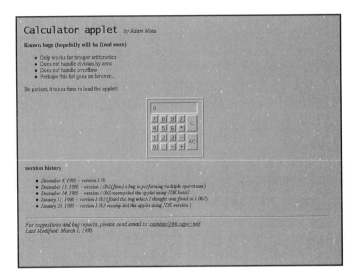

Advertise Scroller

`http://java.elim.net/Advertise/`

Advertise Scroller is a good applet for advertising.

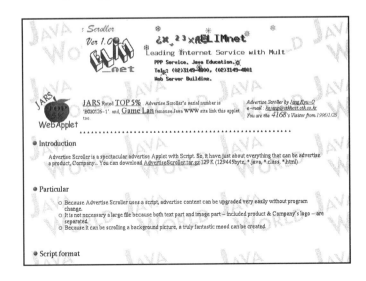

The Advertisement Panel

http://163.121.10.41/java/applets/AdPanel/

The Advertisement Panel is an applet that displays a set of images with different advertisements on your Web page. It offers 11 different effects that can be used to transition from one ad to another.

AmphetiText

http://minyos.its.rmit.edu.au/~s9506190/amphetitext.html

AmphetiText displays text in an unusual fashion.

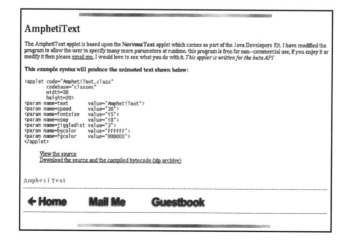

AnimatePLUS22

`http://www.xm.com/cafe/AnimatePLUS/slideshow.html`

AnimatePLUS22 is an applet that can be used to create an animation on a Web page.

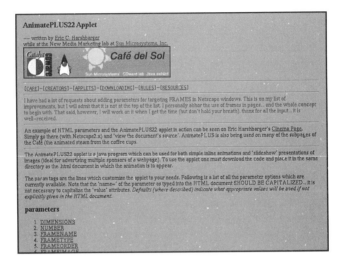

Applets at Kassel

`http://www.uni-kassel.de/fb16/ipm/mt/java/javae.html`

This example is more of a site than an individual applet. Of all the applets at this site, the best one is called Ticker. Ticker creates a scrolling marquee that is one of the best marquee-type programs on the Net.

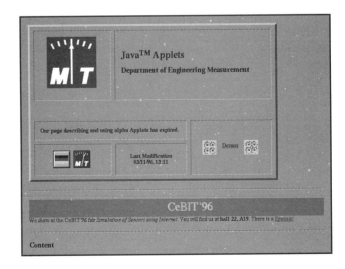

Blue Skies for Java

http://cirrus.sprl.umich.edu/javaweather/

Blue Skies for Java is an applet that displays changing weather maps interactively.

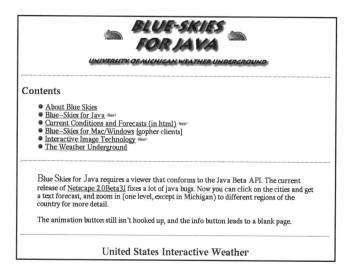

Chart

http://weber.u.washington.edu/~jgurney/java/Chart/

Chart is a applet that draws a simple bar chart with the values that you specify in the HTML file.

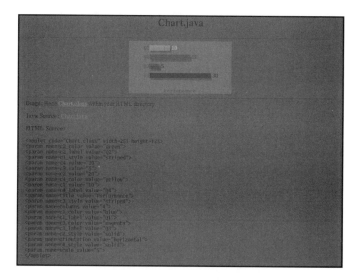

Chat Touring

http://www.cs.princeton.edu/~burchard/www/interactive/chat/express.html

Chat Touring has two purposes. The first is to be a chat system where people can talk to each other interactively. The second is to allow group tours to be conducted.

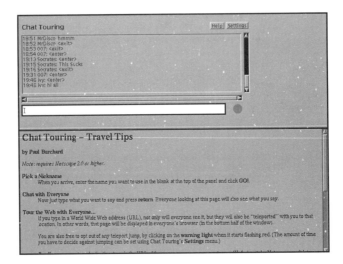

Chinese Fonts

http://phoenix.cs.hku.hk:1234/~jax/C_LED.shtml

This applet enables you to get Chinese characters in an LED sign display.

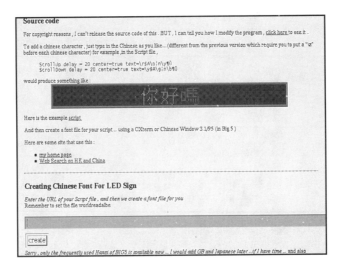

ClickBoard

http://users.aimnet.com/~foureyes/clickboard/ClickBoard.html

ClickBoard is an applet that lets you create your own animation to put on your Web page.

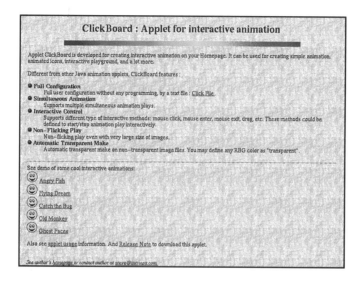

Color Matcher 3

http://www.mcs.anl.gov/home/kwong/JAVA/ColorM.html

This applet lets you enter the RGB values, and it will give you back the six best matches from either the Netscape or the X11 color list.

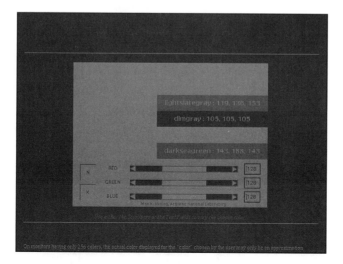

Color(RGB) HTML Tag Generator

`http://www.mindspring.com/~apollo/java/applets/rgb/rgb.html`

This applet generates HTML tags. The user selects a set of colors, and the applet will generate the codes necessary to implement that set of colors on a Web page.

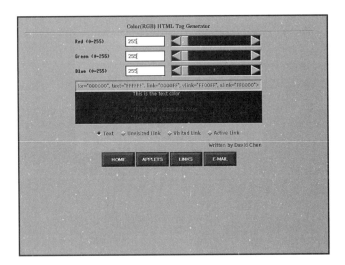

Crossword Puzzle

`http://www6.netscape.com/comprod/products/navigator/version_ 2.0/java_applets/`
`Crossword/`

This applet is a crossword puzzle much like those found in the newspaper.

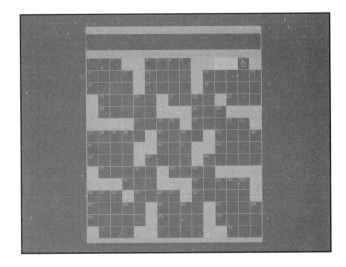

Curve Applet

http://fas.sfu.ca/1/cs/people/GradStudents/heinrica/personal/curve.html

After you select at least four points, this applet draws a curve from the points.

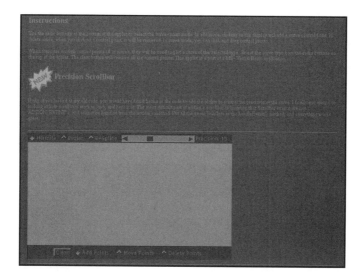

DNA Sequence Display Applet

http://cbil.humgen.upenn.edu/~sdong/sequence.html

This applet lets you annotate biological sequences.

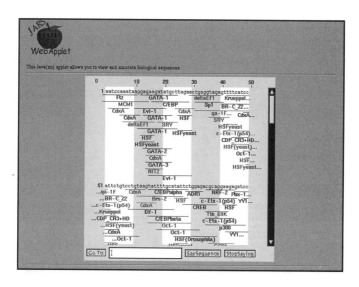

Dynamic Billboard

http://www.db.erau.edu/java/billboard/

Dynamic Billboard is a billboard applet with changing messages.

Gif Slider

http://www.ohiou.edu/~rbarrett/java/rich/gifslider/

Gif Slider slides GIF images around the screen.

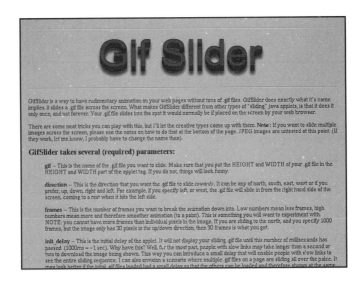

Graph

http://www.sfc.keio.ac.jp/~t93116jk/zemi/test5.html

The Graph applet is a good tool for creating line, bar, and pie graphs.

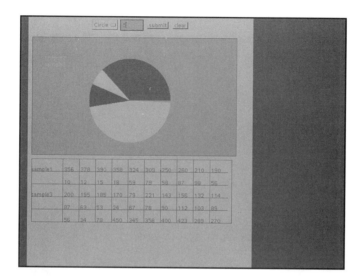

GrowingText Effect

http://www1.mhv.net/~jamihall/java/GrowingText/GrowingText.html

GrowingText is an applet that first displays text very small and then increases its size.

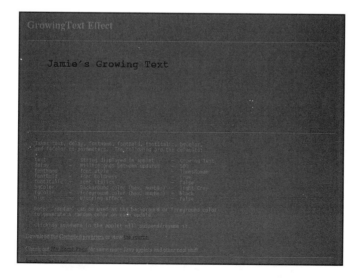

GuestBook

`http://www.nai.net/~rvdi/home.htm#Guestbook`

Want to keep track of people who visit your Web site? Do you also want them to leave comments? GuestBook is an applet that will handle these tasks for you.

HexCalc

`http://www.nrg.org/hexcalc/HexCalc.html`

HexCalc is a hexademical calculator. Programmers will find this applet to be quite useful.

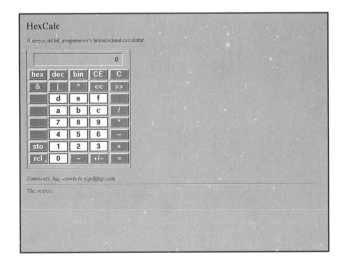

HotTea

http://gpg.com/hottea/

HotTea is an applet that can be used to generated Persian and Arabic text on-screen.

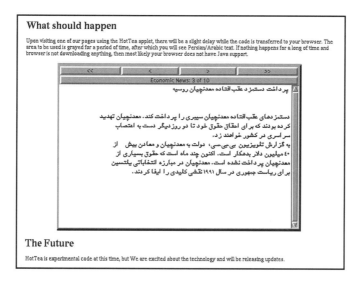

The Impressionist

http://reality.sgi.com/grafica/impression/

This applet is a paint program that lets you create a painting from a photograph.

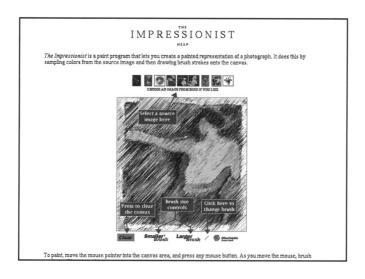

InfoTicker

http://www.panix.com/~erik/InfoTicker.cgi

InfoTicker is an applet that is a simple personal agent. It looks at Internet information in real time and gives you regular updates.

To run InfoTicker, click here. For instructions on how to use InfoTicker, click here. For a FAQ, click here. For a reference manual, click here. Or keep reading.

Introduction

Do you get tired of typing in queries and clicking the submit button again and again? Or having to go out to several different pages to find the information you're usually interested in?

InfoTicker is a simple Java personal agent which allows you to gather, parse, and monitor Internet content in real time. It polls the net with your interests at regular intervals and summarizes the results in one place. Just set InfoTicker up in the corner of your screen, enter what you're interested in, and glance at it every once in a while to see what's up—or be notified by an alert window.

Here's a sample InfoTicker window:

```
File Field Line Settings

BEL                                      69 1/8
LAX                                           71
Fiat Spider rec.autos.marketplace          $1500
http://sun.java.com             Tue Jan 16 08:23:43
```

The first line displays a delayed Bell Atlantic stock price coming from one web page, and the second line a temperature in Los Angeles from another web page. Whenever a field such as price or temperature is updated, it changes color and fades (except under Windows 95, in which there is a Java bug with setting the foreground and background of a Label).

The third line displays a price parsed out of an article containing the pattern Fiat Spider in the newsgroup rec.autos.marketplace. Whenever a new matching article arrives, the price is parsed out of it and an alert window is brought up containing the article (unless alertPopup is set to false).

INOTE

http://jefferson.village.virginia.edu/~mar4g/

INOTE applet is a tool that enables you to put text on an image.

Home Page for the JAVA version of INOTE

Try out INOTE through your WWW browser

(E.G. JAVA Appletviewer or Netscape 2.0b6)

Description

INOTE is an image handling tool which allows the user to construct textual annotations to various regions in an image. This tool has use in educational and medical contexts where certain regions of any type of digital image are to be discussed and evaluated.

Old Version

The previous incarnation of INOTE was written in C++ and Motif++ using HDF libraries. General information about the program itself as well as a forms–based demonstration can be found on the Software page for the Institute for Advanced Technology in the Humanities (IATH).

This Version

With the recent advent of the JAVA programming language by Sun Microsystems, IATH has decided to port INOTE to this new platform independant language. This new version of INOTE can be embedded in a Web page or run as a standalone application on any hardware platform which has a JAVA interpreter.

Currently the JAVA version of INOTE supports GIF and JPEG viewing with image and window resizing features implemented through selections from a menubar. The current version also supports the loading, saving, and construction of text annotations within the image. Additional features under discussion, are forthcoming.

The code runs quite well as a JAVA applet or standalone application. It can be executed using either the JAVA appletviewer, the JAVA interpreter, or a JAVA aware web browser. If you have a "JAVA aware" browser (eg. Netscape 2.0b6 and later), you can run INOTE as an applet through your browser.

Note: As of now, Netscape does not allow the loading and saving of local files. These options have therefore been turned off in the program. However, images can be loaded via the HTTP protocol. For purposes of demonstration, a GIF image of the mask of agamemnon and a few annotations are automatically loaded upon execution. You can use this image to peruse various other

ISO8559 HTML Conversion Machine

http://www.conveyor.com/entity.html

ISO8559 is a standard way to represent foreign characters in U.S. ASCII. This applet will help you convert between ASCII and the HTML entity names for the characters.

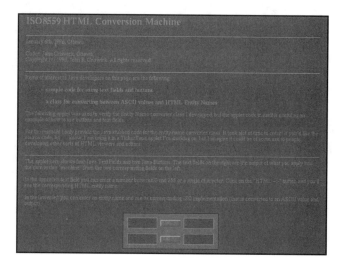

Java Dance

http://tech-www.informatik.uni-hamburg.de/dance/JDance-e.html

Java Dance is a virtual dancing instructor that teaches you how to dance. Only four dances are available.

Java Graffiti Chalkboard

`http://www.tisinc.com/beta/cbapplet.html`

Java Graffiti Chalkboard is an applet that lets a user draw on a chalkboard.

Java Graph Class Library

`http://www-igpp.llnl.gov/people/brookshaw/java/`

This group of Java classes helps you plot graphs using Java applets.

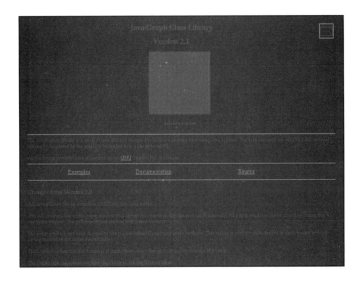

Java Sinus Scroller

http://www.ping.ch/black_sun/sinus.htm

This applet is another strange text display applet.

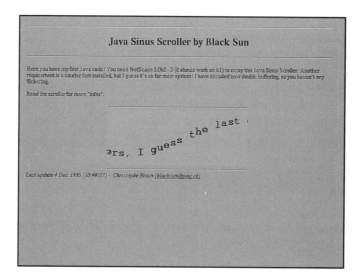

Jmath

http://www.geom.umn.edu:80/~rminer/jmath/

Jmath is an applet that allows you to display mathematical formulas on-screen.

J-Tools

`http://www.crl.com/~integris/j_tools.htm`

The J-tools applet lets you create special effect text, bullets, and rules.

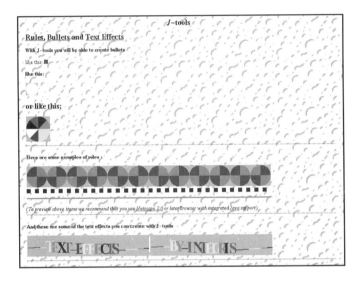

Juggling

`http://www.acm.uiuc.edu/webmonkeys/juggling/`

This animation teaches you how to juggle from one to three balls.

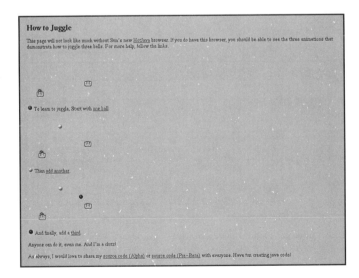

Jumping Frog

http://www.franceway.com/frogjump.htm

Jumping Frog is an applet that displays a frog jumping around the screen.

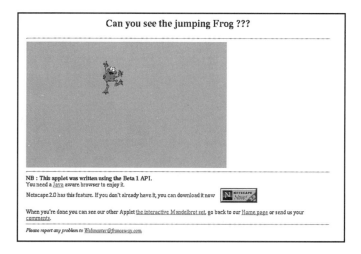

Karl's Mortgage Calculator

http://www.broadcom.ie/~kj/java/mortgage.html

This applet is a very handy way to calculate the payments on any given mortgage.

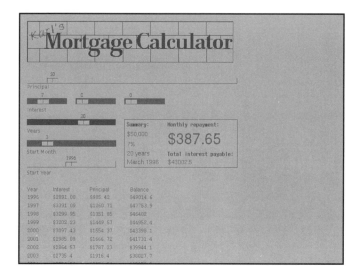

Missile Commando

`http://www.sdsu.edu/~boyns/java/mc/`

Missile Commando is a simple game that is similar to the old arcade game Missile Command. Missile Commando is much simpler though.

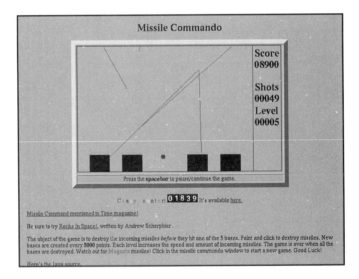

Nizze's HotJava Applets

`http://www-und.ida.liu.se/~d94nilhe/java/applets.html`

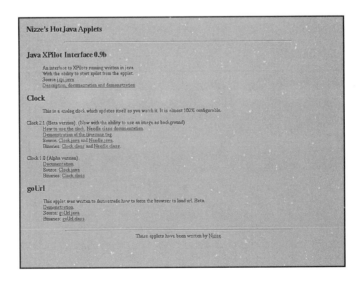

Nuclear Power Plant

http://www.ida.liu.se/~her/npp/demo.html

This applet simulates a nuclear power plant.

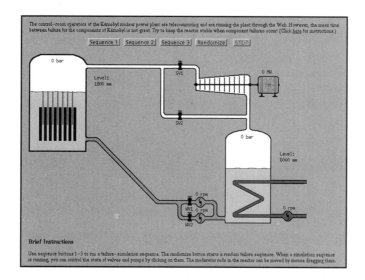

PerspectiveDraw

http://www.ec3.com/

This applet is a package for drawing 3-D models.

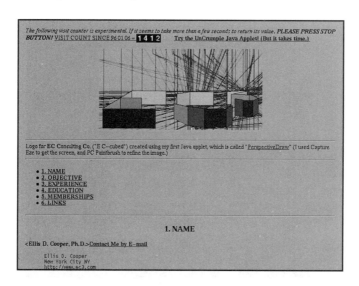

RnbText

http://www.crl.com/~integris/JT_RNBT.htm

RnbText draws text in a rainbow of colors. Also, it gives the text a very slight sine wave effect.

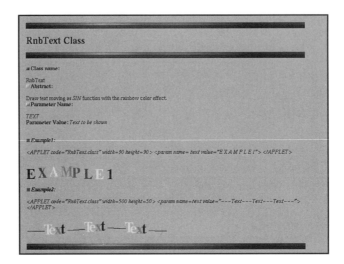

Robert's Online Pricers

http://www.interpid.com/~robert1/

This site contains a series of online pricers. They include options, derivatives, commissions, and loans.

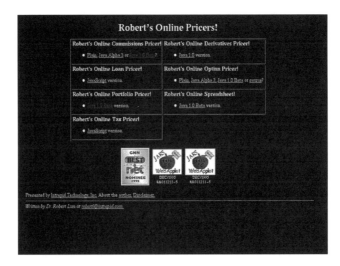

SineWave Text

`http://forte.poly.edu:8000/Sine.html`

SineWave Text is an applet that displays text in an obvious sine wave. The effect is much more stated than the one in RnbText.

Spirograph

`http://www.wordsmith.org/~anu/java/spirograph.html`

Remember Spirograph from when you were a child? You'll be glad to know that there is a Java version of your old favorite.

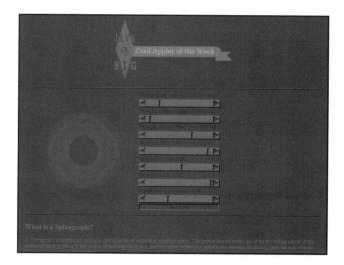

SpreadSheet

`http://weber.u.washington.edu/~jgurney/java/SpreadSheet/`

This applet is no Lotus 1-2-3, but it is a nice small spreadsheet applet.

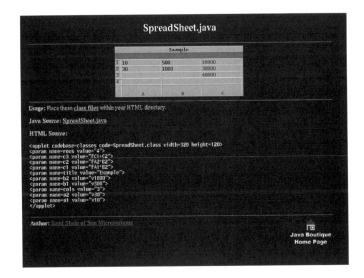

Stock Trace

`http://www.cs.virginia.edu/~cd4v/graph/StockGraph.html`

Stock Trace is a stock market tracking applet. It prints a graph of the history of a stock.

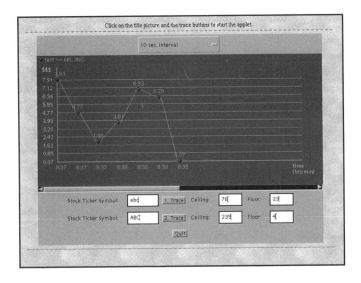

Sunclock

http://www.NeoSoft.com/~forge/java/Sunclock/Sunclock.html

This applet is a map of the world showing where the sun is currently shining.

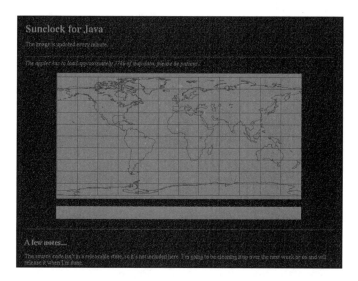

Test Editor

http://www-elec.enst.fr/java/edit-beta/test.html

This applet displays vector graphics that are read in from a file.

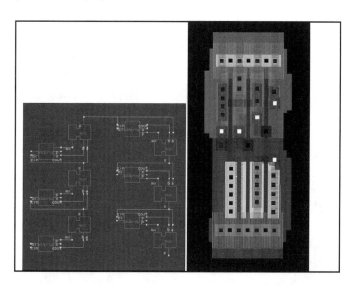

Touch-tone

http://madeira.cc.hokudai.ac.jp/RD/takai/myjava4.html

This applet is a Touch-Tone telephone pad. When its buttons are pressed, it generates the tones needed to place a call.

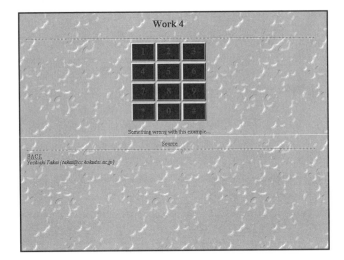

TourGuide

http://weber.u.washington.edu/~jgurney/java/TourGuide/

This applet launches an untrusted applet and another browser screen. The untrusted applet lets you tour the Web page on the new browser screen.

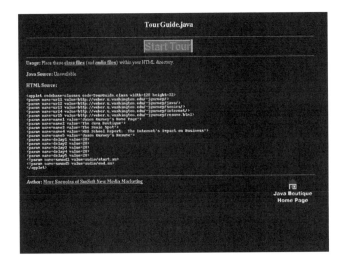

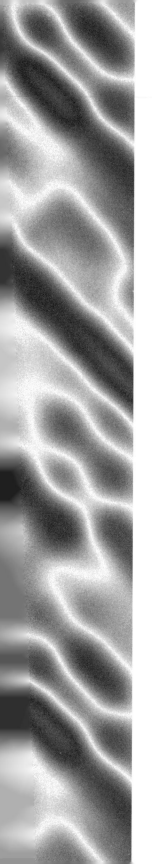

What's on the CD-ROM

The purpose of this appendix is to provide an overview and brief description of the contents of this book's CD-ROM. Because applets and scripts use long filenames, their files have been zipped (compressed) in directories. They may be browsed by using one of the compression utilities also included on this CD-ROM.

Explanation of the CD-ROM Directories

The following is a list of the directories found on the CD-ROM and a brief explanation of their contents. A more detailed description of the applets and scripts is in the following sections:

- \applets—Java applets contributed from the Internet
- \book—Examples and materials from the authors
- \compress—Compression utilities

- \icons—Icons and images for use on Web pages
- \int_apps\adobe—Adobe's Acrobat reader (PDF files)
- \int_apps\graphics—PaintShop and ACDSee graphics shareware programs
- \int_apps\html—HTML shareware: Hotdog, HTML Assistant, and Hot Metal
- \int_apps\sound—WPlany sound utility
- \jdk—The Java Developer's Kit from Sun Microsystems
- \plugins—Plug-Ins for Netscape 2.0 browser
- \scripts—Java scripts contributed from the Internet
- \solaris—Sun's Solaris version of the JDK

Software Development Tools

The following section lists the programming tools included on the CD-ROM, including the Java Developer's Kit.

JDK 1.0

The Java Developer's Kit contains all of the tools necessary to create applications (or Web applets) using the Java programming language, including the following:

javac	The Java compiler
jdb	The Java debugger
javadoc	The Java documentation program
java	The Java Virtual Machine
appletviewer	The Java applet viewer

The JDK also has a variety of sample applets. The JDK is available for the following platforms:

Windows 95
Windows NT
Solaris 2.x
Macintosh Operating System (Note: the Mac version of the JDK is a Beta version)

Utilities

In addition to the JDK, the CD-ROM includes a number of utilities to help you manipulate the sound and image files you might need while creating Java applets. These utilities include the following:

ACDSee

ACDSee is a graphics utility that enables you to view GIF and JPEG file formats and to convert between the two.

Adobe Acrobat

A growing number of Web sites are offering documentation in the PDF format. The Adobe Acrobat reader enables you to read PDF files.

Hotdog, HTML Assistant, and Hot Metal

Hotdog, HTML Assistant, and Hot Metal are HTML editors that you can use to create your Web pages or to edit the HTML files for your Java applets.

PaintShop

PaintShop is a graphics application that enables you to create drawings to incorporate into your Java applets.

WPlany

WPlany is a sound utility that you can use to play sounds you might use in your Java applets.

Sample Applets

The following section lists the sample applets discussed in the book and included on the CD-ROM. Wherever possible, a URL to the applet's home page is included. Keep in mind that these URLs might change over time because the Web is a dynamic environment.

AnimNav
Written by Elijah Dean Meeker
`http://www.realtime.net/~elijah`

Bitsafe imagbutn
Written by Larry Landwehr

ClickBoard: Interactive Animation
Written by Steve Fu
`http://www.intrinsa.com/personal/steve/ClickBoard/ClickBoard.html`

Clock and GoURL
Written by Nils Hedström
`http://www-und.ida.liu.se/~d94nilhe/java/applets.html`

Collections
Written by Doug Lea

Color Picker
Written by Ken Rawlings
`http://www.greyassoc.com`

cmos and kvd
Written by Norman Hendrich
`http://tech-www.informatik.uni-hamburg.de/applets/cmos/cmosdemo.html`

Commissions
Written by Dr. Robert Lum
`http://www.intrepid.com/~robertl/index.html`

Criswick applets (BigTime, WhereToday, TickerTape, PlaySound, Map Apps)
Written by John Criswick

Curve Applet
Written by Michael Heinrichs
`http://fas.sfu.ca:80/1/cs/people/GradStudents/heinrica/personal/curve.html`

Learn to Dance Applet
Written by George Hessmann
`http://tech-www.informatik.uni-hamburg.de/dance/Jdance-e.html`

Documentation and Forms
Written by Thomas Wendt

Frog Jump
Written by Charles-Edouard Ruault
`http://www.franceway.com/frogjump.htm`

GrowText
Written by Jamieson M. Hall
`http://www1.mhv.net/~jamihall/rocham.html`

J-tools
Written by Gene Leybzon

Juggling Applet
Written by Christopher Sequin
`http://www.acm.uiuc.edu/webmonkeys/juggling/`

Missile Commando
Written by Mark Boyns
`http://www.sdsu.edu/~boyns/java/mc/`

Neon
Written by Scott Clark

Nuclear Power Plant
Written by Henrik Eriksson
`http://www.ida.liu.se/~her/npp/demo.html`

Player Piano
Written by Mark Leather
`http://reality.sgi.com/employees/mark/piano/index.html`

Plot2D
Written by Dr. Leigh Brookshaw
`http://www-igpp.llnl.gov/people/brookshaw/java/`

Rock-Paper-Scissors
Written by Jamieson M. Hall
`http://www1.mhv.net/~jamihall/rocham.html`

Server
Written by Mike Fletcher

SlideShow
Written by David Gulbransen
`http://www.fa.indiana.edu/~dgulbran/slideshow.html`

Slot Machine
Written by Jamieson M. Hall
`http://www1.mhv.net/~jamihall/rocham.html`

StockTrace Applet
Written by Christian Dreke
`http://www.cs.virginia.edu/~cd4v/graph/StockGraph.html`

TickerTape
Written by Ken Rawlings
`http://www.greyassoc.com`

User
Written by Scott Clark

WorldClock
Written by Vijay Vaidy
`http://www.webpage.com/~vijay/java/wt/testwt.html`

YARC
Written by Ken Rawlings
`http://www.greyassoc.com`

Sample JavaScript Scripts

The following is a collection of JavaScript scripts included on the CD-ROM:

`bodymass`	You can use this script to calculate your body mass ratio, provide information about proper weight, and so on.
`currency`	This script allows you to convert the value of a currency type to a foreign currency.
`histbutn`	This script provides JavaScript navigation buttons, which can be used on Web pages or inside frames.
`js_maze`	This script is a sample JavaScript maze.
`rclac`	This script is a calculator for running that computes distance and speed.
`snark`	This script enables you to search multiple WWW search engines through a single input form.
`soundex`	This script converts surnames to the standard census Soundex indexing format.
`taxpricr`	This JavaScript script calculates your income taxes based on the 1995 1040EZ.
`telekom`	This script calculates the cost of a telephone call in Germany.

Index

Web Site Administrator's Survival Guide

— Jerry Ablan, et al

The World Wide Web Administrator's Survival Guide is a detailed, step-by-step book that guides the Web administrator through the process of selecting Web server software and hardware, installing and configuring a server, and administering the server on an ongoing basis. Includes a CD-ROM with servers and administrator tools. The book provides complete step-by-step guidelines for installing and configuring a Web server.

Price: $49.99 USA/$67.99 CDN   User Level: Inter-Advanced
ISBN: 1-57521-018-5   700 pages

Web Publishing Unleashed

— Stanek, et al

Includes sections on how to organize and plan your information, design pages, and become familar with hypertext and hypermedia. Choose from a range of applications and technologies, including Java, SGML, VRML, and the newest HTML and Netscape extensions. The CD contains software, templates, and examples to help you become a successful Web publisher.

Price: $49.99 USA/$61.95 CDN   User Level: Casual-Expert
ISBN: 1-57521-051-7   1,000 pages

Web Site Construction Kit for Windows 95

— Christopher Brown and Scott Zimmerman

The Web Site Construction Kit for Windows 95 provides readers with everything you need to set up, develop, and maintain a Web site with Windows 95. It teaches the ins and outs of planning, installing, configuring, and administering a Windows 95–based Web site for an organization, and it includes detailed instructions on how to use the software on the CD to develop the Web site's content: HTML pages, CGI scripts, image maps, etc.

Price: $49.99 USA/$67.99 CDN   User Level: Casual-Accomplished
ISBN: 1-57521-072-X   500 pages

The Internet Business Guide, Second Edition

— Rosalind Resnick & Dave Taylor

Updated and revised, this guide will inform and educate anyone on how they can use the Internet to increase profits, reach a broader market, track down business leads, and access critical information. Updated to cover digital cash, Web cybermalls, secure Web servers, and setting up your business on the Web, *The Internet Business Guide* includes profiles of entrepreneurs' successes (and failures) on the Internet. Improve your business by using the Internet to market products and services, make contacts with colleagues, cut costs, and improve customer service.

Price: $25.00 USA/$39.99 CDN   User Level: All Levels
ISBN: 1-57521-004-5   470 pages

Teach Yourself Netscape Web Publishing in a Week

— *Wes Tatters*

Teach Yourself Netscape Web Publishing in a Week is the easiest way to learn how to produce attention-getting, well-designed Web pages using the features provided by Netscape Navigator. Intended for both the novice and the expert, this book provides a solid grounding in HTML and Web publishing principles, while providing special focus on the possibilities presented by the Netscape environment. Learn to design and create attention-grabbing Web pages for the Netscape environment while exploring new Netscape development features such as frames, plug-ins, Java applets, and JavaScript!

Price: $39.99 USA/ $47.95 CDN   User Level: Beginner-Inter
ISBN: 1-57521-068-1   450 pages

Teach Yourself CGI Programming with Perl in a Week

— *Eric Herrmann*

This book is a step-by-step tutorial of how to create, use, and maintain Common Gateway Interfaces (CGI). It describes effective ways of using CGI as an integral part of Web development. Adds interactivity and flexibility to the information that can be provided through your Web site. Includes Perl 4.0 and 5.0, CGI libraries, and other applications to create databases, dynamic interactivity, and other enticing page effects.

Price: $39.99 USA/$53.99 CDN   User Level: Inter-Advanced
ISBN: 1-57521-009-6   500 pages

Teach Yourself Java in 21 Days

— *Laura Lemay and Charles Perkins*

The complete tutorial guide to the most exciting technology to hit the Internet in years— Java! A detailed guide to developing applications with the hot new Java language from Sun Microsystems, *Teach Yourself Java in 21 Days* shows readers how to program using Java and develop applications (applets) using the Java language. With coverage of Java implementation in Netscape Navigator and Hot Java, along with the Java Development Kit, including the compiler and debugger for Java, *Teach Yourself Java* is a must-have!

Price: $39.99 USA/$53.99 CDN   User Level: Inter-Advanced
ISBN: 1-57521-030-4   600 pages

Presenting Java

— *John December*

Presenting Java gives you a first look at how Java is transforming static Web pages into living, interactive applications. Java opens up a world of possibilities previously unavailable on the Web. You'll find out how Java is being used to create animations, computer simulations, interactive games, teaching tools, spreadsheets, and a variety of other applications. Whether you're a new user, a project planner, or developer, *Presenting Java* provides an efficient, quick introduction to the basic concepts and technical details that make Java the hottest new Web technology of the year!

Price: $25.00 USA/$34.95 CDN   User Level: All Levels
ISBN: 1-57521-039-8   207 pages

Netscape 2 Unleashed

— *Dick Oliver, et al.*

This book provides a complete, detailed, and fully fleshed-out overview of the Netscape products. Through case studies and examples of how individuals, businesses, and institutions are using the Netscape products for Web development, *Netscape 2 Unleashed* gives a full description of the evolution of Netscape from its inception to today, and its cutting-edge developments with Netscape Gold, LiveWire, Netscape Navigator 2.0, Java and JavaScript, Macromedia, VRML, Plug-ins, Adobe Acrobat, HTML 3.0 and beyond, security and Intranet systems.

Price: $49.99 USA/$61.95 CDN   User Level: All Levels
ISBN: 1-57521-007-X   Pages: 800 pages

The Internet Unleashed 1996

— *Barron, Ellsworth, Savetz, et al.*

The Internet Unleashed 1996 is the complete reference to get new users up and running on the Internet while providing the consummate reference manual for the experienced user. *The Internet Unleashed 1996* provides the reader with an encyclopedia of information on how to take advantage of all the Net has to offer for business, education, research, and government. The companion CD-ROM contains over 100 tools and applications. The only book that includes the experience of over 40 of the world's top Internet experts, this new edition is updated with expanded coverage of Web publishing, Internet business, Internet multimedia and virtual reality, Internet security, Java, and more!

Price: $49.99 USA/$67.99 CDN   User Level: All Levels
ISBN: 1-57521-041-X   1,456 pages

The World Wide Web Unleashed 1996

— *December and Randall*

The World Wide Web Unleashed 1996 is designed to be the only book a reader will need to experience the wonders and resources of the Web. The companion CD-ROM contains over 100 tools and applications to make the most of your time on the Internet. Shows readers how to explore the Web's amazing world of electronic art museums, online magazines, virtual malls, and video music libraries, while giving readers complete coverage of Web page design, creation, and maintenance, plus coverage of new Web technologies such as Java, VRML, CGI, and multimedia!

Price: $49.99 USA/$67.99 CDN   User Level: All Levels
ISBN: 1-57521-040-1   1,440 pages

Teach Yourself Web Publishing with HTML in 14 Days, Premier Edition

— *Laura Lemay*

This book teaches everything about publishing on the Web. In addition to its exhaustive coverage of HTML, it also gives readers hands-on practice with more complicated subjects such as CGI, tables, forms, multimedia programming, testing, maintenance, and much more. CD-ROM is Mac- and PC-compatible and includes a variety of applications that help readers create Web pages using graphics and templates.

Price: $39.99 USA/$53.99 CDN   User Level: All Levels
ISBN: 1-57521-014-2   804 pages

Teach Yourself Web Publishing with HTML 3.0 in a Week, Second Edition

— Laura Lemay

Ideal for those people who are interested in the Internet and the World Wide Web—the Internet's hottest topic! This updated and revised edition teaches readers how to use HTML (Hypertext Markup Language) version 3.0 to create Web pages that can be viewed by nearly 30 million users. Explores the process of creating and maintaining Web presentations, including setting up tools and converters for verifying and testing pages. The new edition highlights the new features of HTML, such as tables and Netscape and Microsoft Explorer extensions. Provides the latest information on working with images, sound files, and video, and teaches advanced HTML techniques and tricks in a clear, step-by-step manner with many practical examples of HTML pages.

Price: $29.99 USA/$34.95 CDN   User Level: Beginner-Inter
ISBN: 1-57521-064-9   518 pages

Web Page Construction Kit (Software)

Create your own exciting World Wide Web pages with the software and expert guidance in this kit! Includes HTML Assistant Pro Lite, the acclaimed point-and-click Web page editor. Simply highlight text in HTML Assistant Pro Lite, and click the appropriate button to add headlines, graphics, special formatting, links, etc. No programming skills needed! Using your favorite Web browser, you can test your work quickly and easily without leaving the editor. A unique catalog feature allows you to keep track of interesting Web sites and easily add their HTML links to your pages. Assistant's user-defined toolkit also allows you to add new HTML formatting styles as they are defined. Includes the #1 best-selling Internet book, *Teach Yourself Web Publishing with HTML 3.0 in a Week, Second Edition,* and a library of professionally designed Web page templates, graphics, buttons, bullets, lines, and icons to rev up your new pages!

PC Computing magazine says, "If you're looking for the easiest route to Web publishing, HTML Assistant is your best choice."

Price: $20.00 US/$46.99 CAN   User Level: Beginner-Inter
ISBN: 1-57521-000-2   518 pages

HTML & CGI Unleashed

— John December & Marc Ginsburg

Targeted to professional developers who have a basic understanding of programming and need a detailed guide. Provides a complete, detailed reference to developing Web information systems. Covers the full range of languages—HTML, CGI, Perl C, editing and conversion programs, and more—and how to create commercial-grade Web Applications. Perfect for the developer who will be designing, creating, and maintaining a Web presence for a company or large institution.

Price: $49.99 USA/$53.99 CDN   User Level: Inter-Advanced
ISBN: 0-672-30745-6   830 pages

Web Site Construction Kit for Windows NT

— Christopher Brown and Scott Zimmerman

The Web Site Construction Kit for Windows NT has everything you need to set up, develop, and maintain a Web site with Windows NT—including the server on the CD-ROM! It teaches the ins and outs of planning, installing, configuring, and administering a Windows NT–based Web site for an organization, and it includes detailed instructions on how to use the software on the CD-ROM to develop the Web site's content—HTML pages, CGI scripts, imagemaps, and so forth.

Price: $49.99 USA/$67.99 CDN   User Level: All Levels
ISBN: 1-57521-047-9   430 pages

Add to Your Sams.net Library Today
with the Best Books for Internet Technologies

ISBN	Quantity	Description of Item	Unit Cost	Total Cost
1-57521-039-8		Presenting Java	$25.00	
1-57521-030-4		Teach Yourself Java in 21 Days	$39.99	
1-57521-049-5		Java Unleashed	$49.99	
1-57521-007-X		Netscape 2 Unleashed	$49.99	
1-57521-041-X		The Internet Unleashed 1996	$49.99	
1-57521-040-1		The World Wide Web Unleashed 1996	$49.99	
0-672-30745-6		HTML and CGI Unleashed	$49.99	
1-57521-009-6		Teach Yourself CGI Programming with Perl in a Week	$39.99	
0-672-30735-9		Teach Yourself the Internet in a Week	$25.00	
1-57521-068-1		Teach Yourself Netscape 2 Web Publishing in a Week	$39.99	
0-672-30718-9		Navigating the Internet, Third Edition	$22.50	
1-57521-005-3		Teach Yourself More Web Publishing with HTML in a Week	$29.99	
1-57521-014-2		Teach Yourself Web Publishing with HTML in 14 Days, Premiere Edition	$29.99	
1-57521-072-X		Web Site Construction Kit for Windows 95	$49.99	
1-57521-047-9		Web Site Construction Kit for Windows NT	$49.99	
		Shipping and Handling: See information below.		
		TOTAL		

Shipping and Handling: $4.00 for the first book, and $1.75 for each additional book. If you need to have it NOW, we can ship product to you in 24 hours for an additional charge of approximately $18.00, and you will receive your item overnight or in two days. Overseas shipping and handling adds $2.00. Prices subject to change. Call between 9:00 a.m. and 5:00 p.m. EST for availability and pricing information on latest editions.

201 W. 103rd Street, Indianapolis, Indiana 46290

1-800-428-5331 — Orders   1-800-835-3202 — FAX   1-800-858-7674 — Customer Service

Book ISBN 1-57521-070-3

A V I A C O M S E R V I C E

The Information SuperLibrary™

Bookstore **Search** **What's New** **Reference** **Software** **Newsletter** **Company Overviews**

Yellow Pages **Internet Starter Kit** **HTML Workshop** **Win a Free T-Shirt!** **Macmillan Computer Publishing** **Site Map** **Talk to Us**

CHECK OUT THE BOOKS IN THIS LIBRARY.

You'll find thousands of shareware files and over 1600 computer books designed for both technowizards and technophobes. You can browse through 700 sample chapters, get the latest news on the Net, and find just about anything using our massive search directories.

All Macmillan Computer Publishing books are available at your local bookstore.

We're open 24-hours a day, 365 days a year.

You don't need a card.

We don't charge fines.

And you can be as **LOUD** as you want.

The Information SuperLibrary

http://www.mcp.com/mcp/ ftp.mcp.com

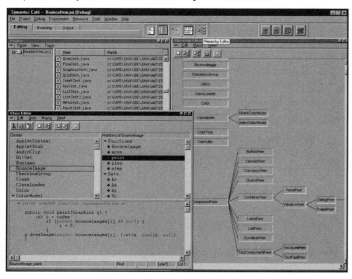

State Sales/Use Tax

In the following states, add sales/use tax: CO–3%; GA, LA, NY–4%; VA–4.5%; KS–4.9%; AZ, IA, IN, MA, MD, OH, SC, WI–5%; CT, FL, ME, MI, NC, NJ, PA, TN–6%; CA, IL, TX–6.25%; MN, WA–6.5%; DC–5.75%.

Please add local tax for: AZ, CA, FL, GA, MO, NY, OH, SC, TN, TX, WA, WI.

Order Information:

- Please allow 2-4 weeks for processing your order.
- Please attach the order form with your payment.
- No P.O. Boxes and no C.O.D.s accepted.
- Order form good in the U.S. only.
- If you are tax-exempt, please include exemption certificate or letter with tax-exempt number.
- Resellers not eligible.
- Offer not valid with any other promotion.
- One copy per product, per order.
- Special offer expires 6/30/96.

HTML in 10 seconds!*

No kidding.
In the time it takes
for a good slurp of coffee, *HTML Transit* generated this Web page.

Say hello to the template.

HTML Transit takes a new approach to online publishing, using a high-speed production template. It's fast and easy. You can turn a 50-page word processing file into multiple, linked HTML pages—complete with graphics and tables—in less than 10 mouse clicks. From scratch.

Customize your template—formatting, backgrounds, navigation buttons, thumbnails—and save even more time. Now in just 4 clicks, you can crank out an entire library of custom Web pages with no manual authoring.

Take a free test drive.

Stop working so hard. Download an evaluation copy of *HTML Transit* from our Web site:

http://www.infoaccess.com

Your download code is **MCML46**. (It can save you money when you order *HTML Transit*.)

Buy HTML Transit risk free.

HTML Transit is just $495, and is backed by a 30-day satisfaction guarantee. To order, call us toll-free at **800-344-9737**.

InfoAccess, Inc.
(206) 747-3203
FAX: (206) 641-9367
Email: info@infoaccess.com

► Automatic HTML from native word processor formats
► Creates HTML tables, tables of contents & indexes
► Graphics convert to GIF or JPEG, with thumbnails
► Template control over appearance and behavior
► For use with Microsoft® Windows®

HTML Transit is a trademark of InfoAccess, Inc. Microsoft and Windows are registered trademarks of Microsoft Corporation.
*Single-page Microsoft Word document with graphics and tables, running on 75MHz Pentium. Conversion speed depends on document length, complexity and PC configuration.

CD
Installation Instructions

What's on the Disc

The companion CD-ROM contains the Java™ Developer's Kit from Sun, other programs mentioned in the book, and many useful examples.

Windows NT Installation Instructions

1. Insert the CD-ROM disc into your CD-ROM drive.

2. From File Manager or Program Manager, choose Run from the File menu.

3. Type **\<drive>CDSETUP** and press Enter, where **\<drive>** corresponds to the drive letter of your CD-ROM. For example, if your CD-ROM is drive D, type **D:CDSETUP** and press Enter.

4. Follow the on-screen instructions in the installation program. Files will be installed to a directory named **\CWA**, unless you choose a different directory during installation.

INSTALL creates a Windows program manager group called Create Web Applets. This group contains icons for exploring the CD-ROM.

Macintosh Installation Instructions

1. Insert the CD-ROM disc into your CD-ROM drive.

2. When an icon for the CD appears on your desktop, open the disc by double-clicking on its icon.

3. Double-click on the icon named Guide to the CD-ROM, and follow the directions that appear.

Windows 95 Installation Instructions

1. If Windows 95 is installed on your computer, and you have the AutoPlay feature enabled, the Guide to the CD-ROM program starts automatically whenever you insert the disc into your CD-ROM drive.

To learn how to use the Guide to the CD-ROM program, press F1 from any screen in the program.

Technical Support from Macmillan

We can't help you with Java problems or software from third parties, but we can assist you if a problem arises with the CD-ROM itself.

E-mail Support: Send e-mail to support@mcp.com.

CompuServe: GO SAMS to reach the Macmillan Computer Publishing forum. Leave us a message addressed to SYSOP. If you want the message to be private, address it to *SYSOP.

Telephone: (317) 581-3833   **Fax:** (317) 581-4773

Mail: Macmillan Computer Publishing
Attention: Support Department
201 West 103rd Street
Indianapolis, IN 46290-1093

Here's how to reach us on the Internet:

World Wide Web *(The Macmillan Information SuperLibrary)*

http://www.mcp.com/samsnet